WOLFMAN
A John Rebus novel

Ian Rankin

ARROW

This edition published by Arrow Books in 1993

1 3 5 7 9 10 8 6 4 2

© Ian Rankin 1992

First published in 1992 by Century

Random House, 20 Vauxhall Bridge Road, London SW1V 2SA

Random House Australia (Pty) Limited
20 Alfred Street, Milsons Point, Sydney,
New South Wales 2061, Australia

Random House New Zealand Limited
18 Poland Road, Glenfield
Auckland 10, New Zealand

Random House South Africa (Pty) Limited
PO Box 337, Bergvlei, South Africa

Random House UK Limited Reg. No. 954009

A CIP catalogue record for this book
is available from the British Library

ISBN 0 09 923091 7

Photoset by Deltatype Ltd, Ellesmere Port
Printed and bound in Great Britain by
Cox & Wyman Ltd, Reading, Berkshire

For Miranda, again,
but this time for
Mugwump too . . .

'How many wolves do we feel on our heels, while our real enemies go in sheepskin'

Malcolm Lowry, *Under the Volcano*

Prologue

She drives home the knife.

The moment, she knows from past experience, is a very intimate one. Her hand is gripped around the knife's cool handle and the thrust takes the blade into the throat up to the hilt until her hand meets the throat itself. Flesh upon flesh. Jacket first, or woollen jersey, cotton shirt or T-shirt, then flesh. Now rent. The knife is writhing, like an animal sniffing. Warm blood covering hilt and hand. (The other hand covers the mouth, stifling screams.) The moment is complete. A meeting. Touching. The body is hot, gaping, warm with blood. Seething inside, as insides become outsides. Boiling. The moment is coming to an end all too soon.

And still she feels hungry. It isn't right, isn't usual, but she does. She removes some of the clothing; in fact, removes quite a lot of it, removes more, perhaps, than is necessary. And she does what she must do, the knife squirming again. She keeps her eyes screwed tightly shut. She does not like this part. She has never liked this part, not then, not now. But especially not *then*.

Finally, she brings out her teeth and sinks them into the white stomach, until they grind together in a satisfying bite, and whispers, as she always does, the same four words.

'It's only a game.'

* * *

It is evening when George Flight gets the call. Sunday evening. Sunday should be his blessed relief, beef and Yorkshires, feet up in front of the television, papers falling from his lap. But he's had a feeling all day. In the pub at lunchtime he'd felt it, a wriggling in his gut like there were worms in there, tiny blind white worms, hungry worms,

1

worms he could not hope to satisfy. He knew what they were and they knew what they were. And then he'd won third prize in the pub raffle: a three-foot high orange and white teddy bear. Even the worms had laughed at him then and he'd known the day would end badly.

As it was doing now, the phone as insistent as last orders. Ringing with whatever bad news couldn't wait until the morning shift. He knew what it meant of course. Hadn't he been expecting it these past weeks? But still he was reluctant to pick up the receiver. At last he did.

'Flight speaking.'

'There's been another one, sir. The Wolfman. He's done ˹nother.'

˹light stared at the silent television. Highlights of the previous day's rugby match. Grown men running after a funny-shaped ball as though their lives depended on it. It was only a bloody game after all. And propped up against the side of the TV that smirking prize, the teddy bear. What the ˹   could he do with a teddy bear?

˹   ay,' he said, 'just tell me where . . .'

'After all, it *is* only a game.'

Rebus smiled and nodded at the Englishman across the table. Then he stared out of the window, pretending once more to be interested in the blur of dark scenery. If the Englishman had said it once, he had said it a dozen times. And during the trip, he had said little else. He also kept stealing precious legroom from Rebus, while his collection of empty beer cans was creeping across the table, invading Rebus's space, pushing against the neatly folded stack of newspapers and magazines.

'Tickets, please!' yelled the guard from the other end of the carriage.

So, with a sigh, and for the third time since leaving Edinburgh, Rebus sought out his ticket. It was never where he thought it was. At Berwick, he'd thought it was in his shirt pocket. It was in the outer top pocket of his Harris tweed jacket. Then at Durham he'd looked for it in his jacket, only to find it beneath one of the magazines on the table. Now, ten minutes out of Peterborough, it had moved to the back pocket of his trousers. He retrieved it, and waited for the guard to make his way forward.

The Englishman's ticket was where it had always been: half-hidden beneath a beer can. Rebus, although he knew every word almost by heart, glanced again at the back page of one of his Sunday papers. He had kept it to the top of the pile for no reason other than a sense of devilment, enjoying the thick black letters of the headline – SCOTS WHA HAE! – beneath which was printed the story of the previous day's Calcutta Cup clash at Murrayfield. And a clash it had been: no day for weak stomachs, but a day for stout hearts and determination. The Scots had triumphed by thirteen points to ten, and now here Rebus was on a late evening Sunday train packed with disappointed English rugby supporters, heading towards London.

London. Never one of Rebus's favourite places. Not that he was a frequent visitor. But this was not pleasure. This was strictly business, and as a representative of the Lothian and Borders Police, he was to be on best behaviour. Or, as his boss had put it so succinctly, 'No fuck ups, John.'

Well, he would do his best. Not that he reckoned there was much he *could* do, right or wrong. But he would do what he could. And if that meant wearing a clean shirt and tie, polished shoes and a respectable jacket, then so be it.

'All tickets, please.'

Rebus handed over his ticket. Somewhere in the corridor up ahead, in the no-man's-land of the buffet car between first and second class, a few voices were raised in a verse of Blake's *Jerusalem*. The Englishman across from Rebus smiled.

'Only a game,' he said to the tins in front of him. 'Only a game.'

The train pulled in to King's Cross five minutes late. It was a quarter past eleven. Rebus was in no hurry. A hotel room had been booked for him in central London, courtesy of the Metropolitan Police. He carried a typed list of notes and directions in his jacket pocket, again sent up from London. He had not brought much luggage with him, feeling that the courtesy of the Met would extend only so far. He expected the trip to last two or three days at most, after which time even they would realise, surely, that he was not going to be of much help to them in their investigations. So: one small suitcase, one sports bag and one briefcase. The suitcase contained two suits, a change of shoes, several pairs of socks and underpants and two shirts (with matching ties). In the sports bag were a small washbag, towel, two paperback novels (one partly read), a travel alarm clock, a thirty-five millimetre camera with flashgun and film, a T-shirt, retractable umbrella, sunglasses, transistor radio, diary, Bible, a bottle containing ninety-seven paracetamol tablets and another bottle (protected by the T-shirt) containing best Islay malt whisky.

The bare essentials, in other words. The briefcase contained notepad, pens, a personal tape recorder, some blank tapes and prerecorded tapes and a thick manila file filled with photocopied sheets of Metropolitan Police paper, ten-by-eight inch colour photographs held together in a small ring-binder affair and newspaper clippings. On the front of this file was a white sticky label with one word typed upon it. The word was WOLFMAN.

Rebus was in no hurry. The night – what was left of it – was his. He had to attend a meeting at ten on Monday morning, but his first night in the capital city could be spent however he chose. He thought he would probably choose to spend it in his hotel room. He waited in his seat until the other passengers had left the train, then slid his bag and briefcase from the luggage rack and made for the sliding door to the carriage, beside which, in another luggage rack, sat his suitcase. Manoeuvring these out of the train door and onto the platform, he paused for a moment and breathed in. The smell was not quite like any other railway station. Certainly it was not like Waverley Station in Edinburgh. The air wasn't quite foetid, but it did seem to Rebus somehow overused and tired. He felt suddenly fatigued. And there was something else in his nostrils, something sweet and revolting at the same time. He couldn't quite think what it reminded him of.

On the concourse, instead of making directly for the Underground, he wandered over to a bookstall. There he purchased an A-Z of London, slipping it into his briefcase. The next morning's editions were just arriving, but he ignored them. This was Sunday, not Monday. Sunday was the Lord's day, which was perhaps why he had packed a Bible along with his other possessions. He hadn't been to a church service in weeks . . . maybe even months. Not since he'd tried the Cathedral on Palmerston Place in fact. It had been a nice place, light and bright, but too far from his home to make for a viable proposition. And besides, it was still organised religion and he had not lost his mistrust of organised religion. If anything, he was warier these days than ever before. He was also hungry. Perhaps he would grab a bite on the way to the hotel. . . .

He passed two women having an animated discussion.

'I heard it on the radio just twenty minutes ago.'

'Done another, has he?'

'That's what they're saying.'

The woman shivered. 'Don't bear thinking about. Did they say it was definitely him?'

'Not definitely, but you just know, don't you?'

There was a truth in that. So, Rebus had arrived in time for another small piece of the drama to unfold around him. Another murder, making four in all. Four in the space of three months. He was a busy little man, this killer they had named the Wolfman. They had named him the Wolfman and then they had sent word to Rebus's boss. Lend us your man, they had said. Let's see what he can do. Rebus's boss, Chief Superintendent Watson, had handed the letter over to him.

'Better take some silver bullets with you, John,' he had said. 'It looks like you're their only hope.' And then he had chuckled, knowing as well as Rebus knew himself that he could be of little help in the case. But Rebus had gnawed on his bottom lip, silent in front of his desk-bound superior. He would do what he could. He would do *everything* he

5

could. Until they saw through him and sent him back home.

Besides, perhaps he needed the break. Watson seemed glad to be rid of him, too.

'If nothing else, it'll keep us out of one another's hair for a while.'

The Chief Superintendent, an Aberdonian, had earned the nickname 'Farmer Watson', a nickname every police officer beneath him in Edinburgh understood. But then one day Rebus, a nip of malt too many beneath his belt, had blurted out the nickname in front of Watson himself, since when he had found himself assigned to more than his fair share of tedious details, desk jobs, lookouts and training courses.

Training courses! At least Watson had a sense of humour. The most recent had been termed 'Management for Senior Officers' and had been a minor disaster – all psychology and how to be nice to junior officers. How to *involve* them, how to *motivate* them, how to *relate* to them. Rebus had returned to his station and tried it for one day, a day of involving, of motivating, of relating. At the end of the day, a DC had slapped a hand onto Rebus's back, smiling.

'Bloody hard work today, John. But I've enjoyed it.'

'Take your hand off my fucking back,' Rebus had snarled. 'And don't call me John.'

The DC's mouth fell open. 'But you said . . .' he began, but didn't bother finishing. The brief holiday was over. Rebus had tried being a manager. Tried it and loathed it.

He was halfway down the steps to the Underground when he stopped, put down his suitcase and briefcase, pulled open the zip on his sports bag and found the transistor radio. Switching it on, he held it to his ear with one hand while the other turned the tuning dial. Eventually, he found a news bulletin, listening as the other travellers passed him, a few of them staring, but mostly ignoring him. At last he heard what he had been waiting for, then switched off the radio and threw it back into the sports bag. Now, he released the two catches on his briefcase and brought out the A-Z. Flipping through the pages of street names at the back, he remembered just how large London really was. Large and populous. Something like ten million, was it? Wasn't that twice the population of Scotland? It didn't bear thinking about. Ten million souls.

'Ten million and one,' Rebus whispered to himself, finding the name he had been looking for.

The Chamber of Horrors

'Not a pretty sight.'

Looking around him, Detective Inspector George Flight wondered whether the sergeant had been referring to the body or to the surrounding area. You could say what you liked about the Wolfman, he wasn't choosy about his turf. This time it was a riverside path. Not that Flight had ever really thought of the Lea as a 'river'. It was a place where supermarket trolleys came to die, a dank stretch of water bordered on one side by marshland and on the other by industrial sites and lo-rise housing. Apparently you could walk the course of the Lea from the Thames to up past Edmonton. The narrow river ran like a mottled black vein from east central London to the most northerly reaches of the capital and beyond. The vast majority of Londoners didn't even know it existed.

George Flight knew about it though. He had been brought up in Tottenham Hale, not far from the Lea. His father had fished on the Navigation section, between Stonebridge and Tottenham Locks. When he was young he had played football on the marshes, smoked illicit cigarettes in the long grass with his gang, fumbled with a blouse or a brassiere on the wasteland just across the river from where he now stood.

He had walked along this path. It was popular on warm Sunday afternoons. There were riverside pubs where you could stand outside supping a pint and watching the Sunday sailors plying their crafts, but at night, only the drunk, the reckless and the brave would use the quiet and ill-lit path. The drunk, the reckless, the brave . . . and the locals. Jean Cooper was a local. Ever since the separation from her husband, she had lived with her sister in a small, recently-built estate just off the towpath. She worked in an off-licence on Lea Bridge Road, and finished work at seven. The riverside path was a quick route home.

8

Her body had been found at nine forty-five by a couple of young lads on their way to one of the pubs. They had run back to Lea Bridge Road and flagged down a passing police car. The operation thereafter had about it a fluid, easy movement. The police doctor arrived, to be met by detectives from Stoke Newington police station, who, recognising the *modus operandi*, contacted Flight.

By the time he arrived, the scene was organised but busy. The body had been identified, questions asked of nearby residents, the sister found. Scene of Crime Officers were in discussion with a couple of people from Forensics. The area around the body had been cordoned off and nobody crossed the tape without first of all donning polythene cover-alls for their feet and hair. Two photographers were busy taking flash photographs under portable lighting powered by a nearby generator. And next to the generator stood an operations van, where another photographer was trying to fix his jammed video camera.

'It's these cheap tapes,' he complained. 'They look like a bargain when you buy them, but then halfway through you find there's a twist or a snag in them.'

'So don't buy cheap tapes,' Flight had advised.

'Thank you, Sherlock,' had been the cameraman's ill-meant response, before once again cursing the tapes, the seller of the tapes and the seller's market stall in Brick Lane. He'd only bought the tapes that day.

Meantime, having discussed their plan of attack, the forensic scientists moved in towards the body armed with sticky tape, scissors and a pile of large polythene bags. Then, with extraordinary care, they began to 'tape' the body in the hope of lifting hairs and fibres from the clothing. Flight watched them from a distance. The portable lights cast a garish white glow over the scene, so that, standing further back in unlit gloom, Flight felt a bit like someone in a theatre, watching a distant play unfold. By God, you had to have patience for a job like this. Everything had to be done by the book and had to be done in meticulous detail. He hadn't gone near the body yet himself. His chance would come later. Perhaps much later.

The wailing started again. It was coming from a police Ford Sierra parked on Lea Bridge Road. Jean Cooper's sister, being comforted in the back of the car by a WPC, being told to drink the hot sweet tea, knowing she would never see her sister alive again. But this was not the worst. Flight knew the worst was still to come, when the sister would formally identify Jean's body in the mortuary.

Jean Cooper had been easy enough to identify. Her handbag lay beside her on the path apparently untouched. In it were letters and house keys with an address tag attached. Flight couldn't help thinking about those house keys. It wasn't very clever to put your address on your keys, was it? A bit late for that now though. A bit late for crime prevention. The crying started again, a long plaintive howl, reaching into the orange glow of the sky above the River Lea and its marshes.

Flight looked towards the body, then retraced the route Jean had taken from Lea Bridge Road. She had walked less than fifty yards before being attacked. Fifty yards from a well-lit and busy main thoroughfare, less than twenty from the back of a row of flats. But this section of path depended for light upon a street lamp which was broken (the council would probably get round to fixing it now) and from whatever illumination was given from the windows of the flats. It was dark enough for the purpose all right. Dark enough for murder most foul.

He couldn't be sure that the Wolfman was responsible, not completely and utterly sure at this early stage. But he could feel it, like a numbing injection in his bones. The terrain was right. The stab wounds reported to him seemed right. And the Wolfman had been quiet for just under three weeks. Three weeks during which the trail had gone stone cold, as cold as a canal path. The Wolfman had taken a risk this time however, striking in late evening instead of at the dead of night. Someone might have seen him. The need for a rapid escape might have led him to leave a clue. Please, God, let him have left a clue. Flight rubbed at his stomach. The worms were gone, consumed by acid. He felt calm, utterly calm, for the first time in days.

'Excuse me.' The voice was muffled, and Flight half-turned to let the diver past him. This diver was followed by another, both of them holding powerful torches. Flight did not envy the police frogmen their job. The river was dark and poisonous, chilled and most probably the consistency of soup. But it had to be searched now. If the killer had dropped something into the Lea by mistake, or had thrown his knife into the river, it had to be recovered as soon as possible. Silt or shifting rubbish might cover it before daybreak. Simply, they couldn't afford the time. And so he had ordered a search just after hearing the news, before he had even left his warm and comfortable home to hurry to the scene. His wife had patted him on the arm. 'Try not to be late.' Both knew the words were meaningless.

He watched the first frogman slip into the water and stared entranced as the water began to glow from the torchlight. The second diver followed the first into the water and disappeared from view. Flight checked the sky. A thick layer of cloud lay still and silent above him. The weather report was for early morning rain. It would dissolve footprints and wash fibres, bloodstains and hair into the hard-packed soil of the path. With any luck, they would complete the initial scene of crime work without the need for plastic tents.

'George!'

Flight turned to greet the newcomer. The man was in his mid-fifties, tall with cadaverous features lit up by a wide grin, or as wide as the long and narrow face would allow. He carried a large black bag in his left hand, and stretched out his right for Flight to shake. By his side walked a handsome woman of Flight's own age. In fact, as far as he could recall she was exactly one month and a day younger than him. Her name was Isobel Penny, and she was, in a euphemistic phrase, the cadaverous man's 'assistant' and 'secretary'. That they had been sleeping together these past eight or nine years was something nobody really discussed, though Isobel had told Flight all about it, for no other reason than that they had been in the same class together at school and had kept in touch with one another ever since.

11

'Hello, Philip,' said Flight, shaking the pathologist's hand.

Philip Cousins was not just a Home Office pathologist: he was by far the *best* Home Office pathologist, with a reputation resulting from twenty-five years' worth of work, twenty-five years during which, to Flight's knowledge, the man had never once 'got it wrong'. Cousins's eye for detail and his sheer bloody doggedness had seen him crack, or help crack, several dozen murder investigations, ranging from stranglings in Streatham to the poisoning of a government official in the West Indies. People who did not know him said that he looked the part, with his dark blue suits and cold grey features. They could not know about his quick and ready humour, his kindness, or the way he thrilled student doctors at his packed lectures. Flight had attended one of those lectures, something to do with arterial sclerosis and hadn't laughed so much in years.

'I thought you two were in Africa,' he said now, pecking Isobel on the cheek by way of greeting.

Cousins sighed. 'We were, but Penny got homesick.' He always called her by her surname. She gave him a playful thump on his forearm.

'You liar!' Then she turned her pale blue eyes to Flight. 'It was Philip,' she said. 'He couldn't bear to be away from his corpses. The first decent holiday we've had in years and he says he's *bored*. Can you believe that, George?'

Flight smiled and shook his head. 'Well, I'm glad you were able to make it. Looks like another victim of the Wolfman.'

Cousins looked over Flight's shoulder towards where the photographers were still photographing, the crouched scientists still sticky-taping, like so many flies about to settle on the corpse. He had examined the first three Wolfman victims, and that sort of continuity helped in a case. It wasn't just that he would know what to look for, what marks were indicative of the Wolfman; he would also spot anything not in keeping with the other killings, anything that might hint at a change of *modus operandi*: a different weapon, say, or a new angle of attack. Flight's

12

mental picture of the Wolfman was coming together piece by tiny piece, but Cousins was the man who could show him where those pieces fitted.

'Inspector Flight?'

'Yes?' A man in a tweed jacket was approaching, carrying several cases and trailing a uniformed constable behind him. He placed the bags on the ground and introduced himself.

'John Rebus.' Flight's face remained blank. 'Inspector John Rebus.' The hand shot out, and Flight accepted it, feeling his grip strongly returned.

'Ah yes,' he said. 'Just arrived, have you?' He glanced meaningfully towards the bags. 'We weren't expecting you until tomorrow, Inspector.'

'Well, I got into King's Cross and heard about . . .' Rebus nodded towards the illuminated towpath. 'So I thought I'd come straight over.'

Flight nodded, trying to appear preoccupied. In fact, he was playing for time while he tried to come to grips with the Scotsman's thick accent. One of the forensic scientists had risen from his squatting position and was coming towards the group.

'Hello, Dr Cousins,' he said, before turning to Flight. 'We're pretty much finished if Dr Cousins wants to take a look.' Flight turned to Philip Cousins, who nodded gravely.

'Come on, Penny.'

Flight was about to follow them, when he remembered the new arrival. He turned back to John Rebus, his eyes immediately drifting down from Rebus's face to his loud and rustic jacket. He looked like something out of *Dr Finlay's Casebook*. Certainly, he looked out of place on this urban towpath at the dead of night.

'Do you want to take a look?' Flight asked generously. He watched as Rebus nodded without enthusiasm. 'Okay, leave your bags where they are then.'

The two men started forward together, Cousins and Isobel a couple of yards in front. Flight pointed towards them. 'Dr Philip Cousins,' he said. 'You've probably heard of him.' But Rebus shook his head slowly. Flight stared at him as though Rebus had just failed to pick out the Queen from a row of postage stamps. 'Oh,' he said coldly. Then, pointing again: 'And that's Isobel Penny, Dr Cousins's assistant.'

Hearing her name, Isobel turned her head back and smiled. She had an attractive face, round and girl-like with a shiny glow to her cheeks. Physically, she was the antithesis of her companion. Though tall, she was well-built – what Rebus's father might have called big boned – and she boasted a healthy complexion to balance Cousins' sickly colour. Rebus couldn't recall ever having seen a really healthy looking pathologist. He put it down to all the time they spent standing under artificial light.

They had reached the body. The first thing Rebus saw was someone aiming a video camera towards him. But the camera moved away again to focus on the corpse. Flight was in conversation with one of the forensics team. Neither looked at the other's face, but concentrated instead on the strips of tape which had been carefully lifted from the corpse and which the scientist now held.

'Yes,' said Flight, 'no need to send them to the lab yet. We'll do another taping at the mortuary.' The man nodded and moved away. There was a noise from the river and Rebus turned to watch as a frogman broke the surface, looked around him, and then dived again. He knew a place like this in Edinburgh, a canal running through the west of the city, between parks and breweries and stretches of nothingness. He'd had to investigate a murder there once, the battered body of a tramp found beneath a road bridge, one foot in the canal. The killer had been easy to find: another tramp, an argument over a can of cider. The court had settled for manslaughter, but it hadn't been man-slaughter. It had been murder. Rebus would never forget that.

'I think we should wrap those hands up right away,' Dr Cousins was saying in a rich Home Counties voice. 'I'll have a good look at them at the mortuary.'

'Right you are,' said Flight, going off to fetch some more

polythene bags. Rebus watched the pathologist at work. He held a small tape recorder in one hand and talked into it from time to time. Isobel Penny meantime had produced a sketch-pad, and was drawing a picture of the body.

'Poor woman was probably dead before she hit the ground,' Cousins was saying. 'Little signs of bruising. Hypostasis seems consistent with the terrain. I'd say she certainly died on this spot.'

By the time Flight returned with some bags, Cousins, watched intermittently by Rebus, had taken readings of the air temperature and of internal temperature. The path on which they all stood was long and reasonably straight. The killer would have had ample visual warning of any approach. At the same time, there were homes and a main road nearby, so any screams would surely have been heard. Tomorrow there would be house-to-house enquiries. The path near the body was littered with rubbish: rusting drinks cans, crisp packets, sweet wrappers, torn and faded sheets of newsprint. In the river itself floated more rubbish and the red handle of a supermarket shopping-trolley broke the surface. Another diver had appeared, head and shoulders bobbing above the water. Where the main road crossed over the river, a crowd had gathered on the bridge, looking down towards the murder scene. Uniformed officers were doing their best to move the sightseers on, cordoning off as much of the area as they could.

'From the marks on the legs, dirt, some grazing and bruising,' continued the voice, 'I would say the victim fell to the ground or was pushed or lowered to the ground on her front. Only later was she turned over.' Dr Cousins's voice was level, disinterested. Rebus took in a few deep breaths and decided he had postponed the inevitable long enough. He had only come here to show willing, to show that he wasn't in London on a joyride. But now that he was here he supposed he should take a good close look at the body for himself. He turned away from the canal, the frogmen, the sightseers, and all the police officers standing behind the cordon. He turned away from the sight of his baggage standing all alone at the end of the path and gazed down on the corpse.

She was lying on her back, arms by her sides, legs together. Her tights and knickers had been pulled down to knee level, but her skirt was covering her, though he could see it was rucked up at the back. Her bright ski-style jacket was unzipped and her blouse had been ripped open, though her bra was intact. She had long straight black hair and wore large circlet earrings. Her face might have been pretty a few years ago, but life had ravaged it, leaving its marks. The killer had left marks, too. There was blood smeared across the face and matting the hair. The source of the blood was a gaping hole in the woman's throat. But there was also blood lying beneath her, spreading out from under the skirt.

'Turning her over,' said Dr Cousins to his tape recorder. He did so, with Flight's help, and then lifted the woman's hair away from the nape of her neck. 'Puncture wound,' he said into his tape recorder, 'consistent with larger wound to the throat. An exit wound, I'd say.'

But Rebus wasn't really listening to the doctor any longer. He was staring in horror at where the woman's skirt was rucked up. There was blood on the body, a lot of blood, staining the small of the back, the buttocks, the tops of the thighs. From the reports in his briefcase, he knew the cause of all this blood, but that didn't make it any easier to face the reality of it, the cold clear horror of it all. He took in more deep breaths. He had never yet vomited at a murder scene and he wasn't about to start now.

'No fuck ups,' his boss had told him. It was a matter of pride. But Rebus knew now that the purpose of his trip to London was very serious indeed. It wasn't to do with 'pride' or 'putting up a good show' or 'doing his best'. It was to do with catching a pervert, a horrifically brutal sadist, and doing so before he could strike again. And if it took silver bullets, by God silver bullets there would be.

Rebus was still shaking when, at the operations van, someone handed him a plastic beaker of tea.

'Thanks.'

He could always blame his gooseflesh on the cold. Not

that it was cold, not really. The cloud cover helped and there was no wind. Of course, London was usually a few degrees warmer than Edinburgh at any time of year and there wasn't the same wind, that bitter and biting wind which whipped across the streets of Edinburgh in summer as well as winter. In fact, if Rebus were asked to describe the weather on this night, the word he would use would be balmy.

He closed his eyes for a moment, not tired, just trying to shut out the sight of Jean Cooper's cooling body. But she seemed etched onto his eyelids in all her grim glory. Rebus had been relieved to note that even Inspector George Flight was not unmoved. His actions, movements and speech had become somehow damped or more muted, as though he were consciously holding back some emotion, the urge to scream or kick out. The divers were coming up from the river, having found nothing. They would look again in the morning, but their voices betrayed a lack of hope. Flight listened to their report and nodded, all the time watched, from behind his beaker of tea, by Rebus.

George Flight was in his late forties, a few years older than Rebus. He wasn't short, yet he had an appearance best described as stocky. There was the hint of a paunch, but a much greater hint of muscle. Rebus didn't rate his own chances against him in a clinch. Flight's wiry brown hair was thin at the crown, but thick elsewhere. He was dressed in a leather bomber jacket and denims. Most men in their forties looked stupid in denims, but not Flight. They fitted his attitude and his brisk, businesslike walk.

A long time before, Rebus had graded CID men into three sartorial groups: the leather-and-denim brigade, who wanted to look as tough as they felt; the suit-and-tie dapper merchants, who were looking for promotion and respect (not necessarily in that order); and the nondescripts, men who wore anything that came to hand of a morning, their year's fashions usually the result of an hour's shopping in a big-name department store.

Most CID men were nondescripts. Rebus reckoned he himself fell into that group. Yet catching a glimpse of himself in a wing-mirror, he noticed that he had a dapper look. Suit-and-ties never got on with leather-and-denims.

Now Flight was shaking hands with an important looking man, who other than for the handshake, kept his hands in his pockets and listened to Flight with head angled downwards, nodding occasionally as though deep in thought. He wore a suit and a black woollen coat. He couldn't have been more crisply dressed if it had been the middle of the day. Most people were beginning to look fatigued, their clothes and faces crumpled. There were only two exceptions: this man and Philip Cousins.

The man was shaking hands with Dr Cousins now and even extended a greeting to Dr Cousins's assistant. And then Flight gestured towards the van . . . no, towards *Rebus*! They were coming towards him. Rebus brought the beaker away from his face, and swapped it from his right to his left hand, just in case a handshake was in the offing.

'This is Inspector Rebus,' Flight said.

'Ah, our man from north of the border,' said the important looking man with a wry, rather superior smile. Rebus returned the smile but looked to Flight.

'Inspector Rebus, this is Chief Inspector Howard Laine.'

'How do you do.' The handshake. Howard Laine: it sounded like a street-name.

'So,' said Chief Inspector Laine, 'you're here to help us with our little problem?'

'Well,' said Rebus, 'I'm not sure what I can do, sir, but rest assured I'll do what I can.'

There was a pause, then Laine smiled but said nothing. The truth hit Rebus like lightning splitting a tree: *they couldn't understand him*! They were standing there smiling at him, but they couldn't understand his accent. Rebus cleared his throat and tried again.

'Whatever I can do to help, sir.'

Laine smiled again. "Excellent, Inspector, excellent. Well, I'm sure Inspector Flight here will show you the ropes. Settled in all right, have you?'

'Well, actually – '

Flight himself interrupted. 'Inspector Rebus came

18

straight here, sir, as soon as he heard about the murder. He's only just arrived in London.'

'Is that so?' Laine sounded impressed, but Rebus could see that the man was growing restless. This was smalltalk, and he did not like to think he had time for smalltalk. His eyes sought some escape. 'Well, Inspector,' he said, 'I'm sure we'll meet again.' And turning to Flight: 'I'd better be off, George. Everything under control?' Flight merely nodded. 'Good, fine, well . . .' And with that the Chief Inspector started back towards his car, accompanied by Flight. Rebus exhaled noisily. He felt completely out of his territory here. He knew when he was not wanted and wondered just whose idea it had been to second him to the Wolfman case. Someone with a warped sense of humour, that was for sure. His boss had passed the letter over to him.

'It seems,' he had said, 'you've become an expert on serial killers, John, and they're a bit short on those in the Met just now. They'd like you to go down to London for a few days, see if you can come up with anything, maybe give them a few ideas.'

Rebus had read the letter through in growing disbelief. It referred to a case from a few years before, the case of a child murderer, a case Rebus had cracked. But that had been personal, not really a serial killer at all.

'I don't know anything about serial killers,' Rebus had protested to his boss.

'Well then, it seems like you'll be in good company, doesn't it?'

And now look at him, standing on a stretch of ground in north-east London, a cup of unspeakably bad tea nursed in both hands, his stomach churning, nerves buzzing, his bags looking as lonely and out of place as he felt. Here to help solve the insoluble, *our man from north of the border*. Whose idea had it been to bring him here? No police force in the country liked to admit failure; yet by lugging Rebus down here the Met was doing precisely that.

Laine had gone and Flight seemed a little more relaxed. He even found time to smile reassuringly across to Rebus before giving orders to two men who, Rebus knew, would be from a funeral parlour. The men went back to their vehicle and returned with a large folded piece of plastic. They crossed the cordon and stopped at the body, laying the plastic out beside it. It was a translucent bag, over six feet long with a zip running from head to toe. Dr Cousins was in close attendance as the two men opened the bag and lifted the body into it, closing the zipper. One photographer had decided to shoot off a few more flash photographs of the spot where the body had lain, while the attendants carried the corpse back through the cordon and up to their vehicle.

Rebus noticed that the crowd of onlookers had disappeared, and only a few curious souls remained. One of them, a young man, was carrying a crash helmet and wore a shiny black leather jacket with shinier silver zips. A very tired constable was trying to move him on.

Rebus felt like an onlooker himself and thought of all the TV dramas and films he'd seen, with detectives swarming over the murder site in minute one (destroying any forensic evidence in the process) and solving the murder by minute fifty-nine or eighty-nine. Laughable, really. Police work was just that: work. Relentless, routine, dull, frustrating, and above all time-consuming. He checked his watch. It was exactly 2 am. His hotel was back in central London, tucked somewhere behind Piccadilly Circus. It would take another thirty to forty minutes to get back there, always supposing a spare patrol car was available.

'Coming?'

It was Flight, standing a few yards in front of him.

'Might as well,' said Rebus, knowing exactly what Flight was talking about, or more accurately *where* he was talking about.

Flight smiled. 'I'll give you this, Inspector Rebus, you don't give up.'

'The famous tenacity of the Scots,' said Rebus, quoting from one of Sunday's newspaper rugby reports. Flight actually laughed. It didn't last long, but it made Rebus feel glad that he'd come here tonight. The ice hadn't been broken completely perhaps, but an important chunk had been chipped away from one corner of the berg.

'Come on then. I've got my car. I'll get one of the drivers to put your bags in his boot. The lock's stuck on mine. Somebody tried to crowbar it open a few weeks back.' He glanced towards Rebus, a rare moment of eye contact. 'Nowhere is safe these days,' he said. 'Nowhere.'

There was already a lot of commotion up at road level. Voices and the slamming shut of car doors. Some officers would stay behind, of course, guarding the site. And a few might be going back to the warmth of the station or – luxury hardly to be imagined! – their own beds. But a few of the cars would be following the funeral van, following it all the way to the mortuary.

Rebus travelled in the front of Flight's own car. Both men spent the journey in desperate pursuit of a conversational opening and as a result said very little until they were near their destination.

'Do we know who she was?' asked Rebus.

'Jean Cooper,' said Flight. 'We found ID in her handbag.'

'Any reason for her to be on that path?'

'She was going home from work. She worked in an off-licence nearby. Her sister tells us she finished work at seven.'

'When was the body found?'

'Quarter to ten.'

'That's a fair gap.'

'We've got witnesses who saw her in the Dog and Duck. That's a pub near where she works. She used to go in there for a drink some evenings. The barmaid reckons she left at nine or thereabouts.'

Rebus stared out of the windscreen. The roads were still fairly busy considering the time of night and they passed groups of youthful and raucous pedestrians.

'There's a club in Stokie,' Flight explained. 'Very popular, but the buses have stopped by the time it comes out so everyone walks home.'

Rebus nodded, then asked: 'Stokie?'

Flight smiled. 'Stoke Newington. You probably passed through it on your way from King's Cross.'

'God knows,' said Rebus. 'It all looked the same to me. I think my taxi driver had me down as a tourist. We took so long from King's Cross I think we might have come via the M25.' Rebus waited for Flight to laugh, but all he raised was a sliver of a smile. There was another pause. 'Was this Jean Cooper single?' Rebus asked at last.

'Married.'

'She wasn't wearing a wedding ring.'

Flight nodded. 'Separated. She lived with her sister. No kids.'

'And she went drinking by herself.'

Flight glanced towards Rebus. 'What are you saying?'

Rebus shrugged. 'Nothing. It's just that if she liked a good time, maybe that's how she met her killer.'

'It's possible.'

'At any rate, whether she knew him or not, the killer could have followed her from the pub.'

'We'll be talking to everybody who was there, don't worry.'

'Either that,' said Rebus, thinking aloud, 'or the killer was waiting by the river for anyone who happened along. Somebody might have seen him.'

'We'll be asking around,' said Flight. His voice had taken on a much harder edge.

'Sorry,' said Rebus. 'A severe case of teaching my granny to suck eggs.'

Flight turned to him again. They were about to take a left through some hospital gates. 'I am not your granny,' he said. 'And any comments you have to make are welcome. Maybe eventually you'll come up with something I haven't already thought of.'

'Of course,' said Rebus, 'this couldn't have happened in Scotland.'

'Oh?' Flight had a half-sneer on his face. 'Why's that then? Too civilised up there in the frozen north? I remember when you had the worst football hooligans in the world. Maybe you still do, only these days they look like butter wouldn't melt in their underpants.'

But Rebus was shaking his head. 'No, it wouldn't have

happened to Jean Cooper, that's all I meant. Our off-licences don't open on Sunday.'

Rebus fell silent and stared fixedly at the windscreen, keeping his thoughts to himself, thoughts which ran along a very simple plane: fuck you, too, pal. Over the years, those four words had become his mantra. Fuck you, too, pal. FYTP. It had taken the Londoner only the length of a twenty-minute car ride to show what he really thought of the Scots.

As Rebus got out of the car, he glanced in through the rear window and saw, for the first time, the contents of the back seat. He opened his mouth to speak, but Flight raised a knowing hand.

'Don't even ask,' he growled, slamming shut the driver's-side door. 'And listen, I'm sorry about what I said . . .'

Rebus merely shrugged, but his eyebrows descended in a private and thoughtful frown. After all, there had to be *some* logical explanation as to why a Detective Inspector would have a huge stuffed teddy bear in the back of his car at the scene of a murder. It was just that Rebus was damned if he could think of one right this second . . .

Mortuaries were places where the dead stopped being people and turned instead into bags of meat, offal, blood and bone. Rebus had never been sick at the scene of a crime, but the first few times he had visited a mortuary the contents of his stomach had fairly quickly been rendered up for examination.

The mortuary technician was a gleeful little man with a livid birthmark covering a full quarter of his face. He seemed to know Dr Cousins well enough and had prepared everything for the arrival of the deceased and the usual retinue of police officers. Cousins checked the post-mortem room, while Jean Cooper's sister was taken quietly into an ante-room, there to make the formal identification. It took only a tearful few seconds, after which she was escorted well away from the scene by consoling officers. They would take her home, but Rebus doubted if she would get any sleep. In fact, knowing how long a scrupulous pathologist could take, he was beginning to doubt that any of them would get to bed before morning.

Eventually, the body bag was brought into the post-mortem room and the corpse of Jean Cooper placed on a slab, beneath the hum and glare of powerful strip lighting. The room was antiseptic but antique. Its tiled walls were cracking and there was a stinging aroma of chemicals. Voices were kept muffled, not so much out of respect but from a strange kind of fear. The mortuary, after all, was one vast memento mori, and what was about to happen to Jean Cooper's body would serve to remind each and every one of them that if the body were a temple, then it was possible to loot that temple, scattering its treasures, revealing its precious secrets.

A hand landed gently on Rebus's shoulder, and he turned, startled, towards the man who was standing there. 'Man' was by way of simplification. This tall and unsmiling individual had cropped fair hair and the acne-ridden face of an adolescent. He looked about fourteen, but Rebus placed him in his mid-twenties.

'You're the Jock, aren't you?' There was interest in the voice, but little emotion. Rebus said nothing. FYTP. 'Yeah, thought so. Cracked the case yet, have you?' The grin accompanying this question was three-quarters sneer and one-quarter scowl. 'We don't *need* any help.'

'Ah,' said George Flight, 'I see you've already met DC Lamb. I was just about to introduce you.'

'Delighted,' said Rebus, gazing stonily at the join-the-dots pattern of spots on Lamb's forehead. Lamb! No surname in history, Rebus felt, had ever been less deserved, less accurate. Over by the slab, Dr Cousins cleared his throat noisily.

'Gentlemen,' he said to the room at large. It was little more than an indication that he was about to start work. The room fell quiet again. A microphone hung down from the ceiling to within a few feet of the slab. Cousins turned to the technician. 'Is this thing on now?' The technician nodded keenly from between arranging a row of clanging metallic instruments along a tray.

Rebus knew all the instruments, had seen them all in action. The cutters and the saws and the drills. Some of them were electrical, some needed a human force to drive them home. The sounds the electrical ones made were horrible, but at least the job was over quickly; the manual tools made similarly revolting sounds that seemed to last forever. Still, there would be an interval before that particular shop of horrors. First of all there was the slow and careful business of removing the clothing and bagging it up for Forensics.

As Rebus and the others watched, the two photographers clicked away, one taking black and white shots and the other colour, recording for posterity each stage of the process. The video cameraman had given up, however, his equipment having jammed irreparably on one of the bargain tapes. Or at least that was the story which kept him away from the mortuary.

Finally, when the corpse was naked, Cousins pointed to a few areas meriting particular close-up shots. Then the Forensics men moved in again, armed with more lengths of sticky tape. Now that the body was unclothed, the same process as was carried out on the tow-path had to be gone through again. Not for nothing were these people known as Sellotape Men.

Cousins wandered over towards the group where Rebus, Flight and Lamb stood.

'I'd kill for a cup of tea, George.'

'I'll see what I can do, Philip. What about Isobel?'

Cousins looked back towards where Isobel Penny stood, making another drawing of the corpse despite the welter of camera shots. 'Penny,' he called, 'care for a cuppa?' Her eyes opened a little and she nodded enthusiastically.

'Right,' said Flight, moving towards the door. Rebus thought the man seemed more than a little relieved to be leaving, albeit temporarily.

'Nasty little chap,' Cousins commented. Rebus wondered for a moment if he were talking about George Flight, but Cousins waved a hand towards the corpse. 'To do this sort of thing time after time, without motive, out of some need for . . . well, pleasure, I suppose.'

'There's always a motive, sir,' said Rebus. 'You just said so yourself. Pleasure, that's his motive. But the way he kills. What he does. There's some other motive there. It's just that we can't see it yet.'

Cousins stared at him. Rebus could see a warm light in his deep eyes. 'Well, Inspector, let us hope *somebody* spots whatever it is before too long. Four deaths in as many months. The man's as constant as the moon.'

Rebus smiled. 'But we all know that werewolves are affected by the moon, don't we?'

Cousins laughed. It was deep and resonant and sounded extraordinarily out of place in this environment. Lamb wasn't laughing, wasn't even smiling. He was following little of this conversation, and the realisation pleased Rebus. But Lamb wasn't going to be left out.

'I reckon he's barking mad. Hee, get it?'

'Well,' said Cousins, as though this joke was too well-worn even to merit acknowledgment, 'must press on.' He turned towards the slab. 'If you've finished, gentlemen?' The Forensics men nodded in unison. 'Jewellery removed?' They nodded again. 'Good. Then if you are ready, I suggest we begin.'

The beginning was never too awful. Measurements, a physical description – five feet and seven inches tall, brown hair, that sort of thing. Fingernail scrapings and clippings were deposited in yet more polythene bags. Rebus made a note to buy shares in whichever company manufactured these bags. He'd seen murder investigations go through hundreds of them.

Slowly but determinedly, things got worse. Swabs were taken from Jean Cooper's vagina, then Cousins got down to some serious work.

'Large puncture wound to the throat. From size of wound, I'd say the knife itself had been twisted in the wound. A small knife. From the extent of the exit wound I would say the blade was about five inches long, perhaps a little less, and about an inch deep, ending in a very fine point. The skin surrounding the entry wound shows some bruising, perhaps caused by the hilt-guard or handle. This would seem to indicate that the knife was driven in with a certain amount of force.

'The hands and arms show no signs of defence wounding, so the victim had no time in which to defend herself. The possibility exists that she was approached from behind. There is some colouring around the mouth and the victim's lipstick had been slightly smeared across her right cheek. If she was approached from behind, a possible scenario would be that the attacker's left hand closed over her mouth to stop her from screaming, thus smearing the lipstick while the attacker stabbed with the right hand. The wound to the throat shows a slight downward angle, which would indicate someone taller than the victim.'

Cousins cleared his throat again. Well, thought Rebus, so far they could strike the mortuary attendant and one of the photographers off the possible list of suspects: everyone else in the room was five feet eight or over.

The pause in proceedings gave the onlookers a chance to shuffle their feet, clear their own throats, and glance at each other, taking note of how pale this or that face was. Rebus was surprised at the pathologist's 'scenarios': that was supposed to be *their* job, not his. All the pathologists Rebus had ever worked with had given the bare facts, leaving the deductions to Rebus himself. But Cousins obviously did not work that way. Perhaps he was a frustrated detective. Rebus still found it hard to believe that people came to pathology through choice.

Tea appeared, carried in three beakers on a plastic tray by Inspector Flight. Cousins and Isobel Penny took a cup each, and Flight himself took the other. There were jealous stares from a few dry-mouthed officers. Rebus was among them.

'Now,' said Cousins between sips, 'I'm going to examine the anal wound.'

It just kept on getting worse. Rebus tried to concentrate on what Cousins was saying, but it wasn't easy. The same knife had been used to make several stabs to the anus. There were friction marks on the thighs from where the tights had been roughly pulled down. Rebus looked over to Isobel Penny, but, apart from some slight heightening of the colour in her cheeks, she seemed dispassionate. A cool customer and no mistake. But then she'd probably seen worse in her time. No, no, she couldn't possibly have seen worse than *this*. Could she?

'The stomach is interesting,' Cousins was saying. 'The blouse has been torn away to expose the stomach, and there are two lines of curved indentations in the skin, enough to have bruised and broken the skin, but there is little actual marking of the skin and no blood, from which I would say that this act was perpetrated only *after* the stabbings. After, in fact, the victim was dead. There are a few dried stains on the stomach near these bite marks. Without prejudging, past evidence from three very similar cases showed these stains to be saline in nature – teardrops or perhaps beads of sweat. I'm now going to take a deep body temperature.'

Rebus felt parched. He was hot, and the tiredness was seeping into his bones, lack of sleep giving everything a hallucinatory quality. There were halos around the pathologist, his assistant, and the technician. The walls seemed to be moving, and Rebus dared not concentrate on them for fear that he would lose his balance. He happened to catch Lamb's eye and the Detective Constable gave him an ugly grin and an uglier wink.

The body was washed now, washed for the first time, freed from a staining of light brown and black, from the pale matt covering of blood. Cousins examined it again, finding nothing new, after which another set of fingerprints was taken. Then came the internal examination.

A deep incision was made down the front of the body. Blood samples were taken and handed to the forensics team, as were samples of urine, stomach contents, liver, body hair (eyebrows included) and tissue. The process used to make Rebus impatient. It was obvious how the victim had died, so why bother with everything else? But he had learned over the years that what you could *see*, the external injuries, often wasn't as important as what you couldn't see, the tiny secrets only a microscope or a chemical test could reveal. So he had learned patience and exercised it now, stifling a yawn every half minute or so.

'Not boring you am I?' Cousins's voice was a polite murmur. He looked up from his work and caught Rebus's eyes, then smiled.

'Not a bit,' said Rebus.

'That's all right then. I'm sure we'd all rather be at home tucked up in bed than in this place.' Only the birthmarked technician seemed doubtful as to the truth of this statement. Cousins was reaching a hand into the corpse's chest. 'I'll be out of here as soon as I can.'

It wasn't the sight of this examination, Rebus decided, that turned men pale. It was the accompanying sound effects. The tearing of flesh, as though a butcher were yanking meat from a flank. The bubbling of liquids and the soft rasping of the cutting tools. If he could somehow block up his ears, maybe everything would be bearable. But on the contrary, his ears seemed extraordinarily sensitive in this room. Next time, he'd bring plugs of cotton wool with him. Next time . . .

The chest and abdominal organs were removed and taken to a clean slab, where a hose was used to wash them clean before Cousins dissected them. The attendant meantime was called into action, removing the brain with the help of a tiny powered circular-saw. Rebus had his eyes shut now, but the room seemed to swirl all the same. Not long to go now though. Not long, thank God. But it wasn't just the sounds now, was it? It was the smell too, that unmistakable aroma of raw meat. It clung to the nostrils like perfume, filling the lungs, catching the back of the throat and clinging there, so that eventually it became a tang in the mouth and he found himself actually tasting it. His stomach moved momentarily, but he rubbed it gently, surreptitiously with a hand. Not surreptitiously enough.

'If you're going to throw up,' it was Lamb again, like a succubus over his shoulder, hissing, 'go outside.' And then the chuckle, throaty and slow like a stalled engine. Rebus half-turned his head and gave a dangerous smile.

Soon enough, the whole mess of matter was being put together again, and Rebus knew that by the time any grieving relatives viewed the mortal remains of Jean Cooper, the body would look quite natural.

As ever, by the end of the autopsy the room had been reduced to silent introspection. Each man and woman present was made of the same stuff as Jean Cooper, and now they stood, momentarily stripped of their individual personalities. They were all bodies, all animals, all collections of viscera. The only difference between them and Jean Cooper was that their hearts still pumped blood. But one day soon enough each heart would stop, and that would be an end of it, save for the possibility of a visit to this butcher's shop, this abattoir.

Cousins removed his rubber gloves and washed his hands thoroughly, accepted from the attendant a proffered sheaf of paper towels. 'That's about it then, gentlemen, until Penny can type up the notes. Murdered between nine o'clock and nine-thirty I'd guess. Same *modus operandi* as our so-called Wolfman. I think I've just examined his fourth victim. I'll get in Anthony Morrison tomorrow, let him have a look at the teeth-marks. See what he says.'

Since everyone seemed to know except Rebus, Rebus asked, 'Who's Anthony Morrison?'

Flight was first to answer. 'A dentist.'

'A dental pathologist,' corrected Cousins. 'And quite a good one. He's got details of the other three murders. His analyses of the bite-marks have been quite useful.' Cousins turned to Flight for confirmation of this, but Flight's eyes were directed towards his shoes, as if to say *I wouldn't go that far*.

'Well,' said Cousins, seeming to take the silent hint, 'at any rate, you know my findings. It's down to your lab chaps now. There's precious little there . . .' Cousins nodded back towards the scooped out husk of the corpse, 'to help with your investigation. That being so, I think I'll go home to bed.'

Flight seemed to realise that Cousins was displeased with him. 'Thank you, Philip.' And the detective lifted a hand to rest it against the pathologist's arm. Cousins looked at the hand, then at Flight, and smiled.

The performance at an end, the audience began to shuffle out into the cold, still darkness of an emerging day. By

Rebus's watch, it was four thirty. He felt completely exhausted, could happily have lain down on the lawn in front of the main building and taken a nap, but Flight was walking towards him, carrying his bags.

'Come on,' he said. 'I'll give you a lift.'

In his fragile state, Rebus felt this to be the nicest, kindest thing anyone had said to him in weeks. 'Are you sure you have room?' he said. 'I mean, with the teddy bear and all.'

Flight paused. 'Or if you'd prefer to walk, Inspector?'

Rebus threw up his hands in surrender, then, when the door was unlocked, slipped into the passenger seat of Flight's red Sierra. The seat seemed to wrap itself around him.

'Here,' said Flight, handing a hip flask to Rebus. Rebus unscrewed the top of the flask and sniffed. 'It won't kill you,' Flight called. This was probably true. The aroma was of whisky. Not great whisky, not a smoky island malt, but a decent enough proprietary brand. Well, it would help keep him awake perhaps until they reached the hotel. Rebus toasted the windscreen and let the liquid trickle into his mouth.

Flight got behind the steering wheel and started the car, then, as the car idled, accepted the flask from Rebus and drank from it greedily.

'How far to the hotel from here?' Rebus asked.

'About twenty minutes at this time of night,' said Flight, screwing tight the stopper and replacing the flask in his pocket. 'That's if we stop for red lights.'

'You have my permission to run every red light you see.'

Flight laughed tiredly. Both men were wondering how to turn the conversation around to the autopsy.

'Best leave it until morning, eh?' said Rebus, speaking for them both. Flight merely nodded and moved off, waving to Cousins and Isobel Penny, who were about to get into their car. Rebus stared out of his side window to where DC Lamb stood beside his own car, a flash little sports model. Typical, thought Rebus. Just typical. Lamb stared back at him, and then gave that three-quarters sneer again.

31

FYTP, Rebus mentally intoned. FYTP. Then he turned in his seat to examine the teddy bear behind him. Flight was resolutely refusing to take the hint, and Rebus, though curious, wasn't about to jeopardise whatever relationship he might be able to strike up with this man by asking the obvious question. Some things were always best left until morning.

The whisky had cleared his nostrils, lungs and throat. He breathed deeply, seeing in his mind the little mortuary attendant, that livid birthmark, and Isobel Penny, sketching like any amateur artist. She might have been in front of a museum exhibit for all the emotion she had shown. He wondered what her secret was, the secret of her absolute calmness, but thought he probably knew in any case. Her job had become merely that: a job. Maybe one day Rebus would feel the same way. But he hoped not.

If anything, Flight and Rebus said less during the drive to the hotel than they had done on the way to the mortuary. The whisky was working on Rebus's empty stomach and the interior of the car was oppressively hot. He tried opening his window a quarter of an inch, but the blast of chill air only made things worse.

The autopsy was being played out again before him. The cutting tools, the lifting of organs out of the body, the incisions and inspections, Cousins's face peering at spongy tissue from no more than an inch away. One twitch and his face would have been smothered in . . . Isobel Penny watching all, recording all, the slice from throat to pubis . . . London sped past him. Flight, true to his word, was cruising through some red lights and slowing merely for others. There were still cars on the streets. The city never slept. Nightclubs, parties, drifters, the homeless. Sleepless dog-walkers, all night bakeries and beigel shops. Some spelt 'beigel' and some spelt 'bagel'. What the hell was a beigel? Wasn't that what they were always eating in Woody Allen films?

Samples from her eyebrows, for Christ's sake. What use were samples from her eyebrows? They should be concentrating on the attacker, not the victim. Those teeth-marks. What was the dentist's name again? Not a dentist, a dental *pathologist*. Morrison. Yes, that was it. Morrison, like the street in Edinburgh, Morrison Street, not too far from the brewery canal, where the swans lived, a single pair of swans. What happened when they died? Did the brewery replace them? So damned hot in this shiny red car. Rebus could feel his insides wanting to become his outsides. The knife twisted in the throat. A small knife. He could almost visualise it. Something like a kitchen knife. Sharp, sour taste in his mouth.

'Nearly there,' said Flight. 'Just along Shaftesbury Avenue. That's Soho on the right. By God, we've cleaned that den up this past few years. You wouldn't believe it. You know, I've been thinking, where the body was found, it's not so far from where the Krays used to live. Somewhere on Lea Bridge Road. I was just a young copper when they were on the go.'

'Please . . .' said Rebus.

'They did somebody in Stokie. Jack McVitie, I think it was. Jack the Hat, they called him.'

'Can you stop here?' Rebus blurted out. Flight looked at him.

'What's up?'

'I need some air. I'll walk the rest of the way. Just stop the car, please.'

Flight began to protest, but pulled over to the kerb. Stepping out of the car, Rebus immediately felt better. There was cold sweat on his forehead, neck and back. He breathed deeply. Flight deposited his bags on the pavement.

'Thanks again,' said Rebus. 'Sorry about this. Just point me in the general direction.'

'Just off the Circus,' Flight said.

Rebus nodded. 'I hope there's a night porter.' Yes, he was feeling much better.

'It's a quarter to five,' said Flight. 'You'll probably catch the day shift coming on.' He laughed, but the laugh died quickly and he gave Rebus a serious nod of his head. 'You made your point tonight, John. Okay?'

Rebus nodded back. *John*. Another chip from the iceberg, or just good management?

'Thanks,' he said. They shook hands. 'Are we still on for a meeting at ten?'

'Let's make it eleven, eh? I'll have someone pick you up from your hotel.'

Rebus nodded and picked up his bags. Then bent down again towards the car's back window. 'Good night, teddy,' he said.

'Watch you don't get lost!' Flight called to him from the car. Then the car moved off, making a screeching u-turn before roaring back the way they had come. Rebus looked around him. Shaftesbury Avenue. The buildings seemed about to swamp him. Theatres. Shops. Litter: the debris from a Sunday night out. A dull roar preceded the arrival, from one of the misty side streets, of a dustcart. The men were dressed in orange overalls. They paid no attention to Rebus as he trudged past them. How long was this street? It seemed to follow a vast curve, longer than he had expected.

Bloody London. Then he spotted Eros atop his fountain, but there was something wrong. The Circus was no longer a Circus. Eros had been paved in, so that traffic had to sweep past it rather than around it. Why the hell had anyone decided to do that? A car was slowing behind him, coming parallel with him. White car with an orange stripe: a police car. The officer in the passenger seat had wound down his window and now called out to him.

'Excuse me, sir, do you mind telling me where you're going?'

'What?' The question stunned Rebus, stopped him in his tracks. The car had stopped too and both driver and passenger were emerging.

'Are those your bags, sir?'

Rebus felt it rise within him, a shining hard steel pole of anger. Then he happened to catch sight of himself in the window of the patrol car. A quarter to five on the streets of London. A dishevelled, unshaven man, a man obviously without sleep, carrying a suitcase, a bag and a briefcase. A *briefcase*? Who the hell would be carrying a briefcase around at this time of the morning? Rebus put down his luggage and rubbed at the bridge of his nose with one hand. And before he knew what was happening, his shoulders began moving, his body convulsing with laughter. The two uniformed officers were looking at one another. Rebus sniffed back the laughter and reached into his inside pocket. One of the officers stepped back a pace.

'Take it easy, son,' Rebus said. He produced his ID. 'I'm on your side.' The less cagey officer, the passenger, took the ID from Rebus, examined it, then handed it back.

'You're a long way off your patch, sir.'

'You don't have to tell me that,' said Rebus. 'What's your name, son?'

The constable was wary now. 'Bennett, sir. Joey Bennett. I mean, Joseph Bennett.'

'All right, Joey. Would you like to do me a favour?' The constable nodded. 'Do you know the Prince Royal Hotel?'

'Yes, sir.' Bennett began to point with his left hand. 'It's about fifty yards – '

'All right,' Rebus interrupted. 'Just show me, will you?' The young man said nothing. 'Will you do that, Constable Bennett?'

'Yes, sir.'

Rebus nodded. Yes, he could handle London. He could take it on and win. 'Right,' he said, moving off towards the Prince Royal. 'Oh,' he said, turning back and taking in both men with his glance, 'and bring my bags, will you?' Rebus had his back to them again, but he could almost hear the sound of two jaws dropping open. 'Or,' he called back, 'shall I just inform Chief Inspector Laine that two of his officers harassed me on my first night as his guest in this fine city?'

Rebus kept on walking, hearing the two officers pick up his luggage and hurry after him. They were arguing as to whether or not they should leave the patrol car unlocked. He was smiling, despite everything. A small victory, a bit of a cheat, but what the hell. This was London, after all. This was Shaftesbury Avenue. And that was showbiz.

★　★　★

Home at last, she had a good wash, and after that she felt a little better. She had brought in a black bin-liner from the boot of her car. It contained the clothes she had been wearing, cheap flimsy things. Tomorrow evening she would tidy the back garden and light a bonfire.

She wasn't crying any more. She had calmed down. She always calmed down afterwards. From a polythene shopping bag she removed another polythene bag, from which she removed the bloodied knife. The kitchen sink was full of boiling, soapy water. The polythene bags went into the bin-liner with the clothes, the knife went into the sink. She washed it carefully, emptying and refilling the washing bowl, all the time humming to herself. It wasn't a recognisable song, nor even really a tune. But it calmed her, it soothed her, the way her mother's hummed lullabies always had.

There, all done. It was hard work, and she was pleased to be finished with it. Concentration was the key. A lapse in concentration, and you could make a slip, then fail to spot that slip. She rinsed the sink three times, sluicing away every last speckle of blood, and left the knife to dry on the draining-board. Then she walked out into the hallway and paused at one of the doors while she found the key.

This was her secret room, her picture gallery. Inside, one wall was all but covered by oil and watercolour paintings. Three of these paintings were damaged beyond repair. A pity, since all three had been favourites. Her favourite now was a small countryside stream. Simple, pale colours and a naive style. The stream was in the foreground and beside it sat a man and a boy, or it could have been a man and a girl. It was hard to tell, that was the problem with the naive style. It was not as though she could even ask the artist, for the artist had been dead for years.

She tried not to look at the other wall, the wall directly opposite. It was a horrid wall. She didn't like what she could see there from the corner of one eye. She decided that what she liked about her favourite painting was its size. It was about ten inches by eight, excluding the rather Baroque gilt frame (which did not suit it at all – her mother had never

36

had much taste in frames). These petite dimensions, added to the washed colours, gave the whole a subtlety and a lack of vision, a humility, a gentleness, which pleased her. Of course, it depicted no great truth, this painting. In fact, it was a monstrous lie, the absolute opposite of the facts. There had been no stream, no touching scene of father and child. There had been only horror. That was why Velasquez was her favourite painter: shadowplay, rich shades of black, skulls and suspicion . . . the dark heart exposed.

'The dark heart.' She nodded to herself. She had seen things, felt things, which few were ever privileged to witness. This was her life. This was her existence. And the painting began to mock her, the stream turning into a cruel turquoise grin.

Calmly, humming to herself again she picked up a pair of scissors from a nearby chair and began to slash at the painting with regular vertical strokes, then horizontal strokes, then vertical again, tearing and tearing its heart out until the scene disappeared forever.

Underground

'And this,' said George Flight, 'is where the Wolfman was born.'

Rebus looked. It was a depressing location for a birth. A cobblestoned alley, a cul-de-sac, the buildings three storeys high, every window either boarded up or barred and grilled. The black bags of rubbish looked to have been languishing by the side of the road for weeks. A few had been impaled on the steel spiked fencing in front of the shut-up windows, and these bags leaked their rank contents the way a cracked sewage pipe would.

'Nice,' he said.

'The buildings are mainly disused. Local bands use the basement of one of them as a practice room, and make quite a racket while they're about it.' Flight pointed to a barred and grilled window. 'And I think that's a clothing manufacturer or distributor. Anyway, he hasn't been back since we started taking an interest in the street.'

'Oh?' Rebus sounded interested, but Flight shook his head.

'Nothing suspicious in that, believe me. These guys use slave labour, Bangladeshis, mostly illegal immigrants. The last thing they want is policemen sniffing around. They'll move the machines and set up again somewhere else.'

Rebus nodded. He was looking around the cul-de-sac, trying to remember, from the photographs he had been sent, just where the body had been found.

'It was there.' Flight was pointing to a gate in the iron railings. Ah yes, Rebus remembered now. Not at street level, but down some stone steps leading to a basement. The victim had been found at the bottom of the steps, same *modus operandi* as last night, down to the bitemarks on the stomach. Rebus opened his briefcase and brought out the manila folder, opening it at the sheet he needed.

'Maria Watkiss, age thirty-eight. Occupation: prostitute. Body found on Tuesday 16th January by council workmen. Estimated that victim had been murdered two to three days prior to being discovered. Rudimentary attempt had been made to conceal body.'

Flight nodded towards one of the impaled bin-liners. 'He emptied a bag of rubbish out over her. It pretty well covered the body. The rats alerted the workmen.'

'Rats?'

'Dozens of them, from all accounts. They'd had a bloody good feed, had those rats.'

Rebus was standing at the top of the steps. 'We reckon,' said Flight, 'the Wolfman must have paid her for a knee-trembler and brought her down here. Or maybe she brought him. She worked out of a pub on Old Street. It's a five minute walk. We interviewed the regulars, but nobody saw her leave with anyone.'

'Maybe he was in a car?'

'It's more than possible. Judging by the physical distance between the murder sites, he must be pretty mobile.'

'It says in the report that she was married.'

'That's right. Her old man, Tommy, he knew she was on the game. It didn't bother him, so long as she handed over the cash.'

'And he didn't report her missing?'

Flight wrinkled his nose. 'Not Tommy. He was on a bender at the time, practically comatose with drink when we went to see him. He said later that Maria often disappeared for a few days, told us she used to go off to the seaside with one or two of her regular johns.'

'I don't suppose you've been able to find these . . . clients?'

'Leave it out.' Flight laughed as though this were the best joke he'd heard all week. 'For the record, Tommy thought one of them might be called Bill or Will. Does that help?'

'It narrows things down,' Rebus said with a smile.

'In any event,' said Flight, 'I doubt Tommy would have come to us for help if she hadn't come back. He's got form as long as your inside leg. To tell you the truth, he was our first suspect.'

'It follows.' Every policeman knew it as a universal truth: most murders happen in the family.

'A couple of years back,' Flight was saying, 'Maria was beaten up pretty badly. A hospital case, in fact. Tommy's doing. She'd been seeing another man and he hadn't been paying for it, if you understand my meaning. And a couple of years before that, Tommy served time for aggravated assault. It would have been rape if we could have got the woman into the witness box, but she was scared seven colours shitless. There were witnesses, but we were never going to pin rape on him. So aggravated assault it was. He got eight months.'

'A violent man then.'

'You could say that.'

'With a record of particular violence against women.'

Flight nodded. 'It looked good at first. We thought we could pin Maria's murder on him and make it stick. But nothing added up. He had an alibi for openers. Then there were the bitemarks: not his size, according to the dentist.'

'You mean Dr Morrison?'

'Yes, that's right. I call him the dentist to annoy Philip.' Flight scratched at his chin. The elbow of his leather jacket gave a creak. 'Anyway, nothing added up. And then when the second murder came along, well, we knew we were working in a different league from Tommy.'

'You're absolutely sure of that?'

'John, I'm not *absolutely* sure what colour of socks I've put on in the morning, I'm sometimes not even sure that I've put socks on at all. But I'm *fairly* sure this isn't Tommy Watkiss's work. He gets his kicks from watching Arsenal, not mutilating dead women.'

Rebus's eyes had not left Flight's. 'Your socks are blue,' he said. Flight looked down, saw that this was indeed the case, and smiled broadly.

'They're also different shades,' Rebus added.

'Bloody hell, so they are.'

'I'd still like to talk to Mr Watkiss,' Rebus continued. 'No hurry, and if it's all right with you.'

Flight shrugged. 'Whatever you say, Sherlock. Now, shall we get out of this shit-hole, or is there anything else you want to see?'

'No,' said Rebus. 'Let's get out of here.' They started back towards the mouth of the cul-de-sac, where Flight's car waited. 'What's this part of town called again?'

'Shoreditch. Remember your nursery rhymes? "When I am rich, say the bells of Shoreditch".'

Yes, Rebus had a vague memory. A memory of his mother, holding him on her knee, or maybe it was his father, singing him songs and bouncing the knee in time. It had never happened that way, but he had a memory of it all the same. They were at the end of the cul-de-sac now. A larger road flowed past, busy with daytime traffic. The buildings were black with grime, windows thick with the stuff. Offices of some kind, warehouses. No shops, save one selling professional kitchenware. No houses or even flats in the upper storeys by the look of it. No one to hear a muffled scream at the dead of night. No one to see, from an unwashed window, the killer slinking away, dappled with blood.

Rebus stared back into the cul-de-sac, then up at the corner of the first building, where a barely legible plaque bore the cul-de-sac's name: Wolf Street E1.

This was the reason why the police had come to call the killer Wolfman. Nothing to do with the savagery of his attacks, or the teethmarks he left at the scene, but simply because, as Flight had said, this was so far as they could know his place of birth, the place where he had defined himself for the very first time. He was the Wolfman. He could be anywhere, but that was relatively unimportant. What was more important was that he could be *anyone*, anyone at all in this city of ten million faces, ten million secret lairs.

'Where next?' he said, opening the passenger door.

'Kilmore Road,' said Flight. He exchanged a glance with Rebus, acknowledging the irony.

'Kilmore Road it is,' said Rebus, getting into the car.

* * *

41

The day had started early. Rebus, waking after three hours' sleep and unable to drop off again, switched on the radio in his room and listened to the morning news programme as he dressed. Not knowing exactly what the day would bring, he dressed casually: caramel cord trousers, light jacket, shirt. No tweeds or tie today. He wanted a bath, but the facilities on his floor of the hotel were locked. He would have to ask in reception. Near the stairs there stood an automatic shoeshine machine. He polished the toes of both well-worn black shoes before starting down to breakfast.

The restaurant area was busy, most of the customers looking like businessmen or tourists. The day's newspapers had been arranged across one vacant table and Rebus lifted a *Guardian* before being directed to a table laid for one by the harassed waitress.

Breakfast was mainly help-yourself, with juices, cereals and fruit crammed onto a large central display. A pot of coffee appeared, unasked for, on his table, as did a toast-rack filled with cool half-slices of lightly tanned bread. Not so much toasted as wafted in front of a lightbulb, Rebus thought to himself as he smeared a portion of butter across one pitiful triangle.

The Full English Breakfast consisted of one slice of bacon, one warm tomato (from a tin), three small mush-rooms, a sickly egg and a curious little sausage. Rebus wolfed down the lot. The coffee wasn't quite strong enough, but he finished the pot anyway and asked for a refill. All the time he was flicking through the paper, but only on a second examination did he find anything about the previous night's murder: a short, bare-bones paragraph near the foot of page four.

Bare bones. He looked around him. An embarrassed looking couple were trying to hush their two vociferous children. Don't, thought Rebus, don't stifle them, let them live. Who could know what might happen tomorrow? They might be killed. The parents might be killed. His own daughter was here in London somewhere, living in a flat with his ex-wife. He should get in touch. He *would* get in touch. A businessman at a corner table rustled his tabloid noisily, drawing Rebus's attention towards the front cover.

WOLFMAN BITES AGAIN.

Ah, that was more like it. Rebus reached for a final half-slice of toast, only to find that he'd run out of butter. A hand landed heavily on his shoulder from behind, causing him to drop the toast. Startled, he turned to see George Flight standing there.

'Morning, John.'

'Hello, George. Sleep okay?'

Flight pulled out the chair across from Rebus and sat down heavily, hands in his lap.

'Not really. What about you?'

'I managed a few hours.' Rebus was about to turn his near-arrest on Shaftesbury Avenue into a morning anecdote, but decided to save it. There might come a time when they would need a funny story. 'Do you want some coffee?'

Flight shook his head. He examined the food on display. 'Some orange juice wouldn't go amiss though.' Rebus was about to rise, but Flight waved him down and rose himself to fetch a glassful, which he promptly downed. He squeezed his eye-lids together. 'Tastes like powdered,' he said. 'Better give me some of that coffee after all.'

Rebus poured another cup. 'Seen that?' he said, nodding towards the corner table. Flight glanced at the tabloid and smiled.

'Well, it's their story now as much as ours. Only difference is, *we'll* keep things in perspective.'

'I'm not sure just what that perspective is.'

Flight stared at Rebus, but said nothing. He sipped at the coffee. 'There's a conference in the Murder Room at eleven o'clock. I didn't think we'd be able to make it, so I left Laine in charge. He likes being in charge.'

'And what are *we* going to be doing?'

'Well, we could go up to the Lea and check on the house-to-house. Or we could visit Mrs Cooper's place of employment.' Rebus didn't look enthusiastic. 'Or I could give you a tour of the other three murder scenes.' Rebus perked up.

'Okay,' said Flight, 'the scenic route it is. Drink up, Inspector. There's a long day ahead.'

'Just one thing,' said Rebus, lifting the cup halfway to his mouth. 'Why the nursemaid treatment? I'd have thought you'd have better things to do with your time than act as my chauffeur?'

Flight examined Rebus closely. Should he tell Rebus the real reason, or invent some story? He opted for invention and shrugged. 'Just easing you into the case, that's all.' Rebus nodded slowly, but Flight knew he didn't wholly believe him.

Out at the car, Rebus glanced in through the back window, seeking the teddy bear.

'I killed it,' Flight said, unlocking the driver's door. 'The perfect murder.'

'So what's Edinburgh like?'

Rebus knew Flight wasn't talking about the tourist Edinburgh, home to the Festival and the Castle. He was talking about criminal Edinburgh, which was another city altogether.

'Well,' he replied, 'we've still got a drug problem, and loan sharks seem to be making a comeback, but other than that things are fairly quiet at the moment.'

'But,' Flight reminded him, 'you did have that child killer a few years back.'

Rebus nodded. 'Five years ago.'

'And you solved it.' Rebus made no reply to this. They'd managed to keep out of the media the fact that it had been personal, had not exactly been 'serial'.

'Thousands of man hours solved it,' he said casually.

'That's not what the chiefs think,' said Flight. 'They think you're some kind of serial killer guru.'

'They're wrong,' said Rebus. 'I'm just a copper, the same as you are. So who exactly *are* the chiefs? Whose idea was it?'

But Flight shook his head. 'I'm not exactly sure. I mean, I know who the chiefs are – Laine, Chief Superintendent Pearson – but not which one of them is responsible for your being here.'

'It was Laine's name on the letter,' said Rebus, knowing this didn't really mean anything.

Then he watched the midday pedestrians scurrying along the pavements. The traffic was at a standstill. He and Flight had come just over three miles in the best part of half an hour. Roadworks, double (and triple) parking, a succession of traffic lights and pedestrian crossings and some maddening tactics from selfish drivers had reduced their progress to a crawl. Flight seemed to read his mind.

'We'll be out of this in a couple of minutes,' he said. He was thinking over what Rebus had said, *just a copper, the same as you are.* But Rebus *had* caught the child killer, hadn't he? The files on the case credited him with the collar, a collar which had earned him the rank of Inspector. No, Rebus was just being modest, that was it. And you had to admire him for that.

A couple of minutes later, they had moved a further fifteen yards and were about to pass a narrow junction with a No Entry sign at its mouth. Flight glanced up this side-street. 'Time to take a few liberties,' he said, turning the steering-wheel hard. One side of the street was lined with market stalls. Rebus could hear the stall-holders sharpening their patter against the whetstone of passing trade. Nobody paid the slightest attention to a car travelling the wrong way down a one-way street, until a boy pulling a mobile stall from one side of the road to the other halted their progress. A meaty fist banged on the driver's side window. Flight rolled down the window, and a head appeared, extraordinarily pink and round and totally hairless.

'Oi, what's your fucking game then?' The words died in his throat. 'Oh, it's you Mister Flight. Didn't recognise the motor.'

'Hello, Arnold,' Flight said quietly, his eyes on the ponderous movement of the stall ahead. 'How's tricks?'

The man laughed nervously. 'Keeping me nose clean, Mister Flight.'

Only now did Flight deign to turn his head towards the man. 'That's good,' he said. Rebus had never heard those

45

two words sound so threatening. Their road ahead was now clear. 'Keep it that way,' Flight said, moving off.

Rebus stared at him, waiting for an explanation.

'Sex offender,' Flight said. 'Two previous. Children. The psychiatrists say he's okay now, but I don't know. With that sort of thing, one hundred per cent sure isn't quite sure enough. He's been working the market now for a few weeks, loading and unloading. Sometimes he gives me good gen. You know how it is.'

Rebus could imagine. Flight had this huge, strong-looking man in the palm of his hand. If Flight told the market-traders what he knew about Arnold, not only would Arnold lose his job, but he'd be in for a good kicking as well. Maybe the man *was* all right now, maybe he was, in psychiatric parlance, 'a fully integrated member of society'. He had paid for his crimes, and now was trying to go straight. And what happened? Policemen, men like Flight and like Rebus himself (if he was being honest), used his past against him to turn him into an informant.

'I've got a couple of dozen snitches,' Flight went on. 'Not all like Arnold. Some are in it for the cash, some simply because they can't keep their gobs shut. Telling what they know to somebody like me makes them feel important, makes them feel like they're in the know. A place this size, you'd be lost without a decent network of snitches.'

Rebus merely nodded, but Flight was warming to his subject.

'In some ways London is too big to take in. But in other ways it's tiny. Everyone knows everyone else. There's north and south of the river, of course, those are like two different countries. But the way the place divides, the loyalties, the same old faces, sometimes I feel like a village bobby on his bicycle.' Because Flight had turned towards him, Rebus nodded again. Inside he was thinking: here we go, the same old story, London is bigger, better, rougher, tougher and more important than anywhere else. He had come across this attitude before, attending courses with Yard men or hearing about it from visitors to London. Flight hadn't seemed the type, but really everybody was the type. Rebus, too, in his time had exaggerated the problems the police faced in Edinburgh, so that he could look tougher and more important in somebody's eyes.

The facts still had to be faced. Police work was all about paperwork and computers and somebody stepping forward with the truth.

'Nearly there,' said Flight. 'Kilmore Road's the third on the left.'

Kilmore Road was part of an industrial estate and therefore would be deserted at night. It nestled in a maze of back streets about two hundred yards from a tube station. Rebus had always looked on tube stations as busy places, sited in populous areas, but this one stood on a narrow back street, well away from high road, bus route or railway station.

'I don't get it,' he said. Flight merely shrugged and shook his head.

Anyone coming out of the tube station at night found themselves with a lonely walk through the streets, past net-curtained windows where televisions blared. Flight showed him that a popular route was to cut into the industrial estate and across the parkland behind it. The park was flat and lifeless, boasting a single set of goalposts, two orange traffic cones substituting for the missing set. On the other side of the park three hi-rise blocks and some lo-rise housing sprang up. May Jessop had been making for one of those houses, where her parents lived. She was nineteen and had a good job, but it kept her late at her office, so it wasn't until ten o'clock that her parents started to worry. An hour later, there was a knock at the door. Her father rushed to answer, relieved, only to find a detective there, bearing the news that May's body had been found.

And so it went. There seemed no connection between the victims, no real geographical link other than that, as Flight pointed out, all the killings had been committed north of the river, by which he meant north of the Thames. What did a prostitute, an office manageress and the assistant in an off- licence have in common? Rebus was damned if he knew.

The third murder had taken place much further west in North Kensington. The body had been found beside a railway line and Transport Police had handled the investigation initially. The body was that of Shelley Richards, forty-one years old, unmarried and unemployed. She was the only coloured victim so far. As they drove through Notting Hill, Ladbroke Grove and North 'Ken' (as Flight termed it) Rebus was intrigued by the scheme of things. A street of extraordinarily grand houses would suddenly give way to a squalid, rubbish-strewn road with boarded up windows and bench-bound tramps, the wealthy and the poor living almost cheek by jowl. It would never happen in Edinburgh; in Edinburgh, certain boundaries were observed. But this, this was incredible. As Flight put it, 'race riots one side, diplomats the other'.

The spot where Shelley Richards had died was the loneliest, the most pathetic so far. Rebus clambered down from the railway line, down the embankment, lowered himself over the brick wall and dropped to the ground. His trousers were smeared with green moss. He brushed them with his hands, but to little effect. To get to the car where Flight was waiting he had to walk under a railway bridge. His footsteps echoed as he tried to avoid the pools of water and the rubbish, and then he stopped, listening. There was a noise all around him, a sort of wheezing, as if the bridge itself were drawing its dying breath. He looked up and saw the dark outlines of pigeons, still against the supporting girders. Cooing softly. That was what he could hear, not wheezing at all. There was a sudden rumble of thunder as a train passed overhead and the pigeons took to the wing, flapping around his head. He shivered and walked back out into sunlight.

Then, finally, it was back to the Murder Room. This was, in fact, a series of rooms covering most of the top floor of the building. Rebus reckoned there to be about twenty men and women working flat out when Flight and he entered the largest of the rooms. There was little to differentiate the scene from that of any murder investigation anywhere in the country. Officers were busy on telephones or working at

48

computer terminals. Clerical staff moved from desk to desk with seemingly endless sheafs of paper. A photocopier was spewing out more paper in a corner of the room and two delivery-men were wheeling a new five-drawer filing cabinet into position beside the three which already stood against one wall. On another wall was a detailed street map of London, with the murder sites pinpointed. Coloured tapes ran from these sites to spaces on the wall where pictures, details and notes had been pinned. A duty roster and progress chart took up what space was left. All very efficient, but the faces told Rebus their own story: everyone here, working hard as they were, was waiting for the Lucky Break.

Flight was immediately in tune with the glaze of efficiency in the office, firing off questions. How did the meeting go? Any word from Lambeth? (He explained to Rebus that the police lab was based there.) Any news on last night? What about house-to-house? Well, does anyone know *anything*?

There were shrugs and shakes of the head. They were simply going through the motions, waiting for that Lucky Break. But what if it didn't come? Rebus had an answer to that: you made your own luck.

A smaller room off this main office was being used as a communications centre, keeping the Murder Room in touch with the investigation, and off this room were two smaller offices yet, each crammed with three desks. This was where the senior detectives worked. Both were empty.

'Sit down,' Flight said. He picked up the telephone on his desk, and dialled. While he waited for an answer, he surveyed with a frown the four-inch high pile of paper which had appeared in his in-tray during the morning. 'Hello, Gino?' he said into the mouthpiece. 'George Flight here. Can I order some sandwiches? Salami salad.' He looked to Rebus for confirmation that this would be acceptable. 'On brown bread, please, Gino. Better make it four rounds. Thanks.' He cut the connection and dialled again. Only two numbers this time: an internal call. 'Gino has a cafe round the corner,' he explained to Rebus. 'He

49

makes great sandwiches, and he delivers.' Then: 'Oh, hello. Inspector Flight here. Can we have some tea? A decent-sized pot should do it. We're in the office. Is it wet milk today or that powdered crap? Great, thanks.' He dropped the receiver back into its cradle and spread his hands, as if some feat of magic had just been performed. 'This is your lucky day, John. We've got real milk for a change.'

'So what now?'

Flight shrugged, then slapped a hand on the bulging in-tray. 'You could always read through this little lot, keep yourself up-to-date with the investigation.'

'Reading about it isn't going to do any good.'

'On the contrary,' said Flight, 'it helps you answer any awkward questions that may be asked by those on high. How tall was the victim? What colour was her hair? Who found her? It's all in there.'

'She was five feet seven and her hair was brown. As to who found her, I don't give a tinker's cuss.'

Flight laughed, but Rebus was being serious. 'Murderers don't just appear,' he continued. 'They're created. To create a serial killer takes time. It's taken this guy years to make himself what he is. What's he been doing during that time? He may well be a loner, but he's probably got a job, maybe even a wife and kids. *Somebody* must know something. Maybe his wife wonders where he goes at night, or how blood got onto the tips of his shoes, or where her kitchen knife disappeared to.'

'All right, John.' Flight spread his hands again, this time in a gesture of peace-making. Rebus realised that his voice had been getting louder. 'Calm down a little. For a start, when you go on like that I can hardly make out a word you're saying, but I get your point. So what are we supposed to do?'

'Publicity. We need the public's help. We need anything they've got.'

'We already get dozens of calls a day. Anonymous tip-offs, nutters who want to confess, people snitching on their next door neighbour, people with grudges, maybe even a few with genuine suspicions. We check them all out. And we've got the media on our side. The Chief Super will be interviewed a dozen times today. Newspapers, magazines, radio, TV. We give them what we can, and we tell them to spread the word. We've got the best bloody Liaison Officer in the country working round the clock to make sure the public knows what we're dealing with here.'

There was a knock on the already open door and a WPC carried a tray into the room and left it on Flight's desk. 'I'll be mother, shall I?' he said, already starting to pour the tea into two plain white mugs.

'What's the Liaison Officer's name?' Rebus asked. He knew a Liaison Officer himself. She, too, was the best there was. But she wasn't in London; she was back in Edinburgh . . .

'Cath Farraday,' said Flight. 'Detective Inspector Cath Farraday.' He sniffed the milk carton, before pouring a dollop into his tea. 'If you stick around long enough, you'll get to meet her. She's a bit of a cracker is our Cath. Mind you, if she heard me talking about her like that, she'd have my head on a plate.' Flight chuckled.

'And salad on the side,' came a voice from just outside the door. Flight, flinching, spilt tea down his shirt and jumped to his feet. The door was swinging open now, to reveal a platinum blonde woman leaning against the jamb, her arms folded, one leg casually crossed over the other. Rebus's gaze was drawn to her eyes, which were slanted like a cat's. They made her whole face seem narrower than it was. Her lips were thin, lined with a thin coat of bright red lipstick. Her hair had a hard, metallic look to it, reflecting the look of the woman herself. She was older than either of the men in the room by several years and if age hadn't withered her, the frequent use of cosmetics had. Her face was lined and puffy. Rebus didn't like a lot of make-up on a woman, but plenty of men did.

'Hello, Cath,' said Flight, trying to regain at least an outer shell of composure. 'We were just . . .'

'. . . talking about me. I know.' She unfolded her arms and took a couple of steps into the room, extending a hand

51

to Rebus. 'You must be Inspector Rebus,' she said. 'I've heard all about you.'

'Oh?' Rebus looked to Flight, whose attention, however, was fixed on Cath Farraday.

'I hope George here is giving you an easy ride.'

Rebus shrugged. 'I've had worse.'

Her eyes became more feline still. 'I'll bet,' she said. She lowered her voice. 'But watch your back, Inspector. Not everyone's as nice as George. How would you feel if someone from London suddenly started to poke his nose into one of your cases, hmm?'

'Cath,' said Flight, 'there's no need for . . .'

She raised a hand, silencing him. 'Just a friendly warning, George, one Inspector to another. We've got to look after our own, haven't we?' She glanced at her watch. 'Must be going. I've a meeting with Pearson in five minutes. Nice to have met you, Inspector. Bye, George.'

And then she was gone, the door left wide open, a strong perfume lingering in the room. Both men were silent for a moment. Rebus was the first to speak.

'I believe your description was "a cracker", George. Remind me never to let you arrange a blind date for me.'

It was late afternoon and Rebus sat in Flight's office alone, a pad of paper in front of him on the desk. He tapped his pen like a drumstick against the edge of the table and stared at the two names he had written so far.

Dr Anthony Morrison. Tommy Watkiss.

These were people he wanted to see. He drew a thick line beneath them and wrote two more names: Rhona. Samantha. These, too, were people he wanted to see, though for personal reasons.

Flight had gone off to see Chief Inspector Laine on another floor of the building. The invitation did not extend to Rebus. He picked up the last remaining quarter of his salami sandwich, but thought better of it and tossed it into the office's metal bin. Too salty. And what kind of meat was salami anyway? He now had a craving for more tea. He thought Flight had dialled 18 to order up the first pot, but decided against trying it. He didn't want to make a fool of himself, did he? It would be just his luck to get through to Chief Superintendent Pearson.

Just a friendly warning. The point was not lost on Rebus. He crumpled up his list and threw that in the bin too, then got up out of his chair and made for the main office. He knew he should be doing something, or should at least *seem* to be doing something. They had brought him four hundred miles to help them. But he couldn't for the life of him see any gaps in their investigation. They were doing everything they could, but to no avail. He was just another straw to be clutched at. Just another chance for that elusive Lucky Break.

He was studying the wall-map when the voice sounded behind him.

'Sir?'

He turned to see one of the Murder Room team standing there. 'Yes?'

'Someone to see you, sir.'

'Me?'

'Well, you're the most senior detective around at the moment, sir.'

Rebus considered this. 'Who is it?'

The officer checked the scrap of paper in his hand. 'A Dr Frazer, sir.'

Rebus considered a moment longer. 'All right,' he said, turning back towards the tiny office. 'Give me a minute and then send him in.' He stopped. 'Oh, and bring some tea, will you?'

'Yes, sir,' said the officer. He waited until Rebus had left the room, then turned to the others, seated at their desks and smiling at him. 'The cheek of these fucking jocks,' he said, loud enough for everyone to hear. 'Remind me to piss in the teapot before I take it in.'

Dr Frazer turned out to be a woman. What was more, as she entered the office, she was attractive enough to have Rebus half-rise from his desk in welcome.

'Inspector Rebus?'

'That's right. Dr Frazer, I presume?'

'Yes.' She showed a row of perfect teeth as Rebus invited her to take a seat. 'Though I'd better explain.' Rebus fixed his eyes on her own and nodded. He kept his eyes fixed on hers for fear that otherwise they would be drawn down to her slim tanned legs, to that point where, an inch above the knee, her cream skirt began, hugging her thighs. He had taken her body in with a single sweeping glance. She was tall, almost as tall as him. Her legs were bare and long, her body supple. She was wearing a jacket to match the skirt and a plain white blouse, set off by a single string of pearls. There was a slight, exquisite scar on her throat just above the pearls and her face was tanned and without make-up, her jaw square, her hair straight and black, tied back with a black band, so that a shock of it fell onto one shoulder. She had brought a soft black leather briefcase into the room, which she now held up in her lap, running her fingers around the handles as she spoke.

'I'm not a medical doctor.' Rebus registered slight surprise. 'I'm a doctor courtesy of my Ph.D. I teach psychology at University College.'

'And you're American,' said Rebus.

'Canadian actually.'

Yes, he should have known. There was a soft lilt to her accent, something few Americans possessed. And she wasn't quite as nasal as the tourists who stopped in Princes Street to get a picture of the Scott Monument.

'I'm sorry,' he said, 'so, what can I do for you, Dr Frazer?'

'Well, I did talk to someone on the telephone this morning and I told them of my interest in the Wolfman case.'

Rebus could see it all now. Another nutter with some crazy idea about the Wolfman, that's probably what the Murder Room had thought. So they'd decided to play a joke on him, arranged a meeting without letting him know, and then Flight, forewarned, had made himself scarce. Well, the joke was on them. Rebus could always find time for an attractive woman, crazy or not. After all, he had nothing better to do, had he?

'Go on,' he said.

'I'd like to try to put together a profile of the Wolfman.'

'A profile?'

'A psychological profile. Like an identikit, but building up a picture of the mind rather than the face. I've been doing some research on criminal profiling and I think I can use similar criteria to help you come to a clearer understanding of the killer.' She paused. 'What do you think?'

'I'm wondering what's in it for you, Dr Frazer.'

'Perhaps I'm just being public spirited.' She looked down into her lap and smiled. 'But really, what I'm looking for is validation of my methods. So far I've been experimenting with old police cases. Now I want to tackle something real.'

Rebus sat back in his chair and picked up the pen again, pretending to study it. When he looked up, he saw that she was studying him. She was a psychologist after all. He put down the pen. 'It isn't a game,' he said, 'and this isn't a lecture theatre. Four women are dead, a maniac is loose somewhere and right now we're quite busy enough following up all the leads and the false trails we've got. Why should we make time for you, Dr Frazer?'

She coloured, her cheekbones blushed a deep red. But she seemed to have no ready answer. Rebus hadn't much to add, so he too sat in silence. His mouth was sour and dry, his throat coated in a layer of resin. Where was the tea?

Eventually she spoke. 'All I want to do is read through the material on the case.'

Rebus found some spare sarcasm. 'That's *all*?' He tapped the mound of paperwork in the in-tray. 'No problem then, it'll only take you a couple of months.' She was ignoring him, fumbling with the briefcase. She produced a slim orange folder.

'Here,' she said stonily. 'Just read this. It'll only take you twenty minutes. It's one of the profiles I did of an American serial killer. If you think it has no validity in helping to identify the killer or target where he might have struck next, fair enough, I'll leave.'

Rebus took the file. Oh God, he thought, not more

55

psychology! *Relating . . . involving . . . motivating*. He'd had his fill of psychology on the management training course. But then again, he didn't want her to leave. He didn't want to be left sitting here on his own with everyone in the Murder Room smirking at their little trick. He opened the folder, drew out a typed and bound thesis about twenty-five pages long and began to read. She sat watching him, waiting for a question perhaps. Rebus read with his chin held up, so that she wouldn't see the sagging folds of flesh on his neck, and with his shoulders back, making the best of his admittedly not very muscular chest. He cursed his parents for not feeding him up as a child. He had grown skinny, and when eventually he had started to put weight on, it had been to his gut and his backside, not his chest and arms.

Backside. Chest. Arms. He gazed hard at the words in front of him, but aware of her body resting in his line of peripheral vision, just above the top edge of the paper. He didn't even know her first name. Perhaps he never would. He frowned as though deep in thought and read through the opening page.

By page five he was interested and by page ten he felt there might be something in it after all. A lot of it was speculative. Be honest, John, it was almost all conjecture, but there were a few points where she made a telling deduction. He saw what it was: her mind worked in a different orbit from a detective's. They circled the same sun, however, and now and then the satellites touched. And what harm could come from letting her do a profile for the Wolfman? At worst, it would lead them up another dead end. At best, he might enjoy some female company during his stay in London. Yes, some pleasant female company. Which reminded him: he wanted to telephone his ex-wife and arrange a visit. He read through the final pages quickly.

'All right,' he said, closing the thesis, 'very interesting.'

She seemed pleased. 'And useful?'

He hesitated before replying. 'Perhaps.'

She wanted more from him than that. 'But worth letting me have a go on the Wolfman?'

He nodded slowly, ruminatively, and her face lit up. Rebus couldn't help returning her smile. There was a knock at the door. 'Come in,' he called.

It was Flight. He was carrying a tray, swimming with spilt tea. 'I believe you asked for some refreshment,' he said. Then he caught sight of Dr Frazer, and Rebus delighted in the stunned look on his face.

'Christ,' said Flight, looking from woman to Rebus to woman, before realising that he had somehow to justify his outburst. 'They told me you were with someone, John, but they didn't, I mean, I didn't know . . .' He tumbled to a halt, mouth still open, and placed the tray on the desk before turning towards her. 'I'm Inspector George Flight,' he said, reaching out a hand.

'Dr Frazer,' she replied, 'Lisa Frazer.'

As their hands met, Flight looked towards Rebus from the corner of his eye. Rebus, beginning to feel a little more at home in the metropolis, gave him a slow, cheerful wink.

'Christ.'

She left him a couple of books to read. One, *The Serial Mind*, was a series of essays by various academics. It included 'Sealing the Bargain: Modes of Motivation in the Serial Killer' by Lisa Frazer, University of London. Lisa: nice name. No mention of her doctorate though. The other book was an altogether heavier affair, dense prose linked by charts and graphs and diagrams: *Patterns of Mass Murder* by Gerald Q MacNaughtie.

MacNaughtie? That had to be a joke of some kind. But on the dustjacket Rebus read that Professor MacNaughtie was Canadian by birth and taught at the University of Columbia. Nowhere could he find out what the Q stood for. He spent what was left of the office day working through the books, paying most attention to Lisa Frazer's essay (which he read twice) and to the chapter in MacNaughtie's book concentrating on 'Patterns of Mutilation'. He drank tea and coffee and two cans of fizzy orange, but the taste in his mouth was sour and as he read on he began to feel physically dirty, made grubby by tale after tale of casual horror. When he got up to visit the bathroom at a quarter to five, everyone in the outer office had already quit for the day, but Rebus hardly registered the fact. His mind was elsewhere.

Flight, who had left him to his own devices for most of the afternoon, came into the office at six. 'Fancy a jar?' Rebus shook his head. Flight sat down on the edge of the chair. 'What's the matter?'

Rebus waved a hand over the books. Flight examined the cover of one. 'Oh,' he said, 'not exactly bedtime reading, I take it?'

'Not exactly. It's just . . . evil.'

Flight nodded. 'Got to keep a perspective though, John, eh? Otherwise they'd go on getting away with it. If it's so horrible, we all shy away from the truth, then everybody gets away with murder. And worse than murder.'

Rebus looked up. 'What's worse than murder?'

'Lots of things. What about someone who tortures and rapes a six-month old child and films the whole thing so he can show it to similarly minded individuals?'

Rebus's words were barely audible. 'You're kidding.' But he knew Flight was not.

'Happened three months ago,' Flight said. 'We haven't caught the bastard, but Scotland Yard have got the video – and a few more besides. Ever seen a thalidomide porn film?' Rebus shook his head wearily. Flight leaned down so that their heads were nearly touching. 'Don't go soft on me, John,' he said quietly, 'that's not going to solve anything. You're in London now, not the Highlands. The top deck of a midday bus isn't safe here, never mind a towpath after dark. Nobody sees any of it. London gives you a thick skin and temporary blindness. You and I can't afford to be blind. But we can afford the occasional drink. Coming?'

He was on his feet now, rubbing his hands, lecture over. Rebus nodded and rose slowly to his feet. 'Only a quick one though,' he said. 'I've got an appointment this evening.'

An appointment reached by way of a packed tube train. He checked his watch: 7.30 pm. Did the rush hour never stop?

The compartment smelt of vinegar and stale air, and three not-so-personal stereos battled it out above the roar of speeding and juddering. The faces around Rebus were blank. Temporary blindness: Flight was right. They shut it all out because to acknowledge what they were going through was to realise the monotony, the claustrophobia and the sheer agony of it all. Rebus was depressed. And tired. But he was also a tourist, so it had to be savoured. Thus the tube journey instead of a closeted taxi ride. Besides, he'd been warned about how expensive the black cabs were and he had checked in his A-Z, and found that his destination was only a quarter of an inch from an Underground station.

So Rebus travelled through the Underground and tried hard not to look out of place, not to gawp at the buskers and the beggars, not to pause in a busy conduit the better to read this or that advertising poster. A tramp actually entered his carriage at one stop and as the doors closed and the train pulled away again he began to rave, but his audience were deaf and dumb as well as blind and they successfully ignored his existence until the next stop where, daunted, he slouched from the carriage onto the platform. As the engine pulled away, Rebus could hear his voice again, coming from the next carriage along. It had been an astonishing performance, not by the tramp but by the passengers. They had closed off their minds, refusing involvement. Would they do the same if they saw a fight taking place? Saw a thick-set man stealing a tourist's wallet? Yes, they probably would. This wasn't an environment of good and evil: it was a moral vacuum and that frightened Rebus more than anything else.

But there were compensations of a sort. Every beautiful woman he saw reminded him of Lisa Frazer. Squeezed into one compartment on the Central Line, he found himself pressed against a young blonde girl. Her blouse was undone to the cleft of her breasts, giving the taller Rebus an occasionally breathtaking view of slopes and swells. She glanced up from her paperback and caught him staring. He looked away quickly, but felt her cold gaze focussing on the side of his head.

Every man is a rapist: hadn't someone said that once? *Traces of salt . . . Bite marks on the . . .* The train slowed into another station: Mile End, his stop. The girl was getting out, too. He lingered on the platform until she was gone, without really knowing why, then headed up towards ground level and a taste of fresh air.

Taste of monoxide, more like. Three lanes of traffic were jammed in either direction, the result of an articulated lorry failing to reverse through the narrow gates of some building. Two exasperated constables were trying to untie this Gordian Knot and for the first time it struck Rebus how silly their tall rounded hats looked. The Scottish-issue flat caps were more sensible. They also made less of a target at football matches.

Rebus wished the constables a silent 'Good luck' and made for Gideon Park – not a park but a road – and for number 78, a three storey house which, according to the front door's entry system, had been split somehow into four flats. He pressed the second-from-bottom buzzer and waited. The door was opened by a tall skinny teenage girl, her long straight hair dyed black, three earrings in each ear. She smiled and gave him an unexpected hug.

'Hello, Dad,' she said.

Samantha Rebus led her father up a narrow staircase to the first floor flat she shared with her mother. If the change in his daughter was striking, then the change in Rebus's ex-wife was doubly so. He had never seen her looking so good. There were strands of grey in her hair, but it had been cut fashionably short and there was a healthy suntanned look to her face, a gleam to her eyes. They studied one another without words, then embraced quickly.

'John.'

'Rhona.'

She had been reading a book. He looked at its cover: *To the Lighthouse*, Virginia Woolf. 'Tom Wolfe's more my style,' he said. The living-room was small, cramped even, but a lot of clever work with shelves and wall-mirrors gave the impression of space. It was a strange sensation, seeing things he recognised, that chair, a cushion-cover, a lamp, things from his life with Rhona, now transported to this pokey flat. But he praised the interior decoration, the snug feel of the place and then they sat down to drink tea. Rebus had brought gifts: record tokens for Samantha, chocolates for Rhona – received with a knowing, coded look between the two women.

Two women. Samantha was no longer a child. Her figure might retain a child's suppleness, but her way of moving, her actions, her face were all fully formed and adult.

'You look good, Rhona.'

She paused, accepting the compliment. 'Thank you, John,' she said at last. He noted her inability to say the same of him. Mother and daughter shared another of their secret looks. It was as though their time together had led to a kind of telepathy between them, so that during the course of the evening Rebus was to do most of the talking, nervously filling the many silent gaps in the conversation.

None of it was very important anyway. He spoke of Edinburgh, without going into detail about his work. This wasn't easy, since work apart he did very little. Rhona asked about mutual friends and he had to admit that he saw none of the old crowd. She talked about her teaching, of property prices in London. (Rebus heard nothing in her tone to suggest that he should pay something towards a bigger place for his kin. After all, it had been her idea to leave him. No real grounds, except, as she'd put it, that she'd loved a man but married a job.) Then Samanatha told him about her secretarial course.

'Secretarial?' said Rebus, trying to sound enthusiastic. Samantha's reply was cool.

'I told you about it in one of my letters.'

'Oh.' There was another break in the conversation. Rebus wanted to burst out: I read your letters, Sammy! I devour your letters! And I'm sorry I so seldom write back, but you know what a lousy letter-writer I am, how much effort it takes, how little time and energy I have. So many cases to solve, so many people depending on me.

But he said nothing. Of course he said nothing. Instead, they played out this little sham scenario. Polite chit-chat in a tiny living-room off Bow Road. Everything to say. Saying nothing. It was unbearable. Truly unbearable. Rebus moved his hands to his knees, spreading the fingers, ready to rise to his feet in the expected manner of one about to leave. Well, it's been nice seeing you, but there's a starched hotel bed waiting for me, and a machine to dispense ice, and another to shine shoes. He started to rise.

And the buzzer sounded. Two short, two long. Samantha fairly flew to the stairs. Rhona smiled.

'Kenny,' she explained.

'Oh?'

'Samantha's current gentleman.'

Rebus nodded slowly, the understanding father. Sammy was sixteen. She'd left school. A secretarial course at college. Not a boyfriend, a gentleman. 'What about you, Rhona?' he said.

She opened her mouth, forming a reply, when the thump of feet climbing the stairs closed it for her. Samantha's face was flushed as she led her gentleman by his hand into the room. Instinctively, Rebus stood up.

'Dad, this is Kenny.'

Kenny was clad in black leather zip-up jacket and black leather trousers, with boots reaching almost to his knees. He squeaked as he moved and in his free hand he carried an upturned crash-helmet, from which poked the fingers of a pair of black leather gloves. Two fingers were prominent, and appeared to be pointing directly at Rebus. Kenny removed his hand from Samanatha's grip and held it out towards her father.

'Wotcher.'

The voice was abrupt, the tone deep and confident. He had lank black hair, almost parted at centre, some residual acne on cheeks and neck, a day's growth of stubble. Rebus shook the hot hand with little enthusiasm.

'Hello, Kenny,' Rhona said. Then, for Rebus's benefit: 'Kenny's a motorcycle messenger.'

'Oh,' said Rebus, taking his seat again.

'Yeah, that's right,' Kenny enthused, 'down the City.' He turned to Rhona. 'Made a fair old packet today, Rhona,' he said, winking. Rhona smiled warmly. This young gentleman, this lad of eighteen or so (so much older, so much more worldly than Samantha) had obviously charmed his way into mother's heart as well as daughter's. He turned now to Rebus with that same winning way. 'I make a hundred quid on a good day. Course, it used to be better, back at Big Bang. There were a lot of new companies then, all of them trying to show off how much dosh they had. Still, there's a killing to be made if you're fast and reliable. A lot of the customers ask for me by name now. That shows I'm getting somewhere.' He sat down on the sofa beside Samantha and waited, as did they all, for Rebus to say something.

He knew what was expected of him. Kenny had thrown down a gauntlet, and the message was, Just you dare disapprove of me now. What did the kid want? A pat on the ego? Rebus's permission to deflower his daughter? A few tips on how to avoid speed-traps? Whatever, Rebus wasn't about to knuckle under.

'Can't be good for your lungs,' he said instead. 'All those exhaust fumes.'

Kenny seemed perplexed by this turn in the conversation. 'I keep myself fit,' he said, sounding slightly piqued. Good, thought Rebus, I can nettle this little bastard. He knew Rhona was warning him to lay off, warning him with her piercing eyes, but Rebus kept his attention on Kenny.

'Must be a lot of prospects for a lad like you.'

Kenny cheered up immediately. 'Yeah,' he said, 'I might even set up my own fleet. All you need's – ' He fell silent as he belatedly noticed that use of 'lad', as though he were dressed in shorts and school-cap. But it was too late to go back and correct it, way too late. He had to push on, but now it all sounded like pipe-dreams and playground fantasies. This rozzer might be from Jockland, but he was every bit as oily as an East End old-timer. He'd have to watch his step. And what was happening now? This Jock, this rough-looking tosser in the ill-fitting gear, the completely uncoordinated gear, this 'man at C&A' type, was reminiscing about a grocery shop from his youth. For a time, Rebus had been the grocer's 'message boy'. (He explained that in Scotland 'messages' meant 'groceries'.) He'd run about on a heavy-framed black bicycle, with a metal rectangle in front of the handlebars. The box of groceries would be held in this rectangle and off he would pedal to do his deliveries.

'I thought I was rich,' Rebus said, obviously coming to a punch line. 'But when I wanted more money, there wasn't any to be had. I had to wait till I was old enough to get a proper job, but I loved running around on that bike, doing errands and delivering messages to the old folk. Sometimes they'd even give me a tip, a piece of fruit or a jar of jam.'

There was silence in the room. A police siren sped past outside. Rebus sat back and folded his arms, a sentimental smile spread across his face. And then it dawned on Kenny: *Rebus was comparing the two of them!* His eyes widened. Everyone knew it. Rhona knew it. Sam knew it. For tuppence, he'd get up and stick the nut on the copper, Sam's dad or not. But he held back and the moment passed. Rhona got up to make more tea, and the big bastard got up and said he had to be going.

It had all happened so fast. Kenny was still trying to unravel Rebus's story and Rebus could see it. The poor half-educated runt was trying to work out just how far Rebus had put him down. Rebus could answer that: as far as was necessary. Rhona hated him for it, of course, and Samantha looked embarrassed. Well to hell with them. He'd done his duty, he'd paid his respects. He wouldn't bother them any more. Let them live in their cramped flat, visited by this . . . gentleman, this mock adult. Rebus had more important things to do. Books to read. Notes to make. And another busy day ahead. It was ten o'clock. He could be back at his hotel by eleven. An early night, that's what was needed. Eight hours' sleep in the last two days. No wonder he was ratty, looking for a fight.

He began to feel a little bit ashamed. Kenny was too easy a target. He'd crushed a tiny fly beneath a tower-block of resentment. Resentment, John, or plain jealousy? That was not a question for a tired man. Not a question for a man like

John Rebus. Tomorrow. Tomorrow, he might start getting some answers. He was determined to pay for his keep now that he had been brought to London. Tomorrow, the task began in earnest.

He shook Kenny's hand again and gave him a man-to-man half-wink before leaving the flat. Rhona offered to see him to the door. They went into the hall, leaving Samantha and Kenny in the living-room, behind a closed door.

'It's okay,' Rebus said quickly. 'I'll see myself out.' He started downstairs, aware that to linger was to invite an argument with Rhona. What was the point? 'Better go keep an eye on Lothario,' he called, unable to resist the parting shot.

Outside, he remembered that Rhona liked her lovers young, too. Perhaps she . . . but no, that thought was unworthy of him. 'Sorry, God,' he said, turning with a steady stride back towards the Underground.

* * *

Something is going wrong.

After the first killing, she had felt horror, remorse, guilt. She had begged forgiveness; she would not kill again.

After a month, a month of not being found, she grew more optimistic, and grew hungry too. So she killed again. This had satisfied for another month, and so it had gone on. But now, only twenty-four hours after the fourth time, she had felt the urge again. An urge more powerful and focussed than ever. She would get away with it, too. But it would be dangerous. The police were still hunting. Time had not elapsed. The public was wary. If she killed now, she would break her patternless pattern, and perhaps that would give the police some clue that she could not predict.

There was only one solution. It was wrong; she knew it was wrong. This wasn't her flat, not really. But she did it anyway. She unlocked the door and entered the gallery. There, tied up on the floor, lay the latest body. She would store this one. Keep it out of sight of the police. Examining it, she realised that now she would have more time with it, more time in which to play. Yes, storage was the answer. This lair was the answer. No fear of being found. After all, this was a private place, not a public place. No fear. She walked around the body, enjoying its silence. Then she raised the camera to her eye.

'Smile please,' she says, snapping her way through the film. Then she has an idea. She loads another film cartridge and photographs one of the paintings, a landscape. This is the one she will carve, just as soon as she has finished playing with her new toy. But now she has a record of it, too. A permanent record. She watches the photograph develop but then starts to scratch across the plate, smearing the colours and the focus until the picture becomes a chemical swirl, seemingly without form. God, her mother would have hated that.

'Bitch,' she says, turning from the wall filled with paintings. Her face is creased with anger and resentment. She picks up a pair of scissors and goes to her plaything again, kneels in front of it, takes a firm hold of the head and brings the scissors down towards the face until they hover a centimetre away from the nose. 'Bitch,' she says again, then carefully snips at the nostrils, her hand shaking. 'Long nosehairs,' she wails, 'are so unbecoming. So unbecoming.'

At last she rises again and crosses to the opposite wall, lifts an aerosol and shakes it noisily. This wall – she calls it her Dionysian wall – is covered in spray-painted black slogans: DEATH TO ART, KILLING IS AN ART, THE LAW IS AN ARSE, FUCK THE RICH, FEEL THE POOR. She thinks of something else to say, something worth the diminishing space. She sprays with a flourish.

'This is art,' she says, glancing over her shoulder towards the Apollonian wall with its framed paintings. 'This is fucking art. This is fuck art.' She sees that the doll's eyes are open and throws herself down to within an inch of those eyes, which suddenly screw themselves shut. Carefully, she uses both hands to prise apart the eyelids. Faces are close now, *so* intimate. The moment is always *so* intimate. Her breath is fast. So is the doll's. The doll's mouth struggles against the tape holding it shut. The nostrils flare.

'Fuck art,' she hisses to the doll. 'This is fuck art.' She has the scissors in her hand again now, and slides one blade into the doll's left nostril. 'Long nosehairs, Johnny, are so unbecoming in a man. So unbecoming in a man.' She pauses, as though listening to something, as though considering this statement. Then she nods. 'Good point,' she says, smiling now.

'Good point.'

Catching a Bite

The telephone woke Rebus. He could not locate it for a moment, then realised that it was mounted on the wall just to the right of his headboard. He sat up, fumbling with the receiver.

'Hello?'

'Inspector Rebus?' The voice was full of zest. He didn't recognise it. Took his Longines (his father's Longines actually) from the bedside table and peered through the badly scratched face to find that it was seven fifteen. 'Did I wake you up? Sorry. It's Lisa Frazer.'

Rebus came to life. Or rather his voice did. He still sat slumped and jangling on the edge of the bed, but heard himself say a bright, 'Hello, Dr Frazer. What can I do for you?'

'I've been studying the notes you gave me on the Wolfman case. Working through most of the night, to be honest. I just couldn't sleep, I was so excited by them. I've made some preliminary observations.'

Rebus touched the bed, feeling its residual warmth. How long since he'd slept with a woman? How long since he'd woken up the following day regretting nothing?

'I see,' he said.

Her laughter was like a clear jet of water. 'Oh, Inspector, I'm sorry, I've wakened you. I'll call back later.'

'No, no. I'm fine, honestly. A bit startled, but fine. Can we meet and talk about what you've found?'

'Of course.'

'But I'm a bit tied up today.' He was trying to sound vulnerable, and thought on the whole that it was probably working. So he played his big card. 'What about dinner?'

'That would be nice. Where?'

He rubbed at a shoulder-blade. 'I don't know. This is your town, not mine. I'm a tourist, remember.'

She laughed. 'I'm not exactly a local myself, but I take your point. Well in that case, dinner's on me.' She sounded set on this. 'And I think I know just the place. I'll come to your hotel. Seven thirty?'

'I look forward to it.'

What a very pleasant way to start the day, thought Rebus, lying down again and plumping up the pillow. He'd just closed his eyes when the telephone rang again.

'Yes?'

'I'm in reception and you're a lazy git. Come down here so I can put my breakfast on your tab.'

Cli-chick. Brrrr. Rebus slapped the receiver back into its cradle and got out of bed with a growl.

'What kept you?'

'I didn't think they'd appreciate a stark naked guest in the dining-room. You're early.'

Flight shrugged. 'Things to do.' Rebus noticed that Flight didn't look well. The dark rings around his eyes and his pale colouring were not due simply to lack of sleep. His flesh had a saggy quality, as though magnets on the floor were drawing it down. But then he wasn't feeling so great himself. He thought he'd probably picked up a bug on the tube. His throat was a little sore and his head throbbed. Could it be true that cities made you sick? In one of the essays Lisa Frazer had given him someone had made that very claim, stating that most serial killers were products of their environment. Rebus couldn't really comment on that, but he did know that there was more mucus in his nostrils than usual. Had he brought enough handkerchiefs with him?

'Things to do,' Flight repeated.

They sat at a table for two. The dining-room was quiet, and the Spanish waitress took their order briskly, the day not yet having had enough time to wear her down.

'What do you want to do today?' Flight seemed to be asking this only in order to get the conversation rolling, but Rebus had specific plans for the day and told him so.

'First off I'd quite like to see Maria Watkiss's man,

Tommy.' Flight smiled at this and looked down at the table. 'Just to satisfy my own curiosity,' Rebus continued. 'And I'd like to talk to the dental pathologist, Dr Morrison.'

'Well, I know where to find both of them,' said Flight. 'Go on.'

'That's about it. I'm seeing Dr Frazer this evening – ' Flight looked up at this news, his eyes widening in appreciation '– to go over her findings on the killer's profile.'

'Uh huh.' Flight sounded unconvinced.

'I've been reading those books she lent me. I think there may be something in it, George.' Rebus used the Christian name carefully, but Flight seemed to have no objections.

The coffee had arrived. Flight poured and drank a cup of it, then smacked his lips. 'I don't,' he said.

'Don't what?'

'Don't think there's anything in all this psychology stuff. It's too much like guesswork and not enough like science. I like something tangible. A dental pathologist, now that's tangible. That's something you can get – '

'Your teeth into?' Rebus smiled. 'The pun's bad enough, but I don't agree anyway. When was the last time a pathologist gave you a precise time of death? They always hedge their bets.'

'But they deal in *facts*, in physical evidence, not in mumbo-jumbo.'

Rebus sat back. He was thinking of the character in a Dickens book he'd read a long time ago, a schoolteacher who wanted facts and nothing but. 'Come on, George,' he said, 'this is the twentieth century.'

'That's right,' said Flight. 'And we don't believe in soothsayers any more.' He looked up again. 'Or do we?'

Rebus paused to pour some coffee. He felt his cheeks tingling. Probably, they were turning red. Arguments did that to him; even casual disagreements like this were sometimes enough. He was careful to make his next utterance in a soft, reasonable voice.

'So what are you saying?'

'I'm saying policework is plodding, John.' (Still on first

70

name terms, thought Rebus: that's good.) 'And shortcuts seldom work. I'm saying don't let your Hampton do your thinking for you.' Rebus thought about protesting, but realised he wasn't exactly sure what Flight meant. Flight smiled.

'Rhyming slang,' he explained. 'Hampton Wick, prick. Or maybe it's dick. Anyway, I'm just warning you not to let a good looking woman interfere with your professional judgment.'

Rebus was still about to protest, but saw that there was little point. Having voiced his thoughts, Flight seemed content. What's more, maybe he was right. Did Rebus want to see Lisa Frazer because of the case, or because she was Lisa Frazer? Still, he felt the need to defend her.

'Listen,' he said, 'like I say, I've been reading the books she gave me and there are some good things in them.' Flight looked unconvinced, goading Rebus into ploughing on. And as he fell for it, beginning to speak, he saw that Flight had played the same trick on him as he himself had played on the motorcycle messenger last night. Too late: he had to defend Lisa Frazer, and himself, even though everything he now said sounded stupid and half-baked to his own ears, never mind to Flight's.

'What we're dealing with is a man who hates women.' Flight looked at him in amazement, as though this were too obvious to need saying. '*Or*,' Rebus went on quickly, 'who has to take out his revenge on women because he's too weak, too scared to take it out on a man.' Flight admitted this possibility with a twitch of the head. 'A lot of so-called serial killers,' continued Rebus, his hand unconsciously grasping the butter-knife, 'are very conservative – small c – very ambitious, but thwarted. They feel rejected from the class immediately above them, and they target this group.'

'What? A prostitute, a shop assistant, an office worker? You're saying they're the same social group? You're saying the Wolfman's social group is lower than a tart's? Leave off, John.'

'It's just a general rule,' Rebus persisted, wishing he'd never started this conversation. He twisted the knife in his hand. 'Mind you, one of the earliest serial killers was a French nobleman.' His voice fell away. Flight was looking impatient. 'All I'm saying is what's in those books. Some of it may make sense, it's just that we don't have enough on the Wolfman yet to allow us to see what sense it's all making.'

Flight finished another cup of coffee. 'Go on,' he said, without enthusiasm. 'What else do the books say?'

'Some serial killers crave publicity,' said Rebus. He paused, thinking of the killer who had taunted him five years ago, who had led them all a merry chase. 'If the Wolfman gets in touch with us, we've a better chance of catching him.'

'Perhaps. So what are you saying?'

'I'm saying we should set some snares and dig some pits. Get Inspector Farraday to pass on a few tidbits to the press, all about how we suspect the Wolfman's gay, or a transvestite. It can be anything, so long as it jars his conservatism, and maybe it'll force him into the open.'

Rebus let go of the knife and waited for Flight's response. But Flight wasn't about to be rushed. He ran a finger around the rim of his cup. 'Not a bad idea that,' he said at last. 'But I'm willing to bet you didn't get it from your books.'

Rebus shrugged. 'Maybe not exactly.'

'I thought not. Well, let's see what Cath says to it.' Flight rose from his chair. 'Meantime, on a less lofty plane of existence, I think I can take you straight to Tommy Watkiss. Come on. And by the way, thanks for breakfast.'

'My pleasure,' said Rebus. He could see Flight was unconvinced by his defence, such as it had turned out to be, of psychology. But then was it Flight he was trying to convince, or himself? Was it Flight he was trying to impress, or Dr Lisa Frazer?

They were passing through the foyer now, Rebus carrying his briefcase. Flight turned to him.

'Do you,' he said, 'know why we're called the Old Bill?' Rebus shrugged, offering no answer. 'Some say it's because we're named after a certain London landmark. You can try guessing on the way there.' And with that Flight pushed

72

hard at the rotating door which served as the hotel's entrance.

The Old Bailey was not quite what Rebus had expected. The famous dome was there, atop which blind folded Justice held her scales, but a large part of the court complex was of much more modern design. Security was the keynote. X-ray machines, cubicle-style doors which allowed only one person at a time into the body of the building and security men everywhere. The windows were coated with adhesive tape so that any explosion would not send lethal shards of glass flying into the concourse. Inside, ushers (all of them women) dressed in flapping black cloaks ran around trying to gather up stray juries.

'Any jurors for court number four?'

'Jurors for court number twelve, please!'

All the time a PA system announced the names of missing single jurors. It was the busy beginning of another judicial day. Witnesses smoked cigarettes, worried-looking barristers, weighed down by documents, held whispered dialogues with dull-eyed clients, and police officers waited nervously to give evidence.

'This is where we win or lose, John,' said Flight. Rebus couldn't be sure whether he was referring to the courtrooms or to the concourse itself. On floors above them were administrative offices, robing rooms, restaurants. But this floor was where cases were held and decided. Through some doors to their left was the older, domed part of the Old Bailey, a darker, more forbidding place than this bright marbled gallery. The place echoed with the squealing of leather soled shoes, the clack-clack-clacking of heels on the solid floor and the constant murmur of conversation.

'Come on,' said Flight. He was leading them towards one of the courtrooms, where he had a word with the guard and one of the clerks before ushering Rebus into the court itself.

If stone and black leather predominated in the concourse, then the courtroom belonged to wood panelling and green leather. They sat on two chairs just inside the door, joining DC Lamb, already seated there, unsmiling, arms folded. He did not greet them, but leaned across to whisper, 'We're going to nail the cunt', before stiffening into his former position.

On the other side of the room sat the twelve jurors, looking bored already, faces numb and unthinking. To the back of the court stood the defendant, hands resting on the rail in front of him, a man of about forty with short, wiry silver and black hair, his face like something hewn from stone, his open-necked shirt a sign of arrogance. He had the dock to himself, there being no police officer on guard.

Some distance in front of him, the lawyers sorted through their papers, watched by assistants and solicitors. The defence counsel was a thick-set and tired-looking man, his face grey (as was his hair), gnawing on a cheap ballpoint. The prosecutor, however, was much more confident look-ing, tall (if stout), dressed immaculately and with the glow of the righteous upon him. His pen was an intricate fountain affair and he wrote with a flourish, his mouth set as defiantly as any Churchill impersonator. He reminded Rebus of how television liked to think of QCs, Rumpole aside.

Directly overhead was the public gallery. He could hear the muffled shuffling of feet. It had always worried Rebus that those in the public gallery had a clear view of the jury. Here, the court had been designed in such a way that they stared directly down and onto the jurors, making intimida-tion and identification that much easier. He'd dealt with several cases of jurors being approached at day's end by some relative of the accused, ready with a wad of notes or a clenched fist.

The judge looked imperious as he pored over some papers in front of him, while just below him the Clerk of Court spoke in hushed tones into a telephone receiver. From the time it was taking to begin proceedings, Rebus realised two things. One was that the case was continuing, not beginning; the other was that some Point of Law had been placed before the judge, which the judge was now considering.

'Here, seen this?' Lamb was offering a tabloid to Flight.

The newspaper had been folded to a quarter of its size and Lamb tapped one column as he passed it to his superior. Flight read quickly, glancing up at Rebus once or twice, then handed the paper to Rebus with a hint of a smile.

'Here you go, expert.'

Rebus read through the unattributed piece. Basically, it concerned itself with the progress or lack of it on the Jean Cooper murder inquiry. But the closing paragraph was the killer: 'The team investigating what have come to be known as the "Wolfman Murders" are being assisted by an expert on serial killers, drafted in from another police force.'

Rebus stared at the newsprint without really seeing it. Surely Cath Farraday wouldn't have? But then how else had the newspaper got to know? He kept his eyes on the page, aware that both Flight and Lamb were looking at him. He couldn't believe it: *him*, an *expert*! Whether it was true or not – and it wasn't – didn't really matter now. What mattered was that results would be expected from him, results above the norm. Yet he knew he couldn't deliver and in not delivering he would be made to look a laughing stock. No wonder those two pairs of eyes burned into his head. No hard-working policeman liked to be usurped by 'experts'. Rebus didn't like it himself. He didn't like any of it!

Flight saw the pained expression on Rebus's face and felt sorry for the man. Lamb, however, was smirking, enjoying Rebus's agony. He accepted his newspaper from Rebus and stuffed it into his jacket pocket.

'Thought you'd be interested,' he said.

The judge finally looked up, his attention fixed on the jury. 'Members of the jury,' he began, 'it has been brought to my attention in the case of Crown versus Thomas Watkiss that the evidence of Police Constable Mills contained a passage which may have lodged in your minds, influencing your objectivity.'

So, the man in the dock was Tommy Watkiss, Maria's husband. Rebus studied him again, shaking his mind clear of the news story. Watkiss's face was a curious shape, the top half much wider than the cheekbones and jaw, which fell almost to a point. He had the look of an old boxer who had suffered one dislocated jaw too many. The judge was going on about some cock-up in the police case. The arresting constable had given evidence stating that his first words on reaching the accused had been 'Hello, Tommy, what's going on here?' By giving this in evidence, he had let the jury know that Watkiss was well known to the local constabulary, something which might well influence their judgment. The judge was therefore ordering the jury to be dismissed.

'Good on ya, Tommy!' came a cry from the public gallery, quickly silenced by a glare from the judge. Rebus wondered where he had heard the voice before.

As the court rose, Rebus stepped forward a few paces and turned to look up at the balcony. The spectators had risen, too, and in the front row Rebus could see a young man dressed in bike leathers and carrying a crash helmet, grinning towards Watkiss. He raised his fist in a gesture of triumph, then turned and began to climb the steps to the gallery's exit. It was Kenny, Samantha's boyfriend. Rebus walked back to where Flight and Lamb were standing, watching him curiously, but Rebus directed his attention towards the dock. The look on Watkiss's face was one of pure relief. DC Lamb, on the other hand, seemed ready to kill.

'Luck of the fucking Irish,' he spat.

'Tommy's no more Irish than you are, Lamb,' Flight said phlegmatically.

'What was the charge?' Rebus asked, his mind still confused by the newspaper story, by Kenny's presence in this place and by his actions. The judge was leaving by a green padded-leather door to the side of the jury box.

'The usual,' said Lamb, calming quickly. 'Rape. When his old woman snuffed it, he needed somebody else on the game. So he tried to "persuade" a girl on his street that she could make a few bob. When that didn't work, he lost his rag and had a go at her. Bastard. We'll get him at the retrial. I still think he did for his old woman.'

'Then find the evidence,' said Flight. 'Meantime, I can think of a certain Police Constable who needs a good kick up the arse.'

'Yeah,' said Lamb. He was grinning evilly at the thought, then took the hint and left the courtroom in search of the unfortunate PC Mills.

'Inspector Flight.' It was the prosecuting counsel, striding briskly towards them with documents and books cradled in his left arm, his right arm outstretched. Flight took the well-groomed hand and shook it.

'Hello, Mr Chambers. This is Inspector Rebus. He's come down from Scotland to help us on the Wolfman investigation.'

Chambers looked interested. 'Ah, yes, the Wolfman. I look forward to prosecuting that particular case.'

'I just hope we can give you the opportunity,' said Rebus.

'Well,' said Chambers, 'meanwhile it's tricky enough landing the little fish like our friend.' He glanced back in the direction of the dock, which now stood empty. 'But we try,' he said with a sigh, 'we try.' Then he paused, and added in an undertone, directed at Flight: 'Get this, George, I don't like being royally shafted by my own team. Okay?'

Flight blushed. Chambers had dressed him down in a way no Superintendent or Chief Constable could ever have done, and he knew it. 'Good day, gentlemen,' he said, moving away, 'and good luck, Inspector Rebus.'

'Thanks,' Rebus called to the retreating figure.

Flight watched as Chambers pushed open the doors of the court, the tail of his wig flicking from side to side, robes flapping behind him. When the doors were closed, Flight chuckled.

'Arrogant prick. But he's the best there is.'

Rebus was beginning to wonder if anyone in London was second-rate. He'd been introduced to the 'top' pathologist, the 'best' prosecuting counsel, the 'crack' forensic team, the 'finest' police divers. Was it part of the city's own arrogance?

'I thought the best lawyers all went in for commercial work these days,' Rebus said.

'Not necessarily. It's only the really greedy bastards who go in for City work. Besides, this sort of stuff is like a drug to Chambers and his ilk. They're actors, bloody good ones at that.'

. Yes, Rebus had known a few Oscar-winning advocates in his time, and had lost a few cases more to their technique than to the strength of their defence. They might earn a quarter of the riches earned by their brothers in the commercial sector, might take home a scant £50,000 each year, but they endured for the sake of their public.

Flight was moving towards the doors. 'What's more,' he said, 'Chambers studied for a time in the USA. They train them to be actors over there. They also train them to be hard-nosed bastards. I'm told he came out top of his class. That's why we like having him on our side.' Flight paused. 'Do you still want a word with Tommy?'

Rebus shrugged. 'Why not?'

Out in the concourse, Watkiss was standing by one of the large windows, relishing a cigarette and listening to his solicitor. Then the two men started to walk away.

'Tell you what,' said Rebus, 'I've changed my mind. Let's skip Watkiss for the moment.'

'Okay,' said Flight. 'You're the *expert* after all.' He saw the sour look on Rebus's face and laughed. 'Don't worry about it,' he said. 'I know you're no expert.'

'That's very reassuring, George,' Rebus said without conviction. He stared after Watkiss, thinking: And I'm not the only one leaving court without conviction.

Flight laughed again, but behind his smile he was still more than a little curious about Rebus's action in the courtroom, walking out into the court like that to peer up at the public gallery. But if Rebus didn't want to talk about it, then that was his privilege. Flight could bide his time. 'So what now?' he asked.

Rebus was rubbing his jaw. 'My dental appointment,' he said.

Anthony Morrison, who insisted that they call him Tony, was much younger than Rebus had been anticipating. No more than thirty-five, he had an underdeveloped body, so that his adult head seemed to have outgrown the rest of him.

Rebus was aware that he was staring at Morrison with more than common interest. The scrubbed and shiny face, the tufts of bristle on chin and cheekbone where a razor had failed to fulfil its duties, the trimmed hair and keening eyes: in the street, he would have taken Morrison for a sixth-year pupil. Certainly, for a pathologist, albeit a dental pathologist, the man was in stark contrast to Philip Cousins.

On learning that Rebus was Scottish, Morrison had started on about the debt modern-day pathology owed to the Scots, 'men like Glaister and Littlejohn and Sir Sydney Smith' though the latter, Morrison had to admit, had been born in the Antipodes. He then said that his own father had been a Scotsman, a surgeon, and asked if Rebus knew that the earliest British Chair of Forensic Medicine had been founded in Edinburgh. Rebus, swept away by the welter of facts, said that this was news to him.

Morrison showed them into his office with an enthusiastic bounce to his walk. Once inside, however, the dentist's demeanour changed from social to professional.

'He's been busy again,' he said without preamble, leading them to the wall behind his desk, where several ten by eight colour and black and white photographs had been pinned. They showed precise close-ups of the bite marks left on Jean Cooper's stomach. Arrows had been drawn in, leading from particular spots on certain photographs out to where pinned notes gave Morrison's technical summary of his findings.

'I know what to look for now, of course,' he said, 'so it didn't take long to establish that these are probably the same teeth used in the previous attacks. A pattern is also emerging, however, perhaps a disturbing one.' He went to his desk and returned with more photographs. 'These are from victim number one. You'll notice that the indents left by the teeth are less marked. They grow a little more marked by victims two and three. And now – ' he pointed to the current crop of pictures.

'They've got even deeper,' Rebus answered. Morrison beamed at him.

'Quite right.'

'So he's becoming more violent.'

'If you can term an attack made on someone who's already dead "violent", then yes, Inspector Rebus, he's getting more violent, or perhaps more unstable would be a better way of phrasing it.' Rebus and Flight exchanged a glance. 'Apart from the change in the relative depth of the bite marks, there's little I can add to my previous findings. The teeth are quite likely to be prosthetic – '

Rebus interrupted. 'You mean false?' Morrison nodded. 'How can you tell?'

Morrison beamed again. The prodigy who liked to show off in front of his teachers. 'How can I best explain this to a layman?' He seemed to consider his own question for a moment. 'Well, one's own teeth – your own, for example, Inspector Rebus – and by the way, you should get them seen to – they get a little ragged over time. The cutting edge gets chipped and worn. The edge on false teeth is more likely to be smoother, more rounded. Less of an edge to the front teeth especially, and less chips and cracks.'

Rebus, lips closed, was running his tongue over his teeth. It was true, they had the serrated feel of a workman's saw. He hadn't visited a dentist in ten years or more, had never felt the need. But now Morrison had commented on them. Did they really look so awful?

'So,' Morrison continued, 'for that reason, as well as for several others, I would say the killer has false teeth. But he also has very curious teeth indeed.'

'Oh?' Rebus tried to speak without showing Morrison any more of his own decaying mouth.

'I've already explained this to Inspector Flight,' Morrison paused so that Flight could nod agreement of this, 'but briefly, the upper set has a greater biting curve than the lower set. From my measurements, I conclude that the person in possession of these teeth must have quite a strangely shaped face. I did draw some sketches, but I've managed to come up with something better. I'm glad you've come this afternoon.' He walked over to a cupboard and opened it. Rebus looked to Flight, who merely shrugged. Morrison was turning towards them again, his right hand supporting a large object covered by an inverted brown paper bag.

'Behold,' he said, lifting the bag from the object. 'I bring you the head of the Wolfman!'

There was silence in the room, so that the traffic noise from outside became conspicuous. Neither Rebus nor Flight could think of anything immediately to say. Instead, they walked across to meet with the chuckling Morrison, who was regarding his creation with a measure of glee. There was a squeal of suddenly braking tyres outside.

'The Wolfman,' Morrison repeated. He was holding the cast of a human head, constructed so far as Rebus could ascertain from pale pink plaster. 'You can ignore the idea from the nose upwards, if you prefer,' said Morrison. 'It's fairly speculative, based on mean measurements taking into account the jaw. But the jaw itself is, I believe, pretty accurate.'

And a strange jaw it was. The upper teeth jutted out from the mouth, so that the lips over them and the skin below the nose was stretched and bulging. The lower jaw seemed tucked in beneath in what seemed to Rebus a Neanderthal display, to the extent that it almost disappeared. The chin had a narrow, pinched look and the cheekbones were swollen in a line with the nose, but concave as the face extended downwards. It was an extraordinary face, the like of which Rebus could not recall having encountered in the real world. But then this was not the real world, was it? It was a reconstruction, depending upon a measure of averages and guesswork. Flight was staring at it in fascination, as though committing the face to memory. Rebus had the chilling notion that Flight would release a photograph to the papers and charge the first poor soul he came across possessing such a physiognomy.

'Would you call that deformed?' Rebus asked.

'Heavens, no,' said Morrison with a laugh. 'You haven't seen some of the medical cases I've had to deal with. No, this couldn't be termed deformed.'

'Looks like my idea of Mr Hyde,' commented Flight.

Don't mention Hyde to me, Rebus thought to himself.

81

'Perhaps,' said Morrison, laughing again. 'What about you, Inspector Rebus? What are your thoughts?'

Rebus examined the cast again. 'It looks prehistoric.'

'Ah! said Morrison enthusiastically. 'That was what I thought at first. The jutting upper jaw especially.'

'How do you know that is the upper jaw?' asked Rebus. 'Couldn't it be the other way round?'

'No, I'm pretty sure this is correct. The bites are fairly consistent. Apart from victim three, that is.'

'Oh?'

'Yes, victim three was a strange one. The lower set, that is the smaller set, seemed more extended than the upper set. As you can see from this cast, the killer would have had to make an extraordinary contortion of his face to produce such a bite.'

He mimed the bite for them, opening his mouth wide, lifting his head, and pushing out his lower jaw, then making a biting motion, the lower jaw doing most of the work.

'In the other bites, the killer has bitten more like this.' Again he put on a dumb show, this time drawing his lips back from his upper jaw and biting down sharply so that the upper teeth closed over the lower teeth, the teeth themselves snapping together.

Rebus shook his head. This wasn't making things clearer. If anything, he was growing more confused. He nodded towards the cast. 'You really believe the man we're looking for looks like this?'

'The man or woman, yes. Of course, I may have exaggerated a little with this cast, but I'm more or less convinced.'

Rebus had stopped listening after the first sentence. 'What do you mean, or woman?' he asked.

Morrison shrugged his shoulders theatrically. 'Again, this is something I've discussed with Inspector Flight. It just seemed to me that, purely on the dental evidence you understand, this head could as easily belong to a woman as to a man. The large upper set of teeth seems to me very male, judging from size and what have you, but the lower set, just as equally, seems very female. A man with a woman's chin, or a woman with a masculine upper jaw?' He shrugged again. 'Take your pick.'

Rebus looked to Flight, who was shaking his head slowly. 'No,' Flight said, 'it's a man.'

Rebus had never considered the possibility that a woman might be behind the killings. It had never entered his head. Until now.

A woman? Improbable, but why impossible? Flight was dismissing it out of hand, but on what grounds? Rebus had read last night that a growing number of multiple murderers were women. But could a woman have stabbed like that? Could a woman so completely have overwhelmed victims of similar height, similar strength?

'I'd like to get some photographs of this,' Flight was saying. He had taken the cast from Morrison and was studying it again.

'Of course,' Morrison said, 'but remember, it's only my idea of the look of the killer's head.'

'We appreciate it, Tony. Thanks for all your work.'

Morrison shrugged modestly. He had fished for a compliment and had hooked one.

Rebus could see that Flight was convinced by this whole piece of theatre, the unveiling of the head and so on. To Rebus it was more showmanship than tangible truth, more the stuff of courtroom melodrama. He still felt that to trap the Wolfman they had to get inside his head, not play with plaster mock-ups of it.

His or her head.

'Would the bite marks be enough to identify the killer?'

Morrison considered this. Then nodded. 'I think so, yes. If you can bring me the suspect, I think I can show that he or she is the Wolfman.'

Rebus persisted, 'But would it stand up in court?'

Morrison folded his arms and smiled. 'I could blind the jury with science.' His face became serious again. 'No, on its own I don't think my evidence would ever be enough to convict. But as part of a larger body of such evidence, we might be in with half a chance.'

'Always supposing the bastard makes it to trial,' Flight

added grimly. 'Accidents have been known to happen in custody.'

'Always supposing,' Rebus corrected, 'we catch him in the first place.'

'That, gentlemen,' said Morrison, 'I leave entirely in your capable hands. Suffice to say, I look forward to introducing my friend here to the real thing.' And he tipped the plaster head backwards and forwards and backwards again, until it seemed to Rebus that the head was mocking them, laughing and rolling its sightless eyes.

As Morrison showed them out, he rested a hand on Rebus's forearm. 'I'm serious about your teeth,' he said, 'you should get them seen to. I could look at them myself if you like?'

When he returned to headquarters Rebus went straight to the wash-room and, in front of a soap-spattered mirror, examined his mouth. What was Morrison talking about? His teeth looked fine. Okay, one of them had a dark line running down it, a crack perhaps, and a few were badly stained from too many cigarettes and too much tea. But they looked strong enough, didn't they? No need for drills and piercing, grinding implements. No need for a dentist's chair, sharp needles, and a spitting out of blood.

Back at his designated desk he doodled on his notebook. Was Morrison just the nervous type, or was he hyperactive? Was he perhaps mad? Or was he merely dealing with the world in his own idiosyncratic way?

So few serial killers were women. Statistically, it was unlikely. Since when had he believed in statistics? Since he had started to read psychology textbooks, last night in his hotel room after the disastrous visit to Rhona and Samantha. Kenny: what the hell was Kenny doing running around with Tommy Watkiss? His daughter's 'gentleman'. A smiling villain? Forget it, John. You don't control that part of your life any more. He had to smile at this: what part of his life did he control? His work gave his life what meaning it had. He should admit defeat, tell Flight he could be of no help and return to Edinburgh, where he could be sure of his villains and his crimes: drug peddlars, protection racketeers, domestic violence, fraud.

A murder each month, regular as the moon. It was only a saying, wasn't it, regular as the moon? He unhooked a calendar from the wall. Portraits of Italy, donated to the station by Gino's Sandwich Bar. Time of the month. Had there been a full moon around 16th January when Maria Watkiss was found? No, but then they reckoned she might have lain undiscovered for two or three days. Thursday 11th January had been the full moon. The full moon affected the Wolfman in the movies, didn't it? But they had named the killer Wolfman after Wolf Street, not because he, or she, killed by the light of the full moon. Rebus was more confused than ever. And weren't women supposedly affected by the moon, something to do with their time of the month?

May Jessop had died on Monday 5th February, four days *before* another full moon. Shelley Richards had died on Wednesday 28th February, nowhere near a full moon. Morrison had said her case was unusual, the bites had seemed different. And then Jean Cooper had died on the night of Sunday 18th March, two days before the vernal equinox.

He threw the calendar onto the desk. There was no pattern, no neat mathematical solution. Who was he trying to kid? This wasn't the movies. The hero didn't stumble upon the answer. There were no shortcuts. Maybe Flight was right. It was all plodding routine and forensic evidence. Psychology was no shortcut, barking at the moon was no shortcut. He couldn't know when the Wolfman would strike again. He knew so little.

Flight wandered exhaustedly into the room and fell onto a chair, causing it to creak in protest.

'I finally got through to Cath,' he said. 'I put your idea to her, and she's giving it some thought.'

'That's big of her.'

Flight gave him a warning look and Rebus raised his hands in apology. Flight nodded towards the calendar. 'What are you up to?'

'I don't know, nothing much. I thought there might be some pattern to the dates when the Wolfman struck.'

'You mean like the stages of the moon, the equinox, that sort of thing?' Flight was smiling. Rebus nodded slowly. 'Hell, John, I've been through all that and more.' He went to a particular manila folder and tossed it towards Rebus. 'Take a look: I've tried number patterns, distance between murder sites, possible means of transport – the Wolfman's pretty mobile, you know, I think he must have a car. I've tried linking the victims, checking which school they went to, which libraries they used, whether they liked sports or discos or classical bloody music. Know what? They don't have *anything* in common, not a single thing linking the four of them save the fact that they were women.'

Rebus flicked through the file. It was an impressive amount of slogging, all to no end save that of clarification. Flight hadn't climbed the ladder to his present rank by a fluke, or by keeping in with his superiors, or by signifying greatness. He had got there by sheer hard work.

'Point taken,' said Rebus. Then, because this didn't seem quite enough: 'I'm impressed. Have you shown this lot to anyone else?'

Flight shook his head. 'It's guesswork, John. Straw-clutching. That's all. It would just confuse the issue. Besides, do you remember the story of the boy who cried wolf? One day, there really was a wolf there, but by then no one believed him because he'd given them so much crap before.'

Rebus smiled. 'Still, it's a lot of work.'

'What did you expect?' Flight asked. 'A chimpanzee in a whistle? I'm a good copper, John. I may be no *expert*, but I'd never claim to be.'

Rebus was about to remonstrate, then frowned. 'What's a whistle?' he said.

Flight threw back his head and laughed. 'A suit, you plonker. Whistle and flute, suit. Rhyming slang. God sakes, John, we're going to have to educate you. Tell you what, why don't we go out for a meal ourselves tonight? I know a good Greek restaurant in Walthamstow.' Flight paused, a gleam in his eye. 'I know it's good,' he said, "cos I've seen a lot of bubbles coming out of it.' His smile was inviting. Rebus thought quickly. Bubbles? Was the food gassy? Did they serve champagne? Rhyming slang. Bubbles.

'Bubble and squeak,' he said. Then a pause. 'Greeks, right?'

'Right!' said Flight. 'You're catching on fast. So what about it? Or Indian, Thai, Italian, you decide.'

But Rebus was shaking his head. 'Sorry, George, prior engagement.'

Flight pulled his head back. 'No,' he said, 'you're seeing *her*, aren't you? That bloody psychiatrist. I forgot you told me at breakfast. You bloody Jocks, you don't waste any time, do you? Coming down here, stealing our women.' Flight sounded in good humour, but Rebus thought he detected something a little deeper down, a genuine sadness that the two of them couldn't get together for a meal.

'Tomorrow night, eh, George?'

'Yeah,' said Flight. 'Tomorrow night sounds fine. One word of advice though?'

'What?'

'Don't let her get you on the couch.'

'No,' said Dr Lisa Frazer, shaking her head vigorously. 'That's psychiatrists. Psychiatrists have couches, not psychologists. We're like chalk and cheese.'

She looked stunning, yet there was no alchemy involved in the process. She was dressed simply and wore no makeup. Her hair had been brushed straight back and tied with a band. Still, casually, elegantly, simply, she was stunning. She had been dead on time at the hotel and had walked with him, her arm linked in his, along Shaftesbury Avenue, past the scene of his run in with the patrol car. The early evening was warm, and Rebus felt good walking with her. Men were glancing towards them, okay, be honest, towards *her*. There might even have been a wolf whistle or two. It made Rebus feel good all the same. He was wearing his tweed jacket with an open-necked shirt and had the sudden fear that she would lead him to some fancy restaurant where men were not admitted without ties. That would be just his luck. The city teemed with nightlife, teenagers mostly, drinking from cans and calling to each other across the busy road. The pubs were doing good business and buses chugged grime into the air. Grime which would be falling unseen on Lisa Frazer. Rebus felt valiant. He felt like stopping all the traffic, confiscating all the keys so that she could walk unsullied through the streets.

Since when did he think like that? Where had this tiny unpolished stone of romance come from? What desperate corner of his soul? Self-conscious, John. You're becoming too self-conscious. And if a psychologist didn't spot it, nobody would. Be natural. Be calm. Be yourself.

She brought him into Chinatown, a few streets off Shaftesbury Avenue, where the telephone boxes were shaped like oriental temples, supermarkets sold fifty-year-old eggs, gateways were decorated like relics from Hong Kong and the street names were given in Chinese as well as English. There were a few tourists about, but mainly the pedestrianised walkway was filled with scuttling Chinese, their voices shrill. It was a different world, like something you would expect to find in New York but never dream of finding in England. Yet he could look back along the street and still see the theatres on Shaftesbury Avenue, the red buses chug-chugging, the punks yelling obscenities at the tops of immature voices.

'Here we are,' she said, stopping outside a restaurant on the corner of the street. She pulled open the door, gesturing for him to precede her into the air-conditioned chill. A waiter was upon them at once, showing them to a dimly-lit booth. A waitress smiled with her eyes as she handed them each a menu. The waiter returned with a wine list, which he placed beside Rebus.

'Would you like a drink while you are deciding?'

Rebus looked to Lisa Frazer for guidance. 'Gin and tonic,' she said without hesitation.

'And the same for me,' said Rebus, then regretted it. He wasn't all that keen on gin's chemical smell.

'I'm very excited about this case, Inspector Rebus.'

'Please, call me John. We're not in the station now.'

She nodded. 'I'd like to thank you for giving me the chance to study the files. I think I'm already forming an interesting picture.' She reached into her clutch-purse and produced a collection of a dozen index cards held together with an outsize paper-clip. The cards were covered in lines of tiny, neat handwriting. She seemed ready to start reading them. 'Shouldn't we at least order first?' Rebus asked. She appeared not to understand, then grinned.

'Sorry,' she said. 'It's just that I'm . . .'

'Very excited. Yes, you said.'

'Don't policemen get excited when they find what they think is a clue?'

'Almost never,' said Rebus, appearing to study the menu, 'we're born pessimists. We don't get excited until the guilty party has been sentenced and locked up.'

'That's curious.' She held her own menu still closed. The index cards had been relegated to the table-top. 'I'd have thought to enjoy police work you would need a level of optimism, otherwise you'd *never* think you were going to solve the case.'

Still studying the menu, Rebus decided that he'd let her order for both of them. He glanced up at her. 'I try not to think about solving or not solving,' he said. 'I just get on with the job, step by step.'

The waiter had returned with their drinks.

'You are ready to order?'

'Not really,' said Rebus, 'could we have a couple more minutes?'

Lisa Frazer was staring across the table at him. It wasn't a large table. Her right hand rested on the rim of her glass, barely an inch from his left hand. Rebus could sense the presence of her knees almost touching his own under the table. The other tables in the restaurant all seemed larger than this one, and the booths seemed better lit.

'Frazer's a Scottish name,' he said. It was as good a line as any.

'That's right,' she replied. 'My great grandfather came from a place called Kirkcaldy.'

89

Rebus smiled. She had pronounced the word the way it looked. He corrected her, then added, 'I was born and brought up not far from there. Five or six miles, to be precise.'

'Really? What a coincidence. I've never been there, but my grandaddy used to tell me it was where Adam Smith was born.'

Rebus nodded. 'But don't hold that against it,' he said. 'It's still not a bad wee town.' He picked up his glass and swirled it, enjoying the sound of the ice chinking on the glass. Lisa was at last studying her menu. Without looking up, she spoke.

'Why are you here?' The question was sudden, catching Rebus off-balance. Did she mean here in the restaurant, here in London, here on this planet?

'I'm here to find answers.' He was pleased with this reply; it seemed to deal with all three possibilities at once. He lifted his glass. 'Here's to psychology.'

She raised her own glass, ice rattling like musical chimes. 'Here's to taking things one step at a time.' They both drank. She studied her menu again. 'Now,' she said, 'what shall we have?'

Rebus knew how to use a pair of chopsticks, but perhaps tonight had just been the wrong time to try. He suddenly found himself unable to pick up a noodle or a sliver of duck without the thing sliding out of his grasp and falling back to the table, splashing sauce across the tablecloth. The more it happened, the more frustrated he became and the more frustrated he became, the more it happened. Finally, he asked for a fork.

'My coordination's all gone,' he explained. She smiled in understanding (or was it sympathy?) and poured more tea into his tiny cup. He could see that she was impatient to tell him what she thought she had discovered about the Wolfman. Over a starter of crabmeat soup the talk had been safe, guarded, had been of pasts and futures, not the present. Rebus stabbed his fork into an unresisting slice of meat. 'So what have you found?'

She looked at him for confirmation that this was her cue. When he nodded, she put down her chopsticks, then pushed aside the paper-clip from her index cards and cleared her throat, not so much reading from the cards, more using them as occasional prompts.

'Well,' she said, 'the first thing I found revealing was the evidence of salt on the bodies of the victims. I know some people think it may be sweat, but I'm of the opinion that these are tear stains. A lot can be learned from any killer's interpersonal relationship with his or her victim.' There it was again: his or her. *Her*. 'To me the tear stains indicate feelings of guilt in the attacker, guilt felt, moreover, not in reflection but at the actual time of the attack. This gives the Wolfman a moral dimension, showing that he is being driven almost against his will. There may well be signs of schizophrenia here, the Wolfman's dark side operating only at certain times.'

She was about to rush on, but already Rebus needed time to catch up. He interrupted. 'You're saying most of the time the Wolfman may seem as normal as you or me?'

She nodded briskly. 'Yes, exactly. In fact, I'm saying that between times the Wolfman doesn't just seem as normal as anyone else, he *is* as normal, which is why he's been hard to catch. He doesn't wander around the streets with the word "Wolfman" tattooed across his forehead.'

Rebus nodded slowly. He realised that by seeming to concentrate on her words, he had an excuse for staring at her face, consuming it with eyes more proficient than any cutlery. 'Go on,' he said.

She flipped one card over and moved to the next, taking a deep breath. 'That the victim is abused *after* death indicates that the Wolfman feels no need to control his victim. In some serial killers, this element of control is important. Killing is the only time when these people feel in any kind of control of their lives. This isn't the case with the Wolfman. The murder itself is relatively quick, occasioning little pain or suffering. Sadism, therefore, is not a feature. Rather, the Wolfman is playing out a scenario upon the corpse.'

Again the rush of words, her energy, her eagerness to

share her findings, all swept past Rebus. How could he concentrate when she was so close to him, so close and so beautiful? 'What do you mean?'

'It'll become clearer.' She stopped to take a sip of tea. Her food was barely touched, the mound of rice in the bowl beside her hardly dented. In her own way, Rebus realised, she was every bit as nervous as he was, but not for the sme reasons. The restaurant, though hectic, might have been empty. This booth was *their* territory. Rebus took a gulp of the still-scalding tea. Tea! He could kill for a glass of cold white wine.

'I thought it interesting,' she was saying now, 'that the pathologist, Dr Cousins, feels the initial attack comes from behind. This makes the attacks non-confrontational and the Wolfman is likely to be like this in his social and working life. There's also the possibility that he cannot look his victims in the eye, out of fear that their fear would destroy his scenario.'

Rebus shook his head. It was time to own up. 'You've lost me.'

She seemed surprised. 'Simply, he's taking out revenge and to him the victims represent the individual against whom he's taking his revenge. If he confronted them face to face, he'd realise they're not the person he bears the grudge against in the first place.'

Rebus still felt a little bit lost. 'Then these women are stand-ins?'

'Substitutes, yes.'

He nodded. This was getting interesting, interesting enough for him to turn his gaze from Lisa Frazer, the better to concentrate on her words. She was still only halfway through her cards.

'So much for the Wolfman,' she said, flipping to the next card. 'But the chosen location can also say a lot about the inner life of the attacker, as can age, sex, race and class of the victims. You'll have noticed that they are all women, that they are mostly older women, women approaching middle age, and that three out of four have been white. I'll admit that I can't make much out of these facts as they stand. In fact, it was just the failure of pattern that made me think a little harder about location. You see, just when a pattern looks to be emerging, an element arises that destroys the precision: the killer attacks a much younger woman, or strikes earlier in the evening, or chooses a black victim.'

Or, Rebus was thinking, kills outside the pattern of the full moon.

Lisa continued, 'I started to give some consideration to the spatial pattern of the attacks. These can determine where the killer may strike next, or even where he lives.' Rebus raised his eyebrows. 'It's true, John, it's been proved in several cases.'

'I don't doubt it. I was raising my eyebrows at that phrase "spatial pattern".' A phrase he'd heard before, on the loathed management course.

She smiled. 'Jargon, yes. There's a lot of it about. What I mean is the pattern of the murder sites. A canal path, a railway line, the vicinity of a tube station. Three out of four take place near travel systems, but again the fourth case defeats the pattern. All four take place north of the river. At least there's *some* evidence of a pattern there. But – and this is my point – the non-emergence of a pattern seems to me in itself a conscious act. The Wolfman is making sure you have as little as possible to go on. This would indicate a high level of psychological maturity.'

'Yes, he's as mature as a hatter all right.'

She laughed. 'I'm being serious.'

'I know you are.'

'There is one other possibility.'

'What's that?'

'The Wolfman knows how *not* to leave a trail because he is familiar with police work.'

'Familiar with it?'

She nodded. 'Especially the way you go about investigating a series of murders.'

'You're saying he's a copper?'

She laughed again, shaking her head. 'I'm saying he may have prior convictions.'

'Yes, well,' he thought of the file George Flight had shown him a few hours earlier, 'we've checked on over a hundred ex-offenders already. No luck there.'

'But you can't possibly have talked to every man who has ever been convicted of rape, violent assault or the like.'

'Agreed. But there's something you seem to have overlooked – the teethmarks. Those are very palpable clues. If the Wolfman is being so clever, why does he leave us a neat set of bite marks every time?'

She blew on her tea, cooling it. 'Maybe,' she said, 'the teeth are a – what do you call it – a red herring?'

Rebus thought about this. 'It's possible,' he conceded, 'but there's something else. I visited a dental pathologist today. From the marks made by the teeth, he said he couldn't rule out the possibility that the Wolfman is a woman.'

'Really?' Her eyes opened wide. 'That's very interesting. I'd never even considered it.'

'Neither had we.' He scooped more rice into his bowl. 'So tell me, why does he, or she, bite the victims?'

'I've given that a lot of thought.' She flipped to her final card. 'The bite is always on the stomach, the female stomach, carrier of life. Maybe the Wolfman has lost a child, or maybe he was abandoned and consequently adopted and resents the fact. I don't know. A lot of serial killers have fragmented upbringings.'

'Mmm. I read all about it in those books you gave me.'

'Really? You read them?'

'Last night.'

'And what did you think?'

'I thought they were clever, sometimes ingenious.'

'But do you think the theories are valid?'

Rebus shrugged. 'I'll tell you if and when we catch the Wolfman.'

She toyed with her food again, but ate nothing. The meat in her bowl had a cold, gelatinous look. 'What about the anal attacks, John. Do *you* have any theories there?'

Rebus considered this. 'No,' he said finally, 'but I know what a psychiatrist might say.'

94

'Yes, but you're not with a psychiatrist, remember. I'm a psychologist.'

'How can I forget? You said in your essay that there are thirty *known* serial killers active in the USA. Is that true?'

'I wrote that essay over a year ago. By now, there are probably more. Frightening, isn't it?'

He shrugged, the shrug disguising a shiver. 'How's the food?' he asked.

'What?' She looked at her bowl. 'Oh, I'm not really very hungry. To tell you the truth, I feel a little bit . . . deflated, I suppose. I was so excited at what I thought I'd managed to piece together, but in telling it all to you, I see that really there's not very much there at all.' She was thumbing through the index cards.

'There's plenty there,' said Rebus. 'I'm impressed, honest. Every little bit helps. And you stick to the known facts, I like that. I was expecting more jargon.' He remembered the terms from one of her books, the one by MacNaughtie. 'Latent psychomania, Oedipal urgings, gobbledygook.'

'I could give you plenty of that stuff,' she said, 'but I doubt it would help.'

'Exactly.'

'Besides, that's more in line with psychiatry. Psychologists prefer drive theories, social learning theory, multiphasic personalities.' Rebus had clamped his hands over his ears.

She laughed again. He could make her laugh so easily. Once upon a time he'd made Rhona laugh too, and after Rhona a certain Liaison Officer back in Edinburgh. 'So what about policemen?' he asked, closing off the memory. 'What can psychologists tell about us?'

'Well,' she said, relaxing into her seat, 'you're extrovert, tough-minded, conservative.'

'Conservative?'

'With a small "c".'

'I read last night that serial killers are conservative, too.'

She nodded, still smiling. 'Oh yes,' she said, 'you're alike in a lot of ways. But by conservative I mean specifically that you don't like anything that changes the status quo. That's why you're reticent about the use of psychology. It interferes with the strict guidelines you've set yourselves. Isn't that so?'

'Well, I suppose I could argue, but I won't. So what happens now you've studied the Wolfman?'

'Oh, all I've done so far is scratch the surface.' Her hands were still on the index cards. 'There are other tests to be done, character analyses and so on. It'll take time.' She paused. 'What about you?'

'Well, we'll plod along, checking, examining, taking it – '

'Step by step,' she interrupted.

'That's right, step by step. Whether I'll be on the case much longer or not I can't say. They may send me back to Edinburgh at the end of the week.'

'Why did they bring you to London in the first place?'

The waiter had come to clear away their dishes. Rebus sat back, wiping his lips with the serviette.

'Any coffees or liqueurs, sir?'

Rebus looked to Lisa. 'I think I'll have a Grand Marnier,' she said.

'Just coffee for me,' said Rebus. 'No, hold on, what the hell, I'll have the same.' The waiter bowed and moved off, his arms heavy with crockery.

'You didn't answer my question, John.'

'Oh, it's simple enough. They thought I might be able to help. I worked on a previous serial killing, up in Edinburgh.'

'Really?' She sat forward in her chair, the palms of her hands pressed to the tablecloth. 'Tell me.'

So he told her. It was a long story, and he didn't know exactly why he gave her as many details as he did – more details than she needed to know, and more, perhaps, than he should be telling to a psychologist. What would she make of him? Would she find a trace of psychosis or paranoia in his character? But he had her complete attention, so he spun the tale out in order to enjoy that attention the more.

It took them through two cups of coffee, the paying of the bill, and a balmy night-time walk through Leicester Square, across Charing Cross Road, up St Martin's Lane and along Long Acre towards Covent Garden. They walked around Covent Garden itself, Rebus still doing most of the talking. He stopped by a row of three telephone boxes, curious about the small white stickers covering every available inch of space on the inside of the booths: Stern corrective measures; French lessons; O and A specialist; TV; Trudy, nymphet, Spank me; S/M chamber; Busty blonde – all of them accompanied by telephone numbers.

Lisa studied them, too. 'Every one a psychologist,' she said. Then: 'That's quite a story you've just told, John. Has anyone written it up?'

Rebus shrugged. 'A newspaper reporter wrote a couple of articles.' Jim Stevens. Christ, hadn't he moved to London, too? Rebus thought again of the newspaper story Lamb had shown him, the *unattributed* newspaper story.

'Yes,' Lisa was saying, 'but has anyone looked at it from your point of view?'

'No.' She looked thoughtful at this. 'You want to turn me into a case study?'

'Not necessarily,' she said. 'Ah, here we are.' She stopped. They were standing outside a shoe shop in a narrow, pedestrianised street. Above the rows of shops were two storeys of flats. 'This is where I live,' she said. 'Thank you for this evening. I've enjoyed it.'

'Thank you for the meal. It was great.'

'Not at all.' She fell silent. They were only two or three feet apart. Rebus shuffled his feet. 'Will you be able to find your way back?' she asked. 'Should I point you in the right direction?'

Rebus looked up and down the street. He was lost. He had not been keeping track of their meanderings. 'Oh, I'll be all right.' He smiled and she smiled back but did not speak. 'So this is it then,' he persisted. 'No offer of a coffee?'

She looked at him slyly. 'Do you really want a coffee?'

He returned the look. 'No,' he admitted, 'not really.'

She turned from him and opened the door to the side of the shoe shop. The shop claimed to specialise in handmade and non-leather shoes. Beside the door to the flats was an entryphone boasting six names. One of them read simply 'L Frazer'. No 'Dr', but then he supposed she wouldn't want to be disturbed by people needing a medical doctor, would she? There were times when a qualification was best kept under wraps.

Lisa drew the mortice key out of the lock. The stairwell was brightly lit, its plain stone painted cornflower blue. She turned back towards him.

'Well,' she said, 'since you don't want a coffee, you'd better come on up . . .'

She later explained, running a hand over his chest as they lay together in bed, that she saw no point in the little games people played, the slow edging towards a moment when both would admit that what they really wanted was to make love.

So instead she led Rebus up to her first floor flat, took him into the darkened room, undressed and got into bed, sitting with her knees tucked up in front of her.

'Well?' she said. So he had undressed, too, and joined her. She lay now with her arms reaching behind her to grab at the bedposts, her body dusky in the light cast from a street-lamp outside. Rebus ran his tongue back up along the inside of her leg, the inner thigh, her legs supple. She smelt of jasmine, tasted of flowers more pungent still. Rebus was self-conscious at first. His own body had become an embarrassment, while hers was in fine, toned condition. (Squash and swimming, she told him later, and a strict diet.) He ran his fingers over the ripples, the corrugations in her flesh. There was some sagging to the skin above her stomach, some creasing to the sides of her breasts and to her throat. He looked down and saw his own distended chest. There was still some muscle to his stomach, but there was also excessive fleshiness; not supple, tired and ageing.

Squash and swimming: he would take up some exercise, join a health club. There were enough of them in Edinburgh.

He was eager to please. Her pleasure became his only goal, and he worked tirelessly. There was sweat in the room now. A lot of sweat. They were working well together, moving fluidly, each seeming to sense what the other was about to do. When he moved slightly too quickly and bumped his nose on her chin, they laughed quietly, rubbing foreheads. And when later he went in search of her fridge and cold liquid, she came too, popping an ice cube into her mouth before kissing him, the kiss extending downwards as she sank to her knees in front of him.

Back in bed, they drank chill white wine from the bottle and kissed some more, then began all over again.

The air between them had lost its nervous charge and they were able to enjoy themselves. She moved on top, rearing above him, her rhythm increasing until all he could do was lie back and watch with his eyes closed, imagining the room in diffuse light, a cold spray of water, a smoothness of skin.

Or a woman. The Wolfman could be a woman. The Wolfman was playing with the police, seemed to know the way they thought and worked. A woman? A woman officer? Cath Farraday came to mind, with her Teutonic face, that wide but angular jaw.

Jesus, here he was with Lisa, thinking of another woman! He felt a sudden pang of guilt, hitting him in the stomach a moment before a very different reaction arched his back and his neck, while her hands pressed down upon his chest, her knees clamped to his hips.

Or a woman. Why the teeth? Leaving not a single clue except those bites. Why? Why not a woman? Why not a policeman? Or . . . or . . .

'Yes, yes.' Her breath escaped with a hiss, the word losing all meaning as she repeated it ten, twenty, thirty times. Yes what?

'Yes, John, yes, John, yes . . .'

Yes.

It had been another busy day for her, a day spent pretending to be what she's not, but now she was out again, prowling. She is beginning to like the way she can move so smoothly through the two worlds. Earlier this evening she was the guest at a dinner party in Blackheath. Mock-Georgian elegance, stripped pine doors, talk of school fees and fax machines, of interest rates and foreign property – and the Wolfman. They asked for her opinion. Her opinion was reasoned, intelligent, liberal. There was chilled Chablis and an exquisite bottle of Chateau Montrose: the '82. She could not choose between the two, so enjoyed a glass of both.

One guest was late arriving, a journalist on one of the better dailies. He apologised. They asked for tidbits from the next day's news, and he supplied them generously. The sister paper to his own was a downmarket tabloid. He told them the next day's front page would have a headline reading SECRET LIFE OF GAY WOLFMAN. Of course, as the journalist knows, this is nothing more than a ruse, to try to bait the killer. And she knows too, naturally. They smile at one another across the table, as she lifts more pasta expertly with her fork. How stupid of them to run a story like that: gay Wolfman indeed! She chuckles into her oversized wine glass. The conversation turns to motorway traffic, wine acquisition, the state of Blackheath Common. Blackheath, of course, is where they buried the plague victims, piling the corpses high. Black Death. Black Heath. One letter separates the two. She smiles at this, too, discreetly.

The meal over, she took a taxi back across the river and got out at the beginning of her street. She intended to go straight home, but walked past her door and kept on walking. She shouldn't be doing this, shouldn't be out here, but it feels right. After all, the toy in the gallery must be lonely. It's always so cold in the gallery. So cold Jack Frost could bite off your nose.

Her mother must have told her that. Her mother. *Long*

nosehairs, Johnny, are so unbecoming in a gentleman. Or her father, singing nonsense songs while she hid herself in the garden. 'Fuck art,' she hisses quietly to herself.

She knows where to go, too. Not far. The intersection of one road with a much larger one. There are many like it in London. Traffic lights, and a few women wandering back and forth, sometimes crossing at the lights so that the drivers can see them, can see their legs and their white bodies. If a car window is rolled down, a woman may lean down close to the driver so that they can discuss terms. Professional, but not very discreet. She knows that sometimes the police will make a rudimentary attempt to close down business, knows too that policemen are among the whores' best customers. That's why it's dangerous for her to come here. Dangerous but necessary: she has an itch, and women like these go missing all the time, don't they? No one gets suspicious. No one starts alarm bells ringing. Alarm bells are the last thing you need in this part of the city. Like with her first victim, by the time they got to her she was a meal for rats. Animal feed. She chuckles again, and makes to walk past one of these women, but stops.

'Hello, love,' says the woman. 'Anything you want?'

'How much for the night?'

'For you, love, a hundred.'

'Very well.' She turns and starts back towards her own street, her own house, so much safer there than out here. The woman follows noisily a yard or two behind, seeming to understand. She does not let the woman catch up until she is at the front door and the key is in the lock. The gallery beckons. Only it doesn't look like a gallery any more.

It looks like a butcher's block.

'Nice place you've got, love.'

She puts a finger to her lips. 'No talking.' The woman begins to look suspicious, looks as though she's thinking twice about being here. So she goes to her and grabs at a breast, planting a clumsy, smeared kiss across puffy lips. The prostitute looks startled for a second, then manages a rehearsed smile.

'Well, you're certainly not a gentleman,' she says.

101

She nods, pleased with this remark. The front door is locked now. And she goes to the door of the gallery, slips the key in, unlocks it.

'In here, love?' The woman is removing her coat as she walks across the threshold. The coat is down past her shoulders by the time she sees the room itself. But by then, of course, it's too late, far too late.

She moves in on her, like a trained worker on a production line. Hand over the mouth, good pressure on the knife and a quick backward arc before the thrust. She has often wondered if they see the knife, or are their eyes closed in terror by then? She imagines them with eyes bulging open, focussing on the knife as, point directed towards them, it swings back and then flies forward towards their face. She can find out, can't she? All she needs is a strategically placed wall-mirror. Must remember that for next time.

Gurgle, gurgle. The gallery is such a marvellous setting, poised between Apollo and Dionysus. The body slips to the floor. Time for the real work now. Her brain is humming – mummydaddymummydaddy mummydaddymummydaddy – as she crouches to her task.

'It's only a game,' she whispers, her voice a mere tremble at the back of her throat. 'Only a game.' She hears the woman's words again: *certainly not a gentleman*. No, certainly not. Her laughter is harsh and abrupt. Suddenly, she feels it again. No! Not already! *Next time*. The knife twitches. She hasn't even finished with this one. She can't possibly do another tonight! It would be madness. Sheer madness. But the craving is there, an absolute and unappeasable hunger. This time with a mirror. She covers her eyes with a bloodstained hand.

'Stop!' she cries. 'Stop it, daddy! Mummy! Make it stop! Please, make it stop!'

But that's the problem, as she knows only too well. Nobody *can* make it stop, nobody *will* make it stop. On it must go, night after night now. Night after night. No letting up, no pausing for breath.

Night after night after night.

Fibs

'You've got to be kidding!'

Rebus was too tired to be truly angry, but there was enough exasperation in his voice to worry the caller on the other end of the telephone, delegated to order Rebus to Glasgow.

'That case isn't supposed to be heard until the week after next.'

'They moved it,' says the voice.

Rebus groaned. He lay back on his hotel bed with the receiver pressed to his ear and checked his watch. Eight-thirty. He'd slept soundly last night, waking at seven, dressed quietly so as not to disturb Lisa and had left her a note before making his exit. His nose had led him to the hotel with only a couple of wrong turnings along the way and now he had walked into this telephone call.

'They brought it forward,' the voice is saying. 'It starts today. They need your testimony, Inspector.'

As if Rebus didn't know. He knows that all he has to do is go into the witness box and say he saw Morris Gerald Cafferty (known in the protection game as 'Big Ger') accept one hundred pounds from the landlord of the City Arms pub in Grangemouth. It's as easy as that, but he needs to be there to say it. The case against Cafferty, boss of a thuggish protection and gaming racket, is not airtight. In fact, it's got more punctures than a blind dressmaker's thumb.

He resigns himself to it. Must it be? Yes, it must be. But there was still the problem of logistics.

'It's all been taken care of,' says the voice. 'We did try phoning you last night, but you were never there. Catch the first available shuttle from Heathrow. We'll have a car meet you and bring you into Glasgow. The prosecution reckons he'll call you about half past three, so there's time enough. With any luck, you can be back in London by tonight.'

'Gee, thanks,' says Rebus, voice so thick with irony the words hardly escape into the air.

'You're welcome,' says the voice.

He found that the Piccadilly Line went to Heathrow, and Piccadilly Circus tube was right outside the hotel. So things started well enough, though the tube ride itself was slow and stifling. At Heathrow, he picked up his ticket and had just enough time for a dash into the Skyshop. He picked up a *Glasgow Herald*, then saw the row of tabloids on another shelf: SECRET LIFE OF GAY WOLFMAN; SICK KILLER 'NEEDS HELP' SAY POLICE; CATCH THIS MADMAN.

Cath Farraday had done well. He bought a copy of all three papers as well as the *Herald* and made for the Departure Lounge. Now that his mind was working, he saw all around him people reading the same headlines and the stories below them. But would the Wolfman see the stories? And if so, would he or she make some kind of move? Hell, the whole thing might be about to crack open and here he was heading four hundred miles north. Damn the judicial system, the judges and advocates and solicitors and all. The Cafferty case had probably been brought forward so that it would not interfere with a golf game or a school sports day. Some spoilt child's involvement with an egg-and-spoon race might be behind this whole breathless journey. Rebus tried to calm down, sucking in gulps of air and releasing them slowly. He didn't like flying as it was. Never since his days in the SAS, when they had dropped him from a helicopter. Jesus! That was no way to calm yourself.

'Will passengers for British Airways Super Shuttle flight –'

The voice was cool and precise, triggering a mass movement. People rose to their feet, checked their baggage and made for the gate just mentioned. Which gate? He'd missed the announcement. Was it his flight? Maybe he should phone ahead so they would have the car waiting. He *hated* flying. That was why he had come down by train on

Sunday. Sunday? And today was Wednesday. It felt like over a week had passed. In fact, he'd been in London only two full days.

Boarding. Oh, Christ. Where was his ticket? He'd no luggage, nothing to worry about there. The newspapers wriggled beneath his arm, trying to break free and fall in a mess on the floor. He pushed them back together again, squeezing them tightly with his elbow. He had to calm down, had to think about Cafferty, had to get everything straight in his mind, so that the defence could find no chink in his story. Keep to the facts, forget about the Wolfman, forget about Lisa, Rhona, Sammy, Kenny, Tommy Watkiss, George Flight . . . Flight! He hadn't notified Flight. They would wonder where he was. He'd have to phone when he landed. He should phone now, but then he might miss the shuttle. Forget it. Concentrate on Cafferty. They would have his notes ready for him when he arrived, so he could go through them before he entered the witness box. There were only the two witnesses, weren't there? The frightened publican, whom they had more or less coerced into giving evidence, and Rebus himself. He had to be strong, confident and believable. He caught sight of himself in a full-length mirror as he made for the Departure Gate. He looked like he'd spent a night on the tiles. The memory of the night made him smile. Everything would be all right. He should phone Lisa, too, just to say . . . what? Thank you, he supposed. Up the ramp now, the narrow doorway in front of him, flanked by smiling steward and stewardess.

'Good morning, sir.'

'Good morning.' He saw they were standing by a stack of complimentary newspapers. Christ, he could have saved himself a few bawbees.

The aisle was narrow too. He had to squeeze past businessmen who were stuffing coats, briefcases and bags into the luggage lockers above their seats. He found his own window seat and fell into it, wrestling with the seatbelt and securing it. Outside, the groundcrew were still working. A plane took off smoothly in the distance, the dull roar perceptible even from here. A plump middle-aged woman sat beside him, spread her newspaper out so that half of it fell onto Rebus's right leg, and began to read. She had offered no greeting, no acknowledgment of his existence.

FYT, madam, he thought to himself, still staring out of the window. But then she gave a loud 'tsk', prompting him to turn towards her. She was staring at him through thick-lensed spectacles, staring and at the same time rapping a finger against the newspaper.

'Nobody's safe these days,' she said, as Rebus examined the news story and saw that it was some fanciful piece about the Wolfman. 'Nobody. I won't let my daughter out these nights. A nine o'clock curfew I told her, until they catch him. Even then you can never be sure. I mean, he could be *anybody*.'

Her look told Rebus that he, too, was not beyond suspicion. He smiled reassuringly.

'I wasn't going to go,' she went on, 'but Frank – that's my husband – he said it was all booked so I should.'

'Visiting Glasgow, are you?'

'Not exactly visiting. My son lives there. He's an accountant in the oil industry. He paid for my ticket, so I could see how he's getting on. I worry about him, what with being so far away and everything. I mean, it's a rough place Glasgow, isn't it? You read about it in the papers. Anything could happen up there.'

Yes, thought Rebus, his smile fixed, so unlike London. There was a sound like an electronic doorbell, and the Fasten Seatbelts sign came on, next to where the No Smoking sign was already lit. Jesus, Rebus could kill for a cigarette. Was he in Smoking or No Smoking? He couldn't make out, and couldn't remember which he'd plumped for at the ticket desk. Was smoking allowed on airplanes these days anyway? If God had meant man to smoke at 20,000 feet, wouldn't he have given us all longer necks? The woman next to him looked to have no neck at all. Pity the poor serial killer who tried cutting his way through *that* throat.

That was a terrible thing to think, God, please forgive me. As penance, he began to concentrate on the woman's

106

conversation, right up until take-off, when even she was forced to stop talking for a moment or two. Rebus, taking advantage of the situation, tucked his newspapers into the pocket on the back of the seat in front of him, leaned his head against the back of his own seat, and promptly fell asleep.

George Flight tried Rebus's hotel again from the Old Bailey, only to be told that Rebus had 'left in a hurry' earlier in the morning after asking how best to get to Heathrow.

'Looks like he's done a runner,' DC Lamb commented. 'Frightened off by our consummate professionalism, I shouldn't wonder.'

'Leave off, Lamb,' growled Flight. 'Mind you, it is a bit mysterious. Why would he leave without saying anything?'

'Because he's a Jock, with all due respect, sir. He was probably worried you were going to drop a bill into his lap.'

Flight smiled obligingly, but his thoughts were elsewhere. Last night Rebus had been seeing that psychologist, Dr Frazer, and now he was in a hurry to leave London. What had happened? Flight's nose twitched. He liked a good honest mystery.

He was in court to have a quiet word with Malcolm Chambers. Chambers was prosecuting counsel in a case involving one of Flight's snouts. The snout had been incredibly stupid, had been caught red-handed. Flight had told the man there was little he could do, but he would do what he could. The snout had given him a lot of very useful tips in the past year, helping put a few fairly nasty individuals behind bars. Flight guessed he owed the man a helping hand. So he would talk to Chambers, not to influence the prosecutor – that was unthinkable, naturally – but to fill in some details on the snout's useful contribution to police work and to society, a contribution which would come to a sad end should Chambers push for the maximum sentence.

Et cetera.

Dirty job, but someone had to do it and besides, Flight was proud of his network of informers. The idea of that network suddenly splintering was . . . well, best not to consider it. He wasn't looking forward to going to Chambers, begging bowl in hand. Especially not after the farce involving Tommy Watkiss. Watkiss was back out on the street, probably telling the story in pubs up and down the East End to a laughing chorus of hangers-on. All about how the arresting constable had said, 'Hello, Tommy, what's going on here?' Flight doubted Chambers would ever forget it, or let Flight forget it. What the hell, best get the begging over and done with.

'Hello there.' It was a female voice, close behind him. He turned to face the cat-like eyes and bright red lips of Cath Farraday.

'Hello, Cath, what are you doing here?'

She explained that she was at the Old Bailey to meet with the influential crime reporter from one of the more upmarket dailies.

'He's halfway through covering a fraud case,' she explained, 'and never strays too far from the courtroom.'

Flight nodded, feeling awkward in her presence. From the corner of his eye he could see that Lamb was enjoying his discomfort, so he tried to be brave and steeled himself to meet the full force of her gaze.

'I saw the pieces you placed in today's press,' he said.

She folded her arms. 'I can't say I'm optimistic about their chances of success.'

'Do the reporters know we're spinning them a yarn?'

'One or two were a bit suspicious, but they've got a lot of hungry readers out there starving for want of another Wolfman story.' She unfolded her arms and reached into her shoulder-bag. 'Ergo, they've got a lot of hungry editors, too. I think they'll take any tidbit we throw them.' She had brought a pack of cigarettes from her bag, and, without offering them out, lit one, dropped the pack back into her bag and snapped the bag shut.

'Well, let's hope something comes of it.'

'You said this was all Inspector Rebus's idea?'

'That's right.'

'Then I'm doubtful. Having met him, I wouldn't say psychology was his strong point.'

'No?' Flight sounded surprised.

'He doesn't *have* a strong point,' broke in Lamb.

'I wouldn't go that far,' said Flight protectively. But Lamb merely gave that insolent grin of his. Flight was part-embarrassed, part-furious. He knew exactly what Lamb's grin was saying: *don't think we don't know why you're sticking so close to him, why you two are so chummy*.

Cath had smiled at Lamb's interruption, but when she spoke her words were directed at Flight: she did not deign to consort with the lower ranks. 'Is Rebus still around?'

Flight shrugged. 'I wish I knew, Cath. I've heard he was last seen heading off towards Heathrow, but he didn't take any luggage with him.'

'Oh well.' She didn't sound disappointed. Flight suddenly shot a hand into the air, waving. Malcolm Chambers acknowledged the signal and came towards them, walking as though no effort whatsoever was involved.

Flight felt the need for introductions. 'Mr Chambers, this is Inspector Cath Farraday. She's the Press Liaison Officer on Wolfman.'

'Ah,' said Chambers, taking her hand momentarily in his. 'The woman responsible for this morning's lurid headlines?'

'Yes,' said Cath. Her voice had taken on a new, soft, feminine edge, an edge Flight couldn't recall having heard before. 'Sorry if they spoiled your breakfast.'

The impossible happened: Chambers' face cracked into a smile. Flight hadn't seen him smile outside of the courtroom in several years. This really was a morning for surprises. 'They did not spoil my breakfast,' Chambers was saying, 'I found them highly entertaining.' He turned to Flight, indicating by this that Cath was dismissed. 'Inspector Flight, I can give you ten minutes, then I'm due in court. Or would you prefer to meet for lunch?'

'Ten minutes should suffice.'

'Excellent. Then come with me.' He glanced towards Lamb, who was still feeling slightly snubbed by Cath. 'And bring your young man with you if you must.'

Then he was gone, striding on noisy leather soles across

the floor of the concourse. Flight winked at Cath, then followed, Lamb silent and furious behind him. Cath grinned, enjoying Lamb's discomfort and the performance Chambers had just put on. She'd heard of him, of course. His courtroom speeches were reckoned to be just about the most persuasive going, and he had even collected what could only be described as 'groupies': people who would attend a trial, no matter how convoluted or boring, just to hear his closing remarks. Her own little coterie of news reporters seemed bland by comparison.

So Rebus had scuttled off home, had he? Good luck to him.

'Excuse me.' A short blurred figure stood before her. She narrowed her eyes until they were the merest slits and peered at a middle-aged woman in a black cloak. The woman was smiling. 'You're not on the jury for court eight by any chance?' Cath Farraday smiled and shook her head. 'Oh well,' sighed the usher, moving off again.

There was such a thing in law as a hung jury, but there were also ushers who would happily see some individual jurors, the rogue jurors, hung. Cath turned on her pointed heels and went off to fulfil her appointment. She wondered if Jim Stevens would remember he was meeting her? He was a good journalist, but his memory was like a sieve at times and seemed especially bad now he was to be a father.

Rebus had time to kill in Glasgow. Time to visit the Horseshoe Bar, or walk through Kelvinside, or even venture down to the Clyde. Time enough to look up an old friend, always supposing he'd had any. Glasgow was changing. Edinburgh had grown corpulent these past few years, during which time Glasgow had been busy getting fit. It had a toned, muscular look to it, a confident swagger rather than the druken stagger which had been its public perception for so long.

It wasn't all good news. Some of the city's character had seeped away. The shiny new shops and wine bars, the bright new office blocks, all had a homogenous quality to them. Go to any prosperous city in the world and you would find buildings just like them. A golden hue of uniformity. Not that Rebus was grieving; anything was better than the old swampland Glasgow had been in the 50s, 60s and early 70s. And the people were more or less the same: blunt, yet wonderfully dry in their humour. The pubs, too, had not changed very much, though their clientele might come more expensively and fashionably dressed and the menu might include chilli or lasagne along with the more traditional fare.

Rebus ate two pies in one pub, standing at the bar with his left foot resting on the polished brass rail. He was biding his time. The plane had landed on schedule, the car had been waiting, the journey into Glasgow had been fast. He arrived in the city centre at twenty minutes past twelve, and would not be called to give his evidence until around three.

Time to kill.

He left the pub and took what he hoped might be a shortcut (though he had no ready destination in mind) down a cobbled lane towards some railway arches, some crumbling warehouse buildings and a rubble-strewn wasteland. There were a lot of people milling about here, and he realised that what he had thought were piles of rubbish lying around on the damp ground were actually articles for sale. He had stumbled upon a flea market, and by the look of the customers it was where the down and outs did their shopping. Dank unclean clothes lay in bundles, thrown down anywhere. Near them stood the vendors, shuffling their feet, saying nothing, one or two stoking up a makeshift fire around which others clustered for warmth. The atmosphere was muted. People might cough and hack and wheeze, but they seldom spoke. A few punks, their resplendent mohicans as out of place as a handful of parrots in a cage of sparrows, milled around, not really looking like they meant to buy anything. The locals regarded them with suspicion. Tourists, the collective look said, just bloody tourists.

Beneath the arches themselves were narrow aisles lined with stalls and trestle tables. The smell in here was worse, but Rebus was curious. No out-of-town hypermarket could have provided such a range of wares: broken spectacles, old wireless sets (with this or that knob missing), lamps, hats, tarnished cutlery, purses and wallets, incomplete sets of dominoes and playing cards. One stall seemed to sell nothing but pieces of used soap, most of them looking as though they had come from public conveniences. Another sold false teeth. An old man, hands shaking almost uncontrollably, had found a bottom set he liked, but could not find a top set to match. Rebus wrinkled his face and turned away. The mohicans had opened a game of Cluedo.

'Hey, pal,' they called to the stallholder, 'there's nae weapons here. Where's the dagger an' the gun an' that?'

The man looked at the open box. 'You could improvise,' he suggested.

Rebus smiled and moved on. London was different to all this. It felt more congested, things moved too quickly, there seemed pressure and stress everywhere. Driving a car from A to B, shopping for groceries, going out for the evening, all were turned into immensely tiring activities. Londoners appeared to him to be on very short fuses indeed. Here, the people were stoics. They used their humour as a barrier against everything Londoners had to take on the chin. Different worlds. Different civilisations. Glasgow had been the second city of the Empire. It had been the first city of Scotland all through the twentieth century.

'Got a fag, mister?'

It was one of the punks. Now, up close, Rebus saw she was a girl. He'd assumed the group had been all male. They all looked so similar.

'No, sorry, I'm trying to give up – '

But she had already started to move away, in search of someone, anyone, who could immediately gratify. He looked at his watch. It was gone two, and it might take him half an hour to get from here to the court. The punks were still arguing about the missing Cluedo pieces.

'I mean, how can you play a game when there's bits missing? Know what I mean, pal? Like, where's Colonel Mustard? An' the board's nearly torn in half, by the way. How much d'ye want for it?'

The argumentative punk was tall and immensely thin, his size and shape accentuated by the black he wore from tip to toe. 'Twa ply o' reek,' Rebus's father would have called him. Was the Wolfman fat or thin? tall or short? young or old? did he have a job? a wife? a husband even? Did someone close to him know the truth, and were they keeping quiet? When would he strike next? And where? Lisa had been unable to answer any of these questions. Maybe Flight was right about psychology. So much of it was guesswork, like a game where some of the pieces are missing and nobody knows the rules. Sometimes you ended up playing a game completely different to the original, a game of your own devising.

That was what Rebus needed: a new set of rules in his game against the Wolfman. Rules which would be to his benefit. The newspaper stories were the start of it, but only if the Wolfman made the next move.

Maybe Cafferty would get off this time, but there'd always be another. The board was always prepared for a fresh start.

Rebus gave his evidence and was out of the court by four. He handed the file on the case back to his driver, a balding middle-aged detective sergeant, and settled into the passenger seat.

'Let me know what happens,' he said. The driver nodded.

'Straight back to the airport, Inspector?' Funny how a Glaswegian accent could be made to sound so sarcastic. The sergeant had managed somehow to make Rebus feel his inferior. Then again, there was little love lost between east and west coasts. There might have been a wall dividing the two, such was their own abiding cold war. The driver was repeating his question, a little louder now.

'That's right,' said Rebus, just as loudly. 'It's a jet-setting life in the Lothian and Borders Police.'

His head was fairly thrumming by the time he got back to the hotel in Piccadilly. He needed a quiet night, a night alone. He hadn't managed to contact Flight or Lisa, but they could wait until tomorrow. For now, he wanted nothing.

Nothing but silence and stillness, lying on the bed and staring at the ceiling, his mind nowhere.

It had been one hell of a week, and the week was only halfway through. He took two paracetamol from the bottle he had brought and washed them down with half a glass of tepid tap-water. The water tasted foul. Was it true that London water had passed through seven sets of kidneys before reaching the drinker? It had an oily quality in his mouth, not the sharp clear taste of the water in Edinburgh. Seven sets of kidneys. He looked at his cases, thinking of the amount of stuff he had brought with him, useless stuff, stuff he would never use. Even the bottle of malt sat more or less untouched.

There was a telephone ringing somewhere. His telephone, but he managed to ignore the fact for fully fifteen seconds. He growled and clawed at the wall with his hand, finally finding the receiver and dragging it to his ear.

'This had better be good.'

'Where the fuck have you been?' It was Flight's voice, anxious and angry.

'Good evening to you too, George.'

'There's been another killing.'

Rebus sat up and swung his legs off the bed. 'When?'

'The body was discovered an hour ago. There's something else.' He paused. 'We caught the killer.'

Now Rebus stood up.

'What?'

'We caught him as he was running off.'

Rebus's knees almost failed him, but he locked them. His voice was unnaturally quiet. 'Is it him?'

'Could be.'

'Where are you?'

'I'm at HQ. We've brought him here. The murder took place in a house off Brick Lane. Not too far from Wolf Street.'

'In a house?' That was a surprise. The other murders had

all taken place out of doors. But then, as Lisa had said, the pattern kept changing.

'Yes,' said Flight. 'And that's not all. The killer was found with money on him stolen from the house, and some jewellery and a camera.'

Another break in the pattern. Rebus sat down on the bed again. 'I see what you're getting at,' he said. 'But the method – ?'

'Similar, to be sure. Philip Cousins is on his way. He was at a dinner somewhere.'

'I'm going to the scene, George. I'll come to see you afterwards.'

'Fine.' Flight sounded as though he had hoped for this. Rebus was scrabbling for paper and a pen.

'What's the address?'

'110 Copperplate Street.'

Rebus wrote the address on the back of his travel ticket from the trip to Glasgow.

'John?'

'Yes, George?'

'Don't go off again without telling me, okay?'

'Yes, George.' Rebus paused. 'Can I go now?'

'Go on then, bugger off. I'll see you here later.'

Rebus put down the telephone and felt an immense weariness take control of him, weighting his legs and arms and head. He took several deep breaths and rose to his feet, then walked to the sink and splashed water on his face, rubbing a wet hand around his neck and throat. He looked up, hardly recognising himself in the wall-mounted mirror, sighed and spread his hands either side of his face, the way he'd seen Roy Scheider do once in a film.

'It's showtime.'

Rebus's taxi driver was full of tales of the Krays, Richardson and Jack the Ripper. With Brick Lane their destination, he was especially vociferous on the subject of 'Old Jack'.

'Done his first prossie on Brick Lane. Richardson, though, he was evil. Used to torture people in a scrapyard.

115

You knew when he was electrocuting some poor bastard, 'cos the bulb across the scrapyard gates kept flickering.' Then a low chuckle. A sideways flick of the head. 'Krays used to drink in that pub on the corner. My youngest used to drink in there. Got in some terrible punch-ups, so I banned him from going. He works in the City, courier sort of stuff, you know, motorbikes.'

Rebus, who had been slouching in the back seat, now gripped the headrest on the front passenger seat and yanked himself forward.

'Motorbike messenger?'

'Yeah, makes a bleeding packet. Twice what I take home a week, I'll tell you that. He's just bought himself a flat down in Docklands. Only they call them "riverside apartments" these days. That's a laugh. I know some of the guys who built them. Every bloody shortcut in the book. Hammering in screws instead of screwing them. Plasterboard so thin you can almost see your neighbours, never mind hear them.'

'A friend of my daughter works as a courier in the City.'

'Yeah? Maybe I know him. What's his name?'

'Kenny.'

'Kenny?' He shook his head. Rebus stared at where the silvery hairs on the driver's neck disappeared into his shirt collar. 'Nah, I don't know a Kenny. Kev, yes, and a couple of Chrisses, but not Kenny.'

Rebus sat back again. It struck him that he didn't know what Kenny's surname was. 'Are we nearly there?' he asked.

'Two minutes, guv. There's a lovely shortcut coming up should save us some time. Takes us right past where Richardson used to hang out.'

A crowd of reporters had gathered outside in the narrow street. Housefront, pavement, then road, where the crowd stood, held back by uniformed constables. Did nobody in London possess such a thing as a front garden? Rebus had yet to see a house with a garden, apart from the millionaire blocks in Kensington.

116

'John!' A female voice, escaping from the scrum of newsmen. She pushed her way towards him. He signalled for the line of uniforms to break momentarily, so as to let her through.

'What are you doing here?'

Lisa looked a little shaken. 'Heard a newsflash,' she gasped. 'Thought I'd come over.'

'I'm not sure that's such a good idea, Lisa.' Rebus was thinking of Jean Cooper's body. If this were similar . . .

'Any comment to make?' yelled one of the newsmen. Rebus was aware of flashguns, of the bright homing lamps attached to video cameras. Other reporters were shouting now, desperate for a story that would reach the first editions.

'Come on then,' said Rebus, pulling Lisa Frazer towards the door of number 110.

Philip Cousins was still dressed in dark suit and tie, suitably funereal. Isobel Penny was in black, too, a full length dress with long, tight sleeves. She did not look funereal. She looked divine. She smiled at Rebus as he entered the cramped living room, nodding in recognition.

'Inspector Rebus,' said Cousins, 'they said you might drop by.'

'Never one to miss a good corpse,' Rebus replied drily. Cousins, stooping over the body, looked up at him.

'Quite.'

The smell was there, clogging up Rebus's nostrils and lungs. Some people couldn't smell it, but he always could. It was strong and salty, rich, clotting, cloying. It smelt like nothing else on earth. And behind it lurked another smell, more bland, like tallow, candle-wax, cold water. The two contrasting smells of life and death. Rebus was willing to bet that Cousins could smell it, but he doubted Isobel Penny could.

A middle-aged woman lay on the floor, an ungainly twist of legs and arms. Her throat had been cut. There were signs of a struggle, ornaments shattered and knocked from their perches, bloody handprints smeared across one wall. Cousins stood up and sighed.

117

'Very clumsy,' he said. He glanced towards Isobel Penny, who was sketching on her notepad. 'Penny,' he said, 'you look quite delightful this evening. Have I told you?'

She smiled again, blushed, but said nothing. Cousins turned to Rebus, ignoring Lisa Frazer's silent presence. 'It's a copycat,' he said with another sigh, 'but a copycat of little wit or talent. He's obviously read the descriptions in the newspapers, which have been detailed but inaccurate. I'd say it was an interrupted burglary. He panicked, went for his knife, and realised that if he made it look like our friend the Wolfman then he might just get away with it.' He looked down at the corpse again. 'Not terribly clever. I suppose the vultures have gathered?'

Rebus nodded. 'When I came in there were about a dozen reporters outside. Probably double that by now. We know what they want to hear, don't we?'

'I fear they are going to be disappointed.' Cousins checked his watch. 'Not worth going back to dinner. We've probably missed the port and cheese. Damned fine table, too. Such a pity.' He waved his hand in the direction of the body. 'Anything you'd like to see? Or shall we wrap this one up, as it were?'

Rebus smiled. The humour was as dark as the suit, but any humour was welcome. The smell in the air had been distilled now to that of raw steak and brown sauce. He shook his head. There was nothing more to be done in here. But outside, outside he was about to create an outrage. Flight would hate him for it, in fact everybody would hate him for it. But hate was fine. Hate was an emotion, and without emotion, what else was left? Lisa had already staggered out into the tiny hallway, where a police officer was trying awkwardly to comfort her. As Rebus came out of the room, she shook her head and straightened up.

'I'm fine,' she said.

'The first one always hits you hard,' said Rebus. 'Come on, I'm going to try out a spot of psychology on the Wolfman.'

The huddle of reporters and cameramen had become a

sizeable crowd, now including the interested and the curious amateurs. The line of uniformed policemen had locked arms in a small but unbreakable chain. The questions began: Over here! Can we ask you who you are? You were at the canal, weren't you? A statement – Anything to say – Wolfman – Is it – The Wolfman? Is it – Just a few words if –

Rebus had walked to within a few inches of them, Lisa by his side. One of the reporters had leaned close to Lisa, asking for her name.

'Lisa, Lisa Frazer.'

'Are you working on the case, Lisa?'

'I'm a psychologist.'

Rebus cleared his throat noisily. The reporters were like mongrels in a dogs' home, calming quickly when they realised it was their turn at last for the feeding bowl. He raised his arms, and they fell quiet.

'A short statement, gentlemen,' said Rebus.

'Can we just ask who you are first?'

But Rebus shook his head. It didn't matter, did it? They would know soon enough. How many Scottish coppers were working on Wolfman? Flight would know, Cath Farraday would know and the journalists would find out. That didn't matter. Then one of them, unable to hold back, asked the question.

'Have you caught him?' Rebus tried to catch the man's eye, but every eye was silently asking the same thing. 'Is it the Wolfman?'

And this time Rebus nodded. 'Yes,' he said emphatically. 'It's the Wolfman. We've caught him.' Lisa looked at him in dumb surprise.

More questions, yelled now, screeched, but the chain in front of them would not break and somehow they did not think simply to walk around it. Rebus had turned away and saw Cousins and Isobel Penny standing just outside the door of the house, rigid, unable to believe what they had just heard. He winked at them and walked with Lisa to where his cab still waited. The driver folded his evening paper and stuck it down the side of his seat.

119

'You fairly got them going, guv. What did you say?'

'Nothing much,' said Rebus, settling back in his seat and smiling towards Lisa Frazer. 'Just a few fibs.'

'Fibs!'

So this was what Flight looked like when he was angry. 'Fibs!'

He seemed unable to believe what he was hearing. 'You call that a few fibs? Cath Farraday's going apeshit trying to calm those bastards down. They're like fucking animals. Half of them are ready to go to print on this! And you call it "fibs"? You're off your trolley, Rebus.'

So it was back to 'Rebus', was it? Well then, so be it. Rebus remembered that they'd promised they'd have dinner together this evening, but somehow he doubted the invitation still stood.

George Flight had been interviewing the murderer. His cheeks were veined with blood, his tie unknotted and hanging loose around his half unbuttoned shirt. He paced what floor there was in the small office. Rebus knew that outside the closed door people were listening in a mixture of fear and amusement: fear at Flight's anger, amusement that Rebus was its sole recipient.

'You're the fucking limit.' Flight's anger had peaked; his voice had dropped by half a decibel. 'What gives you the right – '

Rebus slapped the desk with his hand. He'd had enough of this. 'I'll tell you what gives me the right, George. The mere fact of the Wolfman gives me the right to do anything I think best.'

'Best!' Flight sounded freshly outraged. 'Now I've heard it all. Giving the papers a crock of shit like that is supposed to be "best"? By Christ, I'd hate to see your idea of "worst".'

Rebus's voice was every bit the equal of Flight's now, and rising. 'He's out there somewhere and he's laughing his head off at us. Because he seems to know how we'll play every round, he's knocking hell out of us.' Rebus grew quiet: Flight was listening now, and that was what he wanted. 'We need to get him riled, get him to lift his head over the trench he's hiding in so he can see what the fuck is going on. We need him angry, George. Not angry at the world. Angry at *us*. Because when he raises his head, we'll be ready to bite it off.

'We've already accused him of being everything from gay to a cannibal from Pluto. Now we're telling everyone he's been caught.' Rebus was reaching his point, his defence. He lowered his voice still further. 'I don't think he'll be able to take that, George. Really I don't. I think he'll have to make contact. Maybe with the papers, maybe directly with us. Just to let us know.'

'Or kill again,' countered Flight. '*That* would let us know.'

Rebus shook his head. 'If he kills again, we keep it quiet. Total media blackout. He gets no publicity. Everybody still thinks he's been caught. Sooner or later, he'll have to show himself.'

Rebus was completely calm now, and so was Flight. Flight rubbed both hands over his cheeks and down to his jaw. He was staring into space, thinking it over. Rebus did not doubt the plan would work. It might take time, but it would work. Basic SAS training: if you can't locate your enemy, make the enemy come to you. Besides, it was the only plan they had.

'John, what if the publicity doesn't bother him? Publicity *or* the lack of it?'

Rebus shrugged. He had no answer to that. All he had were case histories and his own instincts.

Finally, Flight shook his head. 'Go back to Edinburgh, John,' he said tiredly. 'Just do it.' Rebus stared at him, not blinking, willing him to say something else. But George Flight simply walked to the door, opened it, and closed it behind him.

That was it then. Rebus released his breath in a long hiss. Go back to Edinburgh. Wasn't that what everyone had wanted all along? Laine? Lamb and the rest of them? Flight too, maybe. Even Rebus himself. He'd told himself he could do no good here. Well, he was doing no good, so why not go home?

The answer was simple: the case had grabbed him by the throat. There was no escaping it. The Wolfman, faceless, bodiless, had pressed a blade to Rebus's ear and was holding it there, ready to slice. And besides, there was London itself, full of its own stories. Rhona. Sammy. Sammy and Kenny. Rebus had to remind himself that he was still interested in Kenny.

And Lisa.

Above all there was Lisa. The taxi had dropped her off at her flat. She had been quite pale, but insisted she was all right, insisted he go on without her. He should ring her, check she really was okay. What? And tell her he was leaving? No, he had to confront Flight. He opened the door and went into the Murder Room. Flight was not there. The curious faces looked at him from their desks, their telephones, their wallcharts and photographs. He looked at no one, but especially not at Lamb, who was grinning from behind a manila file, his eyes peering over at Rebus.

Flight was in the hallway outside, deep in discussion with the Duty Sergeant, who nodded and moved off. Rebus saw Flight sag, leaning his back against the wall, rubbing his face again. He approached slowly, giving George Flight an extra moment or two of peace and quiet.

'George,' he said. Flight looked up, smiled weakly.

'You never give up, John, do you?'

'I'm sorry, George. I should have checked with you before I pulled a stunt like that. Block the story if you want.'

Flight gave a short humourless laugh. 'Too late. It's been on the local radio news already. The other stations can't just sit back. It'll be on every local news report by midnight. It's your snowball, John. You started it running down the hill. All we can do now is watch it getting bigger and bigger.' He stabbed a finger into Rebus's chest. 'Cath is going to be after your guts, lad. She's the one they'll blame, the one who'll have to apologise, who'll have the job of gaining their trust all over again.' Flight now wagged the finger backwards and forwards, then grinned. 'And if anyone can do it, Inspector Cath Farraday can.' He checked his watch. 'Right, I've let the bugger stew long enough. Time to get back to the interview room.'

'How's it going?'

Flight shrugged. 'Singing like Gracie Fields. We couldn't stop him if we wanted to. He thinks we're going to pin all the Wolfman killings on him, so he's telling us everything he knows, and some things he's probably making up besides.'

'Cousins said it was a copycat, done to disguise a cocked-up burglary.'

Flight nodded. 'I sometimes think Philip's in the wrong game. This guy's a petty thief, not the bloody Wolfman. But I'll tell you what is interesting. He's told us he sells the stuff on to a mutual friend.'

'Who?'

'Tommy Watkiss.'

'Well, well.'

'Coming?' Flight pointed along the corridor, towards the stairwell. Rebus shook his head.

'I want to make a couple of phone calls. I might catch you up later.'

'Suit yourself.'

Rebus watched Flight go. Sometimes it was only brute stubbornness that kept humans going, long after their limbs and intellect had told them to quit. Flight was like a footballer playing in extra time. Rebus hoped he could see the game out to its end.

They watched him as he walked back through the Murder Room. Lamb in particular seemed to peer at him from behind a report, eyes gleaming with amusement. There was a noise coming from his office, a strange tapping noise. He pushed open the door and saw on his desk a small toy, a grotesque plastic jaw atop two oversized feet. The jaw was bright red, the teeth gleaming white, and the feet walked to a clockwork whirr while the jaws snapped shut, then open, shut then open. Snap, snap, snap. Snap, snap, snap.

Rebus, furious at the joke, walked to the desk, lifted the contraption and pulled at it, his own teeth bright and gritted, until it snapped in two. But the feet kept on moving, stopping only when the spring had run down. Not that Rebus was noticing. He was staring at the two halves, the upper and lower jaws. Sometimes things weren't what they seemed. The punk at the Glasgow flea market had turned out to be a girl. And at the flea market they had been selling teeth, false plastic teeth. Like a supermarket pick'n' mix counter. Any size you liked. Christ, he should have seen it sooner!

Rebus walked quickly back through the Murder Room. Lamb, doubtless responsible for the joke, seemed ready to say something until he saw the look on Rebus's face, an urgent, don't-mess-with-me look. He ran along the corridor and down the stairs, down towards the euphemism known as an Interview Room. 'A man is helping police with their enquiries.' Rebus loved those euphemisms. He knocked and entered. A detective was changing the tape in a recording machine. Flight was leaning across the table to offer a cigarette to a dishevelled young man, a young man with yellow bruising on his face and skinned knuckles.

'George?' Rubus tried to sound composed. 'Could I have a word?'

Flight pushed back his chair noisily, leaving the cigarette packet with the prisoner. Rebus held open the door, indicating for Flight to move outside. Then he thought of something, and caught the prisoner's eye.

'Do you know somebody called Kenny? he asked.

'Loads.'

'Rides a motorbike?'

The young man shrugged again and reached into the packet for a cigarette. There was no answer forthcoming, and Flight was outside waiting, so Rebus closed the door.

'What was that all about?' asked Flight.

'Maybe nothing,' said Rebus. 'Do you remember when we went to the Old Bailey, how someone shouted out when the case was stopped?'

'Someone in the public gallery.'

'That's right. Well, I recognised the voice. It's a teenager called Kenny. He's one of those motorcycle messengers.'

'So?'

'He's going out with my daughter.'

'Ah. And that bothers you?' Rebus nodded.

'Yes, a bit.'

'And that's what you want to see me about.'

Rebus managed a weak smile. 'No, no, nothing like that.'

'So what's on your mind?'

'I was in Glasgow today, giving evidence. I had a bit of free time and went to a flea market, the sort of place tramps go to do their messages – '

'Messages?'

'Their shopping,' Rebus explained.

'And?'

'And there was a stall selling false teeth. Odds and sods. Top sets and bottom sets, not necessarily matching.' He paused to let those final three words sink home. 'Is there someplace like that in London, George?'

Flight nodded. 'Brick Lane for one. There's a market there every Sunday. The main road sells fruit, veg, clothes. But there are streets off, where they sell anything they've got. Bric-a-brac, old rubbish. It makes for an interesting walk, but you wouldn't buy anything.'

'But you could buy false teeth there?'

'Yes,' said Flight after a moment's thought. 'I don't doubt it.'

'Then he's been cleverer than we thought, hasn't he?'

'You're saying the bite marks aren't real?'

'I'm saying they're not the Wolfman's teeth. The lower set smaller than the upper? You end up with a pretty strange jaw, as Doctor Morrison showed us, remember?'

'How can I forget? I was going to feed the pictures to the press.'

'Which is probably exactly what the Wolfman wanted. He goes to Brick Lane market, or at least to somewhere like it, and buys any upper and lower set. They don't match, but that doesn't matter. And he uses them to make those damned bite marks.'

Flight seemed dismissive, but Rebus knew the man was hooked. 'He can't be that clever.'

'Yes he can,' persisted Rebus. 'He's had everything worked out from the start . . . from *before* the start! He's been playing with us like we were clockwork, George.'

'Then we have to wait until Sunday,' Flight said thoughtfully. 'Search every stall at every market, find the ones selling false teeth – there can't be many – and ask.'

'About the person who bought a set of teeth *without trying them for size*!' Rebus burst out laughing. It was ridiculous. It was absolutely mad. But he was sure it was true, and he was sure the stall-holder would remember, and would give a description. Surely most of the customers would try for size. It was the best lead they'd had so far, and it might just be the only one they'd need.

Flight was smiling too, shaking his head at the dark comic reality of it. Rebus held a closed fist in front of him, and Flight brought his open palm to rest beneath it. When Rebus opened his hand, the plastic chattering teeth fell into Flight's palm.

'Just like clockwork,' said Rebus. 'What's more, we've got Lamb to thank.' He thought about this. 'But I'd rather he didn't get to know.'

Flight nodded. 'Anything you say, John. Anything you say.'

Back at his desk, Rebus sat in front of a fresh sheet of paper. The Wolfman had been too clever. Too clever by half. He thought of Lisa, of her notion that the killer might have a criminal record. It was possible. Possible, too, that the Wolfman simply knew how the police worked. So, he might be a policeman. Or work in forensics. Or be a journalist. A civil rights campaigner. Work in the law. Or write bloody scripts for television. He might just have done his reading. There were plenty of case histories in libraries and bookshops, plenty of biographies of murderers, tracing how they were caught. By studying them, you could learn how *not* to get caught. However hard Rebus tried he just couldn't whittle away at the list of possibilities. The teeth might be yet another dead end. That was why they had to make the Wolfman come to *them*.

He threw down his pen and reached for the telephone, trying Lisa's number. But the phone just rang and rang and rang. Maybe she'd taken a couple of sleeping pills, or gone for a walk, or was a heavy sleeper.

'You stupid prick.'

He looked towards the open door. Cath Farraday was standing there, in her favourite position, against the jamb, arms folded. As if to let him know she'd been there for some time.

'You incredibly stupid little man.'

Rebus pinned a smile to his face. 'Good evening, Inspector. How can I help you?'

'Well,' she said, coming into the room, 'you can start by keeping your gob shut and your brain in gear. You never speak to the press. Never!' She was rearing over him now, looking ready to butt him in the face. He tried to avoid her eyes, eyes sharp enough to cut a man open, and found himself staring instead at her hair. It, too, looked dangerous.

'Do you understand me?'

'FYTP,' said Rebus, speaking without thinking.

'What?'

'Loud and clear,' he said. 'Yes, loud and clear.'

She nodded slowly, not seeming completely convinced, then threw a newspaper onto the desk. He hadn't noticed the paper till now, and glanced towards it. There was a photograph on the front, not large but large enough. It showed him talking to the reporters, Lisa standing nervously by his side. The headline was larger: WOLFMAN CAUGHT? Cath Farraday tapped the photograph.

'Who's the bimbo?'

Rebus felt his cheeks growing red. 'She's a psychologist. She's helping on the case.'

Cath Farraday looked at Rebus as though he were something more than merely stupid, then shook her head and turned to leave. 'Keep the paper,' she said. 'There are plenty more where it came from.'

* * *

She sits with the newspaper in front of her. There are several more piled on the floor. She has the scissors in her hand. One of the reports mentions who the policeman is: Inspector John Rebus. The report calls him an 'expert' on serial murders. And another report mentions that standing to his left is a 'police psychologist, Lisa Frazer'. She cuts around the photograph, then cuts another line, splitting Rebus from Frazer. Time and again she does this, until she has two new neat piles, one of John Rebus, one of Lisa Frazer. She takes one of the photographs of the psychologist and snips off her head. Then, smiling, she sits down to write a letter. A very difficult letter, but that doesn't matter. She has all the time in the world.

All the time.

Churchill

Rebus woke to his radio-alarm at seven, sat up in bed and rang Lisa. No reply. Maybe something was wrong.

Over breakfast, he skimmed the newspapers. Two of the quality titles carried bold front page stories recounting the capture of the Wolfman, but they were couched in speculative prose: Police are believed . . . it is thought that . . . ; Police may have already captured the evil cut-throat killer. Only the tabloids carried pictures of Rebus at his little press conference. Even they, despite the shouting headlines, were being cagey; probably they didn't believe it themselves. That didn't matter. What mattered was that somewhere the Wolfman might be reading about his capture.

His. There was that word again. Rebus couldn't help but think of the Wolfman as a man, yet part of him was wary of narrowing the possible identity in this way. There was still nothing to indicate that it could not be a woman. He needed to keep an open mind. And did the sex of the beast really matter? Actually yes, probably it did. What was the use of women waiting hours just so that they could travel home from a pub or party in a mini-cab driven by another woman, if the killer they were so afraid of turned out to be a woman? All over London people were taking protective measures. Housing estates were patrolled by neighbourhood vigilantes. One group had already beaten up a completely innocent stranger who'd wandered onto the estate because he was lost and needed directions. His crime? The estate was white, and the stranger was coloured. Flight had told Rebus how prevalent racism was in London, 'especially the south-east corner. Go into some of those estates with a tan and you'll end up being nutted.' Rebus had encountered it already, thanks to Lamb's own particular brand of xenophobia.

Of course, there wasn't nearly so much racism in Scotland. There was no need: the Scots had bigotry instead.

He finished the papers and went to HQ. It was early yet, a little after half past eight. A few of the murder team were busy at their desks, but the smaller offices were empty. The office Rebus had taken over was stuffy, and he opened the windows. The day was mild, a slight breeze wafting in. He could hear the distant sound of a computer printer, of telephones starting to ring. Outside, the traffic flowed in slow motion, a dull rumbling, nothing more. Without realising he was doing it, Rebus rested his head on his arms. This close to the desk, he could smell wood and varnish, mixed with pencil-lead. It reminded him of primary school.

A knock, echoing somewhere, jarred his sleep. Then a cough, not a necessary cough, a diplomatic cough.

'Excuse me, sir.'

Rebus lifted his head sharply from the desk. A WPC was standing, her head around the door, looking in at him. He had been sleeping with his mouth open. There was a trail of saliva on the side of his mouth, and a tiny pool of the stuff on the surface of the desk.

'Yes,' he said, still muzzy. 'What is it?'

A sympathetic smile. They weren't all like Lamb, he had to remember that. On a case like this, you became a team, came to feel as close to the others as you would to your best friend. Closer than that even, sometimes.

'Someone to see you, sir. Well, she wants to speak to someone about the murders, and you're about the only one here.'

Rebus looked at his watch. Eight forty-five. He hadn't been asleep long then. Good. He felt he could confide in this WPC. 'How do I look?' he asked.

'Well,' she said, 'one side of your face is red from where you've been lying on it, but otherwise you'll do.' Then the smile again. A good deed in a naughty world.

'Thanks,' he said. 'Okay, send her in, please.'

'Right you are.' The head disappeared, but only momentarily. 'Can I get you a coffee or something?'

'Coffee would hit the spot,' said Rebus. 'Thanks.'

'Milk? Sugar?'

'Just milk.'

The head disappeared. The door closed. Rebus tried to look busy: it wasn't difficult. There was a mound of fresh paperwork to be gone through. Lab reports and the like. Results (negative) from door-to-door on the Jean Cooper murder from the interviews with everyone who'd been in the pub with her that Sunday night. He picked up the first sheet and held it in front of him. There was a knock on the door, so soft that he only just caught it.

'Come in,' he called.

The door opened slowly. A woman was standing there, looking around her as though her timidity might be about to turn to fright. She was in her late twenties, with closely cropped brown hair, but other than that she defied description. She was more a collection of 'nots' than anything else: not tall, but not exactly short; not slim, but by no means overweight, and her face lacked anything approaching a personality.

'Hello,' Rebus said, half-rising to his feet. He indicated a chair on the other side of the desk, and watched as, with breathtaking slowness, she closed the door, testing it afterwards to make sure it was going to stay shut. Only then did she turn to look at him – or at least towards him, for she had a way of focussing just to the side of his face, so that her eyes never met his.

'Hello,' she said. She seemed ready to stand throughout proceedings. Rebus, who had seated himself again, gestured once more with his hand.

'Please. Sit down.'

At last, she poised herself above the chair and lowered herself into it. Rebus had the feeling that he was the boss at some job interview, and that she wanted the job so much she'd worked herself into a good and proper state about it.

'You wanted to speak to someone,' he said, in what he hoped were soft and sympathetic tones.

'Yes,' she said.

Well, it was a start. 'My name is Inspector Rebus. And yours is. . . ?'

'Jan Crawford.'

'Okay, Jan. Now, how can I help you?'

She swallowed, gazing at the window behind Rebus's left ear. 'It's the killings,' she said. 'They call him the Wolfman.'

Rebus was undecided. Maybe she was a crank, but she didn't seem like one. She just seemed jumpy. Perhaps she had good reason.

'That's right,' he cajoled. 'The papers call him that.'

'Yes, they do.' She had become suddenly excitable, the words spilling from her. 'And they said last night on the radio, this morning in the paper . . .' She pulled a news-paper clipping from her bag. It was the photograph of Rebus and Lisa Frazer. 'This is you, isn't it?'

Rebus nodded.

'Then you'll know. I mean, you must. The paper says he's done it again, they're saying you've caught him, or maybe you've caught him, nobody's sure.' She paused, breathing heavily. All the time her eyes were on the window. Rebus kept his mouth shut, letting her calm down. Her eyes were filling, becoming glossy with tears. As she spoke, one droplet squirmed out from the corner of an eye and crept down towards her lips, her chin. 'Nobody's sure whether you've caught him, but I could be sure. At least, I think I can be sure. I didn't get, I mean, I've been scared so long now, and I haven't said anything. I didn't want anybody to know, my mum and dad to know. I just wanted to shut it out, but that's stupid, isn't it?, when he could do it again if he's not caught. So I decided to, I mean, maybe I can. . .' She made to stand up, thought better of it, and squeezed her hands together instead.

'Can what, Miss Crawford?'

'Identify him,' she said, her voice almost a whisper now. She searched in the sleeve of her blouse, found a tissue, and blew her nose. The tear dripped onto one knee. 'Identify him,' she repeated, 'if he's here, if you've caught him.'

Rebus was staring hard at her now, and at last his eyes found hers. Her brown eyes, covered with a film of liquid. He'd seen cranks before, plenty of them. Maybe she was, and maybe she wasn't.

'What do you mean, Jan?'

She sniffed again, turned her eyes to the window, swallowed. 'He almost got me,' she said. 'I was the first, before all the others. He almost got me. I was almost the first.'

And then she lifted her head. At first Rebus couldn't understand why. But then he saw. Under her right ear, running in a crescent shape towards her white throat, there was a dark pink scar, no more than an inch long.

The kind of scar you made with a knife.

The first intended kill of the Wolfman.

'What do you think?'

They faced one another across the desk. Four inches of fresh paperwork had appeared in the in-tray, threatening to overbalance the pile and send it slewing down across the floor. Rebus was eating a cheese and onion sandwich from Gino's. Comfort food. One of the nice things about being a bachelor was that you could eat, without fear of regrets, onions, Branston pickle, huge sausage, egg and tomato sauce sandwiches, curried beans on toast and all the other delicacies favoured by the male.

'What do you think then?'

Flight sipped from a can of cola, giving slight closed-mouth burps between times. He had listened to Rebus' story and had met with Jan Crawford. She had now been taken to an interview room to be fed tea and sympathy by a WPC while a detective took her statement. Flight and Rebus both hoped she would not have to deal with Lamb.

'Well?'

Flight rubbed a knuckle against his right eye. 'I don't know, John. This case has gone ga-ga. You're off telling porkies to the press, your picture's all over the front pages, we've got our first – maybe not our last – copycat killing, then you come up with some idea of flea markets and false teeth. And now this.' He opened his arms wide, pleading for help to put his world back into some semblance of order. 'It's all a bit much.'

Rebus bit into the sandwich, chewing slowly. 'But it fits

the pattern, doesn't it? From what I've read about serial killers, the first attempt is often botched. They're not quite ready, they haven't planned well enough. Somebody screams, they panic. He didn't have his technique honed. He didn't go for the mouth, so she was able to scream. Then he found that human skin and muscle is tougher than it looks. He'd probably seen too many horror films, thought it was like cutting through butter. So he scraped her, but not enough to do serious damage. Maybe the knife wasn't sharp enough, who knows. The point is, he got scared and he ran.'

Flight merely shrugged. 'And she didn't come forward,' he said. 'That's what bothers me.'

'She's come forward now. Tell me this, George. How many rape victims do we actually *see*? I heard tell somebody reckons it's less than one in three. Jan Crawford is a timid little woman, scared half to death. All she wanted to do was forget about it, but she couldn't. Her conscience wouldn't let her. Her conscience brought her to us.'

'I still don't like it, John. Don't ask me why.'

Rebus finished the sandwich and made a show of wiping his hands together. 'Your copper's instinct?' he suggested, just a little sarcastically.

'Maybe,' said Flight, appearing to miss, or at least to ignore, Rebus's tone. 'There's just something about her.'

'Trust me. I've talked to her. I've been through it all with her. And, George, I believe her. I think it was him. Twelfth of December last year. That was his first time.'

'Maybe not,' said Flight. 'Maybe there are others who haven't come forward.'

'Maybe. What matters is, one did.'

'I still don't see what good this does us.' Flight picked up a sheet of paper from the desk and read the scribbled details. ' "He was about six feet tall, white, and I think he had brown hair. He was running away with his back to me, so I couldn't see his face." ' Flight put down the paper. 'That narrows things down nicely, doesn't it?'

Yes, Rebus wanted to say, it does. Because now I think I'm dealing with a man, and before this I wasn't sure. But he kept that particular thought to himself. He'd given George Flight enough grief in the past few days.

'That's still not the point,' he said instead.

'Then what in God's name *is* the point?' Flight had finished the can of cola and now tossed it into a metal wastepaper bin, where it rang against the side, the reverberation lasting for what seemed like an age.

When all was quiet again, Rebus spoke. 'The point is, the Wolfman doesn't know she didn't get a good look at him. We've got to persuade Miss Crawford to go public. Let the TV cameras feast on her. The One Who Got Away. Then we say that she's given us a good description. If that doesn't panic the bastard, nothing will.'

'Panic! Everything you do is designed to panic him. What good does that do? What if it simply frightens him off? What if he just stops killing and we never find him?'

'He's not the type,' Rebus said with authority. 'He'll go on killing because it's taken him over. Haven't you noticed how the murders are coming at shorter and shorter intervals? He may even have killed again since Lea Bridge, we just haven't found the body yet. He's possessed, George.' Flight looked at him as though seeking a joke, but Rebus was in deadly earnest. 'I mean it.'

Flight stood up and walked to the window. 'It might not even have been the Wolfman.'

'Maybe not,' Rebus conceded.

'What if she won't go public?'

'It doesn't matter. We still issue the news story. We still say we've got a good description.'

Flight turned from the window. 'You believe her? You don't think she's a crank?'

'It's possible, but I really don't think so. She's very plausible. She kept the details just vague enough to be convincing. It *was* three months ago. We can check on her if you like.'

'Yes, I'd like that very much.' The emotion had left Flight's voice. This case was draining him of every reserve he had. 'I want to know about her background, her present, her friends, her medical records, her family.'

'I could even get Lisa Frazer to give her some psychological tests?' Rebus suggested, not altogether without tongue in cheek. Flight smiled faintly.

'No, just the checks I've mentioned. Get Lamb onto it. It'll keep him out of our hair.'

'You don't like him then?'

'Whatever gives you that idea?'

'Funny, he says you're like a father to him.'

The moment of tension was over. Rebus felt he had won another small victory. They both laughed, using their dislike of Lamb to strengthen the link between them.

'You're a good policeman, John,' Flight said. Rebus, despite himself, blushed.

'Sod off, you old fart,' he replied.

'That reminds me,' said Flight. 'I told you yesterday to go home. Have you any intention of doing so?'

'None at all,' said Rebus. There was a pause before Flight nodded.

'Good,' he said. 'That's good.' He walked to the door. 'For now.' He turned back towards Rebus. 'Just don't go rogue on me, John. This is my turf. I need to know where you are and what you're up to.' He tapped at his own head. 'I need to know what's going on up here. Okay?'

Rebus nodded. 'Fine, George. No problem.' But the fingers behind his back were crossed. He liked to work alone, and had the feeling Flight wanted to stick close to him for reasons other than traditional Cockney chumminess. Besides, if the Wolfman did turn out to be a policeman, nobody could be discounted, nobody at all.

Rebus tried Lisa again, but without success. At lunchtime, he was wandering around the station when he bumped into Joey Bennett, the constable who had stopped him on Shaftesbury Avenue that first night in London. Bennett was wary at first. Then he recognised Rebus. 'Oh, hello, sir. Was that your picture I saw in the papers?'

Rebus nodded. 'This isn't your patch, is it?' he asked.

'No, not exactly, sir. Just passing through, you might

say. Dropping off a prisoner. That woman in the photo with you. She looked a bit of all – '

'Do you have your car with you?'

Bennett was wary again. 'Yes, sir.'

'And you're going back into town now?'

'To the West End, yes, sir.'

'Good. Then you won't mind giving me a lift, will you?'

'Er, no, sir. Of course not, sir.' Bennett broke into the least convincing smile Rebus had seen outside a synchronised swimming event. On their way out to the car, they passed Lamb.

'Teeth stopped chattering yet?' he asked, but Rebus was in no mood to respond. Lamb, undaunted, tried again. 'Going somewhere?' He managed even to make this simple question sound like a threat. Rebus stopped, turned and walked up to him, so that their faces were a couple of inches apart.

'If that's all right with you, Lamb, yes, I'm going somewhere.' Then he turned away again and followed Bennett. Lamb watched them go, half his teeth showing in a parody of a grin.

'Mind how you go!' he called. 'Shall I phone ahead and get the hotel to pack your bags?'

Rebus's reply was a two-fingered salute, a more determined stride, and a whispered 'FYTP'. Bennett heard him.

'Sorry, sir?'

'Nothing,' said Rebus. 'Nothing at all.'

It took them half an hour to reach Bloomsbury. Every second building seemed to sport a blue circular plaque commemorating some writer's having lived there. Rebus recognised few of the names. Finally, he found the building he was looking for, and waved Bennett goodbye. It was the Psychology Department of University College in Gower Street. The secretary, who appeared to be the only living soul around at one o'clock, asked if she could help him.

'I hope so,' he said. 'I'm looking for Lisa Frazer.'

'Lisa?' The secretary seemed unsure. 'Oh, Lisa. Dear me, I don't think I can help. I haven't seen her in over a week. You might try the library. Or Dillon's.'

'Dillon's?'

'It's a bookshop, just around the corner. Lisa seems to spend a lot of her time in there. She loves bookshops. Or there's always the British Library. It's just possible she might be there.'

He left the building with a new puzzle. The secretary had seemed very distant, very fuzzy. Maybe it was just him. He was starting to read things into every situation. He found the bookshop and went inside. 'Shop' was something of an understatement. It was huge. He read on a wall that psychology books were to be found three floors up. So many books. One man could not hope to read them all in a lifetime. He tried to walk through the aisles without focussing. If he focussed, he would become interested, and if he became interested he would buy. He already had over fifty books at home, piled beside his bed, waiting for that elusive weeklong break when he could concentrate on something other than police work. He collected books. It was just about his only hobby. Not that he was precious about it. He did not lust after first editions, signed copies and the like. Mostly, he bought paperbacks. And he was nothing if not catholic in his tastes: any subject matter would do.

So he tried to pretend he was wearing blinkers, pondered the essential difference between catholic and Catholic and finally reached the psychology section. It was a room joined onto other rooms as in a chain, but there was no sign of Lisa in any of the links. He did, however, find where some of her own library of books had no doubt originated. There was a shelf next to the cashier's desk, dedicated to crime and violence. One of the books she had loaned him was there. He picked it up and turned it over to look at the price. Then blinked twice in astonishment. So much money! And it wasn't even a hardback! Still, academic books always did carry steep price tickets. Strange really: weren't students, the intended readership after all, least able to afford these titles? It might take a psychologist to explain that one, or perhaps a shrewd economist.

Next to the criminology section were books on the occult

138

and witchcraft, along with various packs of Tarot cards and the like. Rebus smiled at this curious marriage: policework and hocus-pocus. He picked up a book on rituals and flipped through it. A young, slender woman, in billowing satin dress and with long fiery hair, paused beside him to lift a Tarot set, which she took to the cash desk. Well, it took all sorts, didn't it? She looked serious enough, but then these were serious times.

Ritual. He wondered if there was an element of ritual to the Wolfman's particular spree. So far he had been seeking an explanation from the killer's psyche: what if the whole thing were some kind of rite? Slaughter and defilement of the innocent, that sort of thing. Charlie Manson and his swastika-tattooed forehead. Some said there was a Masonic element to Jack the Ripper's methods. Madness and evil. Sometimes you found a cause, and sometimes you just didn't.

Slash the throat.

Gouge the anus.

Bite the stomach.

The two ends of the human trunk, and something like the mid-point. Could there be a clue in that particular pattern? *There are clues everywhere.*

The monster from his past, rearing up out of the dark deep waters of memory. That case had tied him up all right, but not half as much as this. He had thought the Wolfman might be a woman. Now a woman had conveniently appeared to tell him the Wolfman was a man. Very conveniently. George Flight was right to be wary. Perhaps Rebus could learn something from him. Flight did everything by the book, and in scrupulous detail. He didn't go running down the bloody hall with a pair of toy false teeth clutched in his sweaty hand. He was the type to sit down and think things through. That was what made him a good copper, better than Rebus, because he didn't snap at every red herring that came along. Better because he was methodical, and methodical people never let anything escape them.

Rebus left Dillon's Bookshop with his own little

thundercloud hanging above his head and a plastic carrier-bag full of newly purchased books swinging from his right hand. He walked down Gower Street and Bloomsbury Street, took a fortuitous left at a set of traffic lights and found himself outside the British Museum, inside which, he knew from memory, was to be found the British Library. Unless, that was, they'd already moved it, as he'd read they were planning to.

But the British Library itself was off-limit to 'non-readers'. Rebus tried to explain that he was a reader, but apparently what this meant was that he had to be in possession of a reader's card. With hindsight, he supposed he could have flashed his ID and said he was on the trail of a maniac, but he didn't. He shook his head, shrugged his shoulders and went instead for a walk around the museum.

The place seemed full almost to bursting with tourists and school parties. He wondered if the children, their imaginations still open, were as thunderstruck as he was by the Ancient Egyptian and Assyrian rooms. Vast stone carvings, huge wooden gates, countless exhibits. But the real throng was around the Rosetta Stone. Rebus had heard of it, of course, but didn't really know what it was. Now he found out. The stone contained writing in three languages and thus helped scholars to work out for the first time what Egyptian hieroglyphics actually meant.

He was willing to bet they hadn't solved it overnight, or even over a weekend. Slow, painstaking graft, just like police work, toil as difficult as anything a bricklayer or miner could endure. And in the end it usually still came down to the Lucky Break. How many times had they interviewed the Yorkshire Ripper and let him go? That sort of thing happened more often than the public would ever be allowed to know.

He walked through more rooms, rooms airy and light and containing Greek vases and figurines, then, pushing open a glass double-door, he found himself confronted by the Sculptures of the Parthenon. (For some reason they had stopped advertising them as the Elgin Marbles.) Rebus walked around this large gallery, feeling almost as though he were in some modern-day place of worship. At one end, a gabble of school-kids squatted before some statues, trying to draw them, while their teacher walked around, trying to keep the grudging artists quiet. It was Rhona. Even at this distance he recognised her. Recognised her walk and the slant of her head and the way she held her hands behind her back whenever she was trying to make a point. . . .

Rebus turned away, and found himself face to face with a horse's head. He could see the veins bulging from the marble neck, the open mouth with its teeth worn away to an indeterminate smoothness. No bite. Would Rhona thank him for walking over and interrupting her class, just to make smalltalk? No, she would not. But what if she spotted him? If he were to slink away, it would look like the action of a coward. Hell, he was a coward, wasn't he? Best to face facts and move back towards the doors. She might never spot him, and if she did she was hardly likely to announce the fact. But then he wanted to know about Kenny, didn't he? Who better to ask than Rhona? There was a simple answer: better to ask *anyone*. He'd ask Samantha. Yes, that's what he'd do. He'd ask Samantha.

He crept back to the doors and walked briskly towards the exit. Suddenly all the exquisite vases and statues had become ridiculous. What was the point in burying them behind glass for people to glance at in passing? Wasn't it better to look forward, forget about ancient history? Wouldn't it be better if he just took Lamb's ill-meant advice? There were too many ghosts in London. Way too many. Even the reporter Jim Stevens was down here somewhere. Rebus fairly flew across the museum courtyard only pausing when he reached the gates. The guards stared at him strangely, glancing towards his carrier-bag. They're just books, he wanted to say. But he knew you could hide anything in a book, just about anything. Knew from painful personal experience.

When feeling depressed, be rash. He stuck a hand out into the road and at the first attempt managed to stop an empty black cab. He couldn't remember the name of the street he wanted, but that didn't matter.

'Covent Garden,' he said to the driver. As the cab did what Rebus assumed was a fairly illegal u-turn, he dipped into his bag to claim the first prize.

He wandered around Covent Garden proper for twenty minutes, enjoying an open-air magic act and a nearby fire-eater before moving off in search of Lisa's flat. It wasn't too difficult to find. He surprised himself by recalling a kite shop and another shop which seemed to sell nothing but teapots. Took a left and a right and another right and found himself in her street, standing outside the shoe shop. The shop itself was busy. The clientele, like the serving staff, was very young, probably not yet out of teens. A jazz saxophone played. A tape perhaps, or someone busking in the distance. He looked up at the window to Lisa's flat, with its bright yellow roller blind. How old was she really? It was hard to tell.

And then, only then, he went to the door and pressed her buzzer. There was noise from the intercom, a crackle of movement. 'Hello?'

'It's me, John.'

'Hello? I can't hear you!'

'It's John,' he said loudly into the door frame, looking around him in embarrassment. But no one was interested. People glanced into the shop window as they passed, eating strange-looking snacks, vegetable-looking things.

'John?' As though she had forgotten him already. Then: 'Oh, John.' And the buzzer sounded beside him. 'Door's open. Come on up.'

The door to her flat was open, too, and he closed it behind him. Lisa was tidying the studio, as she called it. In Edinburgh it wouldn't have been called a studio. It would have been called a bedsit. He supposed Covent Garden didn't have such things as bedsits.

'I've been trying to get in touch,' he said.

'Me too.'

'Oh?'

She turned to him, noting the hint of disbelief in his voice. 'Didn't they tell you? I must've left half a dozen messages with, what was his name, Shepherd?'

142

'Lamb?'

'That's it.'

Rebus's hate for Lamb intensified.

'About an hour ago,' she went on, 'I called and they said you'd gone back to Scotland. I was a bit miffed at that. Thought you'd gone without saying goodbye.'

Bastards, thought Rebus. They really did hate his guts, didn't they? *Our expert from north of the border.*

Lisa had finished making a neat stack from the newspapers lying on the floor and the bed. She had straightened the duvet and the cover on the sofa. And now, a little out of breath, she was standing close to him. He slid his arms around her and pulled her to him.

'Hello,' he murmured, kissing her.

'Hello,' she said, returning the kiss.

She broke away from his hug and walked into the alcove which served as a kitchen. There was the sound of running tap water, a kettle filling. 'I suppose you've seen the papers?' she called.

'Yes.'

Her head came out of the alcove. 'A friend called me up to tell me. I couldn't believe it. My picture on the front page!'

'Fame at last.'

'Infamy more like: a "police psychologist" indeed! They might have done their research. One paper even called me Liz Frazier!' She plugged the kettle in, switched it on, then came back into the room. Rebus was sitting on the arm of the sofa.

'So,' she asked, 'how goes the investigation?'

'A few interesting developments.'

'Oh?' She sat on the edge of the bed. 'Tell me.'

So he told her about Jan Crawford, and about his false teeth theory. Lisa suggested that Jan Crawford's memory might be helped by hypnosis. 'Lost memory' she called it. But Rebus knew this sort of thing was inadmissable as evidence. Besides, he'd experienced 'lost memory' for himself, and shivered now at the memory.

They drank Lapsang Souchong, which he said reminded him of bacon butties, and she put on some music, something soft and classical, and they ended up somehow sitting next to one another on the Indian carpet, their backs against the sofa, shoulders, arms and legs touching. She stroked his hair, the nape of his neck.

'What happened the other night between us,' she said, 'are you sorry?'

'You mean sorry it happened?'

She nodded.

'Christ, no,' said Rebus. 'Just the opposite.' He paused. 'What about you?'

She thought over her answer. 'It was nice,' she said, her eyebrows almost meeting as she concentrated on each word.

'I thought maybe you were avoiding me,' he said.

'And I thought you were avoiding me.'

'I went looking for you this morning at the university.'

She sat back, the better to study his face. 'Really?'

He nodded.

'What did they say?'

'I spoke to some secretary,' he explained. 'Glasses on a string around her neck, hair in a sort of a bun.'

'Millicent. But what did she tell you?'

'She just said you hadn't been around much.'

'What else?'

'That I might find you in the library, or in Dillon's.' He nodded over towards the door, where the carrier-bag stood propped against a wall. 'She said you liked bookshops. So I went looking there, too.'

She was still studying his face, then she laughed and pecked him on the cheek. 'Millicent's a treasure though, isn't she?'

'If you say so.' Why did her laugh have so much relief in it? Stop looking for puzzles, John. Just stop it right now. She was crawling away from him towards the bag.

'So what did you buy?'

He couldn't honestly remember, with the exception of the book he'd started reading in the taxi. *Hawksmoor*. Instead, he watched her behind and her legs as she moved away from him. Spectacular ankles. Slim with a prominent hemisphere of bone.

144

'Well!' she said, lifting one of the paperbacks from the bag. 'Eysenck.'

'Do you approve?'

She thought this question over, too. 'Not entirely. Probably not at all, in fact. Genetic inheritance and all that. I'm not sure.' She lifted out another book, and shrieked. 'Skinner! The beast of behaviourism! But what made you – ?'

He shrugged. 'I just recognised some names from those books you loaned me, so I thought I'd – '

Another book was lifted high for him to see. *King Ludd*. 'Have you read the first two?' she asked.

'Oh,' he said, disappointed, 'is it part of a trilogy? I just liked the title.'

She turned and gave him a quizzical look, then laughed. Rebus could feel himself going red at the neck. She was making a fool of him. He turned away from her and concentrated on the pattern of the rug, brushing the rough fibres with his hand.

'Oh dear,' she said, starting to crawl back. 'I'm sorry, I didn't mean to. I'm sorry.' And she placed a hand on either of his legs, kneeling in front of him, angling her head until his eyes were forced to meet hers. She was smiling apologetically. 'Sorry,' she mouthed. He managed a smile which said: 'that's okay'. She leaned across him and placed her lips on his, one of her hands sliding up his leg towards the thigh, and then a little higher still.

It was evening before he escaped, though 'escape' was perhaps putting it too harshly. The effort of easing himself from beneath Lisa's sleeping limbs was almost too much. Her body perfume, the sweet smell of her hair, the flawless warmth of her belly, her arms, her behind. She did not waken as he slid from the bed and tugged on his clothes. She did not waken as he wrote her another of his notes, picked up his carrier-bag of books, opened the door, cast a glance back towards the bed and then pulled the door shut after him.

He went to Covent Garden tube station, where he was offered a choice: the queue for the elevator, or the three hundred-odd spiralling stairs. He opted for the stairs. They seemed to go on forever, turning and turning in their gyre. His head became light as he thought of what it must have been like to descend this corkscrew during the war years. White tiled walls like those of public lavatories. Rumble from above. The dull echo of footsteps and voices.

He thought, too, of Edinburgh's Scott Monument, with its own tightly winding stairwell, much more constricted and unnerving than this. And then he was at the bottom, beating the elevator by a matter of seconds. The tube train was as crowded as he had come to expect. Next to a sign proclaiming 'Keep your personal stereo personal', a white youth wearing green parka with matching teeth shared his musical taste with the rest of the carriage. His eyes had a distant, utterly vacant look and from time to time he swigged from a can of strong lager. Rebus toyed with the notion of saying something, but held back. He was only travelling one stop. If the glowering passengers were content to suffer silently, that was how it should be.

He prised himself out of the train at Holborn, only to squeeze into another compartment, this time on the Central Line. Again, someone was playing a Walkman at some dizzying level, but they were somewhere over towards the far end of the carriage, so all Rebus had to suffer was the Schhch-schch-schch of what he took to be drums. He was becoming a seasoned traveller now, setting his eyes so that they focussed on space rather than on his fellow passengers, letting his mind empty for the duration of the journey.

God alone knew how these people could do it every day of their working lives.

He had already rung the doorbell before it struck him that he did not have a pretext for coming here. Think quickly, John.

The door was pulled open. 'Oh, it's you.' She sounded disappointed.

'Hello, Rhona.'

'To what do we owe the honour?' She was standing her ground, just inside the front door, keeping him on the doorstep. She was wearing a hint of make-up and her clothes were not after-work, relaxing-at-home clothes. She was going out somewhere. She was waiting for a gentleman.

'Nothing special,' he said. 'Just thought I'd pop round. We didn't get much of a chance to talk the other night.' Would he mention that he had seen her in the British Museum? No, he would not.

Besides, she was shaking her head. 'Yes we did, it was just that we had nothing to talk about.' Her voice wasn't bitter; she was simply stating a fact. Rebus looked at the doorstep.

'I've caught you at a bad time,' he said. 'Sorry.'

'No need to apologise.'

'Is Sammy in?'

'She's out with Kenny.'

Rebus nodded. 'Well,' he said, 'enjoy wherever it is you're going.' My God, he actually felt jealous. He couldn't believe it of himself after all these years. It was the make-up that did it. Rhona had seldom worn make-up. He half-turned to leave, then stopped. 'I couldn't use your loo, could I?'

She stared at him, seeking some trick or plan, but he smiled back with his best impersonation of a crippled dog and she relented.

'Go on then,' she said. 'You know where it is.'

He left his carrier at the door, squeezed past her and began to climb the steep stairs. 'Thanks, Rhona,' he said.

She was lingering downstairs, waiting to let him out again. He walked across the landing to the bathroom, opened and closed the door loudly, then opened it again very quietly and crept back across the landing to where the telephone sat on a small and quite grotesque confection of brass, green glass and red hanging tassels. There were London phone books piled beneath this table, but Rebus went straight to the smaller 'Telephone & Addresses' book on the top of the table. Some of the entries were in Rhona's writing. Who, he wondered, were Tony, Tim, Ben and Graeme? But most were in Sammy's grander, more confident script. He flipped to the K section and found what he wanted.

'KENNY', printed in capitals with a seven figure number scribbled below the name, the whole enclosed by a loving ellipse. Rebus took pen and notepad from his pocket and copied down the number, then closed the book and tiptoed back to the bathroom, where he flushed the toilet, gave his hands a quick rinse and boldly started downstairs again. Rhona was looking along the street, no doubt anxious that her beau should not arrive and find him here.

'Bye,' he said, picking up the carrier, walking past her and setting off in the direction of the main road. He was nearly at the end of her street when a white Ford Escort turned off the main drag and moved slowly past him, driven by a canny-looking man with thin face and thick moustache. Rebus stopped at the corner to watch the man pull up outside Rhona's building. She had already locked the door and fairly skipped to the car. Rebus turned away before she could kiss or hug the man called Tony, Tim, Ben or Graeme.

In a large pub near the tube station, a barn of a place with walls painted torrid red, Rebus remembered that he had not tried the local brews since coming south. He'd gone for a drink with George Flight, but had stuck to whisky. He looked at the row of pumps, while the barman watched him, a proprietorial hand resting on one pump. Rebus nodded towards this resting hand.

'Is it any good?'

The man snorted. 'It's bloody Fuller's, mate, of course it's good.'

'A pint of that then, please.'

Th stuff turned out to have a watery look, like cold tea, but it tasted smooth and malty. The barman was still watching him, so Rebus nodded approval, then took his glass to a distant corner where the public telephone stood. He dialled HQ and asked for Flight.

'He's left for the day,' he was told.

'Well then, put me through to anyone from CID, anyone who's helpful. I've got a telephone number I want tracing.' There were rules and regulations about this sort of thing, rules at one time ignored but of late enforced. Requests had to be made and were not always granted. Some forces could pull more weight than others when it came to number tracing. He reckoned the Met and the Yard ought to carry more weight than most, but just in case he added: 'It's to do with the Wolfman case. It might be a very good lead.'

He was told to repeat the number he wanted tracing. 'Call back in half an hour,' said the voice.

He sat at a table and drank his beer. It seemed silly, but it appeared to be going to his head already, with only half a pint missing from the glass. Someone had left a folded, smudged copy of the midday *Standard*. Rebus tried to concentrate on the sports pages and even had a stab at the concise crossword. Then he made the call and was put through to someone he didn't know, who passed him on to someone else he didn't know. A boisterous crowd, looking like a team of bricklayers, had entered the bar. One of them made for the jukebox, and suddenly Steppenwolf's *Born to be Wild* was booming from the walls, while the men urged the unwilling barman to 'wick it up a bit'.

'If you'll just hold a minute, Inspector Rebus, I believe Chief Inspector Laine wants a word.'

'But, Christ, I don't want – ' Too late, the voice at the other end had gone. Rebus held the receiver away from him and scowled.

Eventually, Howard Laine came on the line. Rebus pushed a finger into one ear, pressing his other ear hard against the earpiece.

'Ah, Inspector Rebus. I wanted a quiet word. You're a hard man to catch. About that business last night.' Laine's was the voice of reasoned sanity. 'You're about a bollock-hair's breadth away from an official reprimand, understand? Pull a stunt like that again and I'll personally see to it that you're shipped back to Jockland in the boot of a National Express bus. Got that?'

Rebus was silent, listening closely. He could almost hear Cath Farraday sitting in Laine's office, smirking.

'I said, have you got that?'

'Yes, sir.'

'Good.' A rustling of paper. 'Now, you want an address I believe?'

'Yes, sir.'

'It's a lead, you say?'

'Yes, sir.' Rebus suddenly wondered if this would be worth it. He hoped so. If they found out he was abusing the system like this, they'd have him in the dole office with prospects roughly equivalent to those of a shoeshine boy on a nudist beach.

But Laine gave him the address and, as a bonus, supplied Kenny's surname.

'Watkiss,' said Laine. 'The address is Pedro Tower, Churchill Estate, E5. I think that's Hackney.'

'Thank you, sir,' said Rebus.

'Oh by the way,' said Laine, 'Inspector Rebus?'

'Yes, sir?'

'From what I've been told of Churchill Estate, if you're intending to visit, tell us first. We'll arrange for an SPG escort. All right?'

'Bit rough is it then, sir?'

'Rough doesn't begin to tell the story, son. We train the SAS in there, pretend it's a mock-up of Beirut.'

'Thanks for the advice, sir.' Rebus wanted to add that he'd been in the SAS and he doubted Pedro Tower could throw anything at him that the SAS HQ in Hereford hadn't. All the same, it paid to be cautious. The brickies were playing pool, their accents a mix of Irish and Cockney. *Born to be Wild* had finished. Rebus finished his pint and ordered another.

Kenny Watkiss. So there was a connection and rather a large one at that, between Tommy Watkiss and Samantha's boyfriend. How was it that in a city of ten million souls, Rebus had suddenly begun to feel an overwhelming sense of claustrophobia? He felt like someone had wrapped a muffler around his mouth and pulled a Balaclava down over his head.

'I'd be careful, mate,' said the barman as Rebus took delivery of his second pint. 'That stuff can kill you.'

'Not if I kill it first,' said Rebus, winking as he raised the glass to his lips.

* * *

150

The taxi driver wouldn't take him as far as the Churchill Estate. 'I'll drop you off a couple of streets away and show you where to go, but there's no way I'm going in there.'

'Fair enough,' said Rebus.

So he took the taxi as far as the taxi would take him, then walked the remaining distance. It didn't look so bad. He'd seen worse on the outskirts of Edinburgh. A lot of dull concrete, nuggets of glass underfoot, boarded windows and spray-painted gang names on every wall. Jeez Posse seemed to be the main gang, though there were other names so fantastically contrived that he could not make them out. Young boys skateboarded through an arena constructed from milk-crates, wooden planks and bricks. You couldn't muzzle the creative mind. Rebus stopped to watch for a moment; it only took a moment to appreciate that these boys were masters of their craft.

Rebus came to the entrance of one of the estate's four hi-rises. He was busy looking for an identifying mark when something went splat on the pavement beside him. He looked down. It was a sandwich, a salami sandwich by the look of it. He craned his neck to look up at the various levels of the tower block, just in time to catch sight of something large and dark growing larger and darker as it hurtled towards him.

'Jesus Christ!' He leapt into the safety of the block's entrance hall, just as the TV set landed, flattening itself with an explosion of plastic, metal and glass. From their arena, the boys cheered. Rebus moved outside again, but more warily now, and craned his neck. There was no one to be seen. He whistled under his breath. He was impressed, and a little scared. Despite the thunderous sound, nobody seemed curious or interested.

He wondered which television show had so angered the person somewhere above him. 'Everyone's a critic,' he said. And then: 'FYTP.'

He heard a lift opening. A young woman, greasy dyed-blonde hair, gold stud in her nose and three in each ear, spider-web tattoo across her throat. She wheeled a push-chair out onto the concrete. Seconds earlier she would have been beneath the television.

151

'Excuse me,' said Rebus above the noise of her wailing passenger.

'Yeah?'

'Is this Pedro Tower?'

'Over there,' she said, pointing a sharpened fingernail towards one of the remaining blocks.

'Thank you.'

She glanced towards where the television had landed. 'It's the kids,' she said. 'They break into a flat, and throw a sandwich out of the window. A dog comes to eat it, and they chuck a telly after it. Makes a helluva mess.' She sounded almost amused. Almost.

'Lucky I don't like salami,' Rebus said.

But she was already manoeuvring the pushchair past the fresh debris. 'If you don't shut up I'll fucking kill you!' she yelled at her child. Rebus walked on unsteady legs towards Pedro Tower.

Why was he here?

It had all seemed to make sense, had seemed logical. But now that he stood in the sour-smelling ground-floor hallway of Pedro Tower he found that he had no reason at all to be here. Rhona had said that Sammy was out with Kenny. The chances of them choosing to spend the evening in Pedro Tower must be slim, mustn't they?

Even supposing Kenny were here, how would Rebus locate the flat? The locals would sniff an enquiring copper from fifty paces. Questions would go unanswered, knocked doors would stay unopened. Was this what intellectuals called an impasse? He could always wait, of course. Kenny would be sure to return at some point. But wait where? In here? Too conspicuous, too unappealing. Outside? Too cold, too open, too many armchair critics high above him in the now-dark sky.

Which left him where precisely? Yes, this probably was an impasse. He walked from the block, his eyes on the windows above him, and was about to make off in the direction of the skateboarders when a scream split the air from the other side of Pedro Tower. He walked quickly towards the source of the sound and was in time to see the butt-end of a burning argument. The woman – no more than a girl really, seventeen, eighteen – hit the bedenimed man with a good right hand, sending him spinning. Then she stalked off as he, holding one side of his face, tried to hurl obscenities at her while at the same time feeling in his mouth for damaged teeth.

They did not interest Rebus particularly. He was looking past them to a low-built, dimly illuminated building, a prefabricated construction surrounded by grass and dirt. A weathered board, lit by a single bulb, proclaimed it The Fighting Cock. A pub? Here? That was no place for a policeman, no place for a *Scots* policeman. But what if. . . ? No, it couldn't be so simple. Sammy and Kenny couldn't be in there, wouldn't be in there. His daughter deserved better. Deserved the best.

But then she reckoned Kenny Watkiss was the best. And maybe he was. Rebus stopped dead. Just what the hell was he doing? Okay, so he didn't like Kenny. And when he had seen Kenny cheering in the Old Bailey, he had put two and two together and come to the conclusion that Kenny was in deep with Tommy Watkiss. But now it turned out the two were related in some way and that would explain the cheer, wouldn't it?

The psychology books told him that coppers read the worst into every situation. It was true. He didn't like the fact that Kenny Watkiss was dating his daughter. If Kenny had been heir apparent to the throne, Rebus would still have been suspicious. She was his daughter. He'd hardly seen her since she had entered her teens. In his mind she was still a child, a thing to be cosseted, loved, and protected. But she was a big girl now, with ambition, drive, good looks and a grown up body. She was grown up, there was no escaping it, and it scared him. Scared him because she was Sammy, his Sammy. Scared him because he hadn't been there all these years to warn her, to tell her how to cope, what to do.

Scared because he was getting old.

There, it was out. He was growing old. He had a sixteen-year-old daughter and she was old enough to leave school and get a job, to have sex, to get married. Not old enough to go into pubs, but that wouldn't stop her. Not old enough for street-wise eighteen year olds like Kenny Watkiss. But grown up all the same; grown up without him, and now he too was old.

And by God he felt it.

He plunged his left hand deep into his pocket, his right hand still wrapped around the handle of the carrier bag, and turned from the pub. There was a bus stop near where the taxi had dropped him. He'd go where the bus would take him. The skateboarders were coming along the path in front of him. One of them seemed very proficient, weaving without losing balance. As the boy approached, he suddenly flipped the board up so that it spun in the air in front of him. Both hands neatly grabbed the board by its running-tail and swung the board itself in a backward arc. Too late, Rebus saw the manoeuvre for what it was. He tried to duck but the heavy wooden board hit the side of his head with a sharp crack.

He staggered, dropped to his knees. They were on him immediately, seven or eight of them, hands gouging into his pockets.

'Fuckin split my board, man. Lookatit. Fuckin six inch split.'

A training shoe caught Rebus on the chin and sent him flying. He was concentrating on not losing consciousness, so much so that he forgot to fight or to scream or to defend himself. Then a loud voice:

'Oi! What the fuck d'you think you're up to?'

And they ran, rolling their boards until they had gained enough speed, the hard wheels crackling on the tarmac as they fled. Like a posse in an old western, Rebus thought with a smile. Like a posse.

'You all right, mate? Come on, let's get you up.'

The man helped Rebus to his feet. When his eyes regained their powers of focus, he saw blood on the man's lip, smeared across his chin. The man noticed him looking.

'My bird,' he said, his breath rich with alcohol. 'She

fuckin' clocked me, didn't she? Got me a good one, too. Couple of loose teeth. Still, they was rotten anyway, probably saved me a fortune at the dentist's.' He laughed. 'Come on, let's get you into the Cock. A couple of brandies'll see you right.'

'Took my money,' Rebus said. He was clutching the carrier bag to him like a shield.

'Never mind that,' said his Samaritan.

They were kind to him. They sat him down at a table, and every now and again a drink would appear, and someone would say 'That one's from Bill', or 'That one's from Tessa,' or 'That one's from Jackie', or 'That one's from. . .'

They were kind to him. They collected a fiver so he could get a taxi back to his hotel. He explained that he was a tourist, down here for a bit of sightseeing. He'd managed to get lost, had jumped off a bus and ended up here. And they, kind souls, believed him.

They didn't bother phoning the police.

'Those bastards,' they spat. 'Waste of time. Wouldn't turn up till tomorrow morning and then they'd do nothing. It's the cops round here that are behind half the crimes, believe me.'

And he did. He did believe them. And another drink arrived, another brandy in a small schooner.

'All the best, eh?'

And they were playing cards and dominoes, a lively crowd, a regular crowd. The TV blared – a musical quiz show – and the jukebox sang and the one-armed bandit bleeped and buzzed and spat out an occasional win. He thanked God Sammy and Kenny weren't here. How would it have looked to them? He dreaded to think.

At one point he excused himself and went to the toilet. There was a jagged triangle of mirror nailed to one wall. The side of his head, jaw and ear, were red and would probably bruise. The jaw would ache for some time. Where the shoe had connected, there was already a red and purple welt. Nothing more. Nothing worse. No knives or razor blades. No massed assault. It had been a clean, professional hit. The way that kid had flipped the board, caught it and swung it. Professional. An absolute pro. If Rebus ever caught him, he would congratulate him on one of the sweetest moves he had ever seen.

Then he'd kick the little bastard's teeth so far down his throat they'd bite his small intestine.

He reached down the front of his trousers and drew out his wallet. The warning from Laine and the knowledge that he was on uncharted ground, had been enough to persuade Rebus that he should hide his wallet. Not to save him from muggers, no. So that no one would find his ID. It was bad enough being a stranger in this place, but being a copper. . . . So he had hidden the wallet, ID and all, down the front of his underpants, tucked into the elasticated waistband. He slipped it back there now. After all, he was not yet clear of Churchill Estate. The night might turn out to be a long one.

He pulled open the door and headed back to his table. The brandy was working. His head was numb, his limbs pleasantly flexible.

'You all right there, Jock?'

He hates that name, absolutely loathes it, but he smiles nevertheless. 'I'm all right. Oh yes, I'm quite all right.'

'Great. By the way, this one's from Harry at the bar.'

* * *

After she has posted the letter, she feels a lot better. She does some work, but soon begins to twitch inside. It's like feeding a habit now. But it's also an art form. Art? Fuck art. So unbecoming in a man. So art unbecoming fuck in a man. So fuck a man in unbecoming art. They used to quarrel, squabble, argue all the time. No, that's not true. She remembers it that way but it wasn't that way. For a while it was, but then they just stopped communicating altogether. Her mother. Her father. Mother, strong, domineering, determined to be a great painter, a great watercolourist. Every day busy at an easel, ignoring her child who needed her, who would creep into the studio and sit quietly in a

156

corner, crouched, trying not to be noticed. If noticed, she would be sent out of the room fiercely, red hot tears streaming down her face.

'I never wanted you!' her mother would screech. 'You were an accident! Why can't you be a *proper* little girl?'

Run, run, run. Out of the studio and down the stairs, through the morning room, and out of the doors. Father, quiet, innocuous, cultured, civilised father. Reading the newspapers in the back garden, one trousered leg crossed over the other as he reclined in his deckchair.

'And how's my little sweet this morning?'

'Mummy shouted at me.'

'Did she? I'm sure she didn't mean anything. She's a bit crochety when she's painting, isn't she? Come and sit here on my lap, you can help me read the news.'

Nobody visited, nobody came. No family, no friends. At first she went to school, but then they kept her at home, educating her themselves. It was all the rage with a certain section of a certain class. Her father had been left money by a great aunt. Enough money for a comfortable life, enough to keep the wolf from the door. He pretended to be a scholar. But then his painstakingly researched essays started to be rejected and he saw himself for what he was. The arguments grew worse. Grew physical.

'Just leave me alone will you? My art's what matters to me, not you.'

'Art? Fuck art!'

'How dare you!'

A dull, solid thump. A blow of some kind. From anywhere in the house she could hear them, anywhere but the attic. But she daren't go to the attic. That was where . . . Well, she just couldn't.

'I'm a boy,' she whispered to herself, hiding beneath her bed. 'I'm a boy, I'm a boy, I'm a boy.'

'Sweetness, where are you?' His voice, all sugar and summery. Like a slide-projector show. Like an afternoon car-ride.

They said the Wolfman was homosexual. It wasn't true. They said they'd caught him. She almost whooped when she read it. Wrote them a letter and posted it. See what they'd make of that! Let them find her, she didn't care. He and she didn't care. But he cared that she was taking over his mind as well as his body.

Sweetness . . . Oranges and lemons say the bells of . . .

So unbecoming in a man. Long nosehairs, her mother had been talking about Daddy's nosehairs. Long nosehairs, Johnny, are so unbecoming in a man. Why did she remember that utterance above all others? Long. Nose. Hairs. So. Unbecoming. In. A. Man. Johnny.

Daddy's name: Johnny.

Her father, who had sworn at her mother. Fuck art. Fuck was the dirtiest word there was. At school it had been whispered, a magic word, a word to conjure up demons and secrets.

And she's on the streets now, although she knows that really she should do something about the Butcher's Gallery. It needs cleaning badly. There are torn canvases everywhere. Torn and spattered. It doesn't matter: nobody visits. No family, no friends.

So she finds another one. This one's stupid. 'As long as you're not the Wolfman,' she says with a laugh. The Wolfman laughs too. He? She? It doesn't matter now. He and she are one and the same. The wound has healed. He feels whole, feels complete. It is not a good feeling. It is a bad feeling. But it can be forgotten for a moment.

Back in his house.

'Some gaff you've got here,' she says. He smiles, takes her coat and hangs it up. 'Bit of a smell though. You haven't got a gas leak, have you?'

No, not a gas leak. But a leak, yes. He slips his hand into his pocket, checks that the teeth are there. Of course they are, they're always there when he needs them. To bite with. The way he was bitten.

'Only a game, sweet.'

Only a game. Bitten in fun. On the stomach. Bitten. Not hard, more like blowing a raspberry. But that didn't stop it hurting. He touches his gut. It still hurts, even now.

'Where do you want me, love?'

'In here will do,' he says, taking out the key and beginning to unlock the door. The mirror was a bad idea. The last one had seen what was happening behind her, had almost screamed. The mirror has been taken down. The door is unlocked.

'Keep it locked, do you? What you got in there, the crown jewels?'

And the Wolfman, showing teeth, smiles.

Know This, Womin

He woke up in his hotel room, which was something in itself, bearing in mind that he had no idea how he'd got there. He was lying on his bed, fully clothed, his hands pressed between his legs. Beside him lay the carrier-bag full of books. It was seven o'clock and by the quality of the light streaming in through the uncurtained window, it was morning rather than evening. So far so good. The bad news was that his head seared with two kinds of pain, bad when he opened his eyes, unbearable when he closed them. With eyes closed, the world spun at an awkward tilt. With eyes opened, it merely floated on a different plane.

He groaned, attempted to unglue his furred tongue from the roof of his mouth. Staggered to the sink and ran the cold tap for some moments, then splashed his face and cupped his hand, lapping water from it the way a mongrel might. The water was sweet, chlorinated. He tried not to think of kidneys . . . seven sets of kidneys. Knelt by the toilet-pan and retched. The big white telephone receiver to God. What was the score? Seven brandies, six dark rums – he'd lost count after that. He squeezed an inch-long strip of toothpaste onto his brush and scrubbed at his teeth and gums. Then, only then, did he have the courage to examine himself in the wall mirror.

There were two kinds of pain. One from the hangover, the other from the mugging. He'd lost twenty quid, maybe thirty. But the loss to his pride was above price. He held in his head a good description of a couple of the gang and especially the leader. This morning, he would give what he knew to the local station. His message would be clear: seek out and destroy. Who was he kidding? They'd rather protect their own villains than help an intruder from north of the border. *Our man from north of the border. Jockland. Jock.* But to let the gang get away with it was worse. What the hell.

He rubbed his jaw. It felt worse than it looked. There was a pale mustard bruise down one cheek and a graze on his chin. Good thing training shoes were all the rage. In the early 70s it would have been a steel-capped Airwear boot and he would not have been so chipper.

He was running out of clean clothes. Today, he would have either to buy some new bits and pieces or else find himself a laundrette. He had come to London intending to stay no more than two or three days. He'd thought that after that the Met would come to see that he could add nothing to the case. But instead here he was, coming up with possible leads, making himself useful, getting beaten up, turning into an overprotective father, having a holiday romance with a psychology lecturer.

He thought about Lisa, about the way the secretary at University College had acted. Something jarred about the whole incident. Lisa, who slept so soundly, the sleep of a clear conscience. What was that smell? That smell creeping into his room? The smell of cooking fat mingled with toast and coffee. The smell of breakfast. Somewhere downstairs they were busy perspiring over the griddles, breaking eggs to sizzle beside thick sausages and grey-pink bacon. The thought sent Rebus's stomach on a tiny rollercoaster ride. He was hungry, but the thought of fried food repelled him. He felt his just-cleaned mouth turning sour.

When had he last eaten? A sandwich on the way to Lisa's. Two packets of crisps in the Fighting Cock. Christ, yes, he was hungry. He dressed quickly, making a mental note of what needed buying – shirt, pants, socks – and headed down to the dining-room clutching three paracetamol tablets in his hand. A fistful of dullers.

They weren't quite ready to start serving, but when he announced that he needed only cereal and fruit juice, the waitress (a different face each day) relented and showed him to a table set for one.

He ate two small packets of cereal. A cereal killer. Smiled grimly and went to the trestle table to help himself to more juice. Lots more juice. It had a funny artificial smell to it, and a taste best described as 'wersh'. But it was cold and wet

161

and the vitamin C would help his head. The waitress brought him two daily papers. Neither contained anything of interest. Flight had not yet used Rebus's idea of the detailed description. Maybe Flight had passed it on to Cath Farraday. Would she sit on it out of spite? After all, she hadn't been too happy about his last little stunt, had she? Maybe she was holding back on this one, just to show him that she could. Well, sod them. He didn't see anyone coming up with better ideas, with any ideas at all, come to that. Nobody wanted to make a mistake; they'd all rather sit on their hands than be seen to get it wrong. Jesus Christ.

When the first customer proper of the morning ordered bacon, eggs and tomatoes, Rebus finished his orange juice and left the restaurant.

In the Murder Room, he sat at one of the typewriters and prepared detailed descriptions of the gang members. His typing had never been proficient at the best of times, but today's hangover was compounded by an electronic typewriter of infernal complexity. He couldn't get the thing to set a reasonable line length, the tabs appeared not to work and every time he pressed a wrong key the thing bleeped at him.

'Bleep yourself,' he said, trying again to set it for single space typing.

Eventually, he had a typed description. It looked like the work of a ten-year-old, but it would have to do. He took the sheets of paper through to his office. There was a note from Flight on his desk.

'John, I wish you wouldn't keep disappearing. I've run a check on missing persons. Five women have been reported missing north of the river in the past forty-eight hours. Two of these could be explicable, but the other three look more serious. Maybe you're right, the Wolfman's getting hungrier. No feedback from the press stories yet though. See you when you've finished shagging the Prof.'

It was signed simply 'GF'. How did Flight know where he'd been yesterday afternoon? An inspired guess, or something more cunning and devious? It didn't really matter. What mattered were the missing women. If Rebus's hunch were true, then the Wolfman was losing some of his previous control and that meant that sometime soon he was bound to make a mistake. They need only goad him a little more. The Jan Crawford story might just do that particular trick. Rebus had to sell the idea to Flight – and to Farraday. They had to be made to see that it was the right move at the right time. Three missing women. That would bring the count to seven. Seven murders. There was no telling where it would stop. He rubbed at his head again. The hangover was returning with a steel-tipped vengeance.

'John?'

She was standing in the doorway, trembling, her eyes wide.

'Lisa?' He rose slowly to his feet. 'Lisa, what is it? What's wrong?'

She stumbled towards him. There were tears in her eyes and her hair was slick with sweat. 'Thank God,' she said, clinging to him. 'I thought I'd never . . . I didn't know what to do, where to go. Your hotel said you'd already left. The Sergeant on the desk downstairs let me come up. He recognised me from the photo in the papers. My photo.' And then the tears came: hot, scalding, and loud. Rebus patted her on the back, trying to calm her, wanting to know just what the hell had happened.

'Lisa,' he said quietly, 'just tell me about it.' He manoeuvred her onto a chair, with his hand rubbing soothingly at her neck. Every bit of her seemed damp with perspiration.

She pulled her bag onto her lap, opened it, and drew from one of the three compartments a small envelope, which she handed silently to Rebus.

'What is it?' he asked.

'I got it this morning,' she said, 'addressed to me by name and sent to my home.'

Rebus examined the typed name and address, the first class stamp, and the postmark: London EC4. The frank stated that the letter had been posted the previous morning.

'He knows where I live, John. When I opened it this

morning, I nearly died on the spot. I had to get out of the flat, but all the time I knew that maybe he was watching me.' Her eyes filled with water again, but she threw back her head so that the tears would not escape. She fished in her bag and came out with some paper tissues, peeling off one so that she could blow her nose. Rebus said nothing.

'It's a death threat,' she explained.

'A *death threat?*'

She nodded.

'Who from? Does it say?'

'Oh yes, it says all right. It's from the Wolfman, John. He says I'm going to be next.'

It was a rush job, but the lab, when they heard the circumstances, were happy to cooperate. Rebus stood with hands in pockets watching them at work. There was the crackle of paper in his pocket. He had folded the description of the gang members and tucked it away, perhaps for future use: for now, there were more important matters to attend to.

The story was straightforward enough. Lisa had been scared out of her wits by the letter, and more so by the fact that the Wolfman knew where she lived. She had tried contacting Rebus and when that failed had panicked, fleeing from her flat, aware that *he* might be watching her, might be about to pounce at any moment. The pity was, as the lab had already explained, she'd messed up the letter, gripping it in her hand as she fled, destroying any fingerprints or other evidence that there might have been on the envelope itself. Still, they'd do their best.

If the letter was from the Wolfman and not from some new and twisted crank, then there might well be clues to be had from the envelope and its contents: saliva (used to stick down both flap and stamp), fibres, fingerprints. These were the physical possibilities. Then there were more arcane elements: the typewriter itself might be traceable. Were there oddities of speech or misspellings which might yield a clue? And what about that postmark? The Wolfman had outwitted them in the past, so was the postal address another red herring?

The various processes involved would take time. The lab was efficient, but the chemical analyses could not be hurried. Lisa had come to the lab, too, as had George Flight. They were off in another part of the building drinking tea and going over the details for the fourth or fifth time, but Rebus liked to watch the lab boys at work. This was his idea of sleuthing. It also helped calm him to watch someone working in such painstaking detail. And he certainly needed calming.

His plan had worked. He had prodded and teased the Wolfman into action. He should, though, have realised the danger Lisa might be in. After all, her photo had been in the papers, as had her name. They had even mistakenly termed her a police psychologist – the very people who, according to the earlier planted story, had come to the conclusion that the Wolfman might be gay, or transsexual, or any of the other barbs they had used. Lisa Frazer had become the Wolfman's enemy, and he, John Rebus, had led her into it by the nose. Stupid, John, oh so very stupid. What if the Wolfman had actually tracked her to her flat and . . . ? No, no, no: he couldn't bear to think of it.

But though Lisa's name had appeared in the newspapers, her address had not. So how had the Wolfman found out her address? That was much more problematic.

And much more chilling.

She was ex-directory, for a start. But as he knew only too well, this was no barrier to someone in authority, someone like a police officer. Jesus: was he *really* talking about another police officer? There had to be other candidates: staff and students at University College, other psychologists – they would know Lisa. Then there were those groups who could have linked an address to a name: civil servants, the local council, taxmen, gas and electricity boards, the postman, the guy next door, numerous computers and mailshot programmes, her local public library. Where could he start?

'Here you are, Inspector.'

One of the assistants handed him a photocopy of the typed letter.

'Thanks,' said Rebus.

'We're testing the original at the moment, scanning for traces of anything interesting. We'll let you know.'

'Right. What about the envelope?'

'The saliva tests will take a little longer. We should have something for you in the next couple of hours. There was also the photograph, of course, but it won't photocopy too well. We know which paper it was from, and that it was cut out with a pair of fairly sharp scissors, perhaps as small as manicure scissors judging from the length of each cut.'

Rebus nodded, staring at the photostat. 'Thanks again,' he said.

'No problem.'

No problem? That wasn't right; there were plenty of problems. He read through the letter. The typing seemed nice and even, as though the typewriter used was a new one, or a good quality model, something like the electronic machine he'd been using this morning. As for the content, well, that was something else again.

GET THIS, I'M NOT HOMOSEXUL, O.K.? WOLF-MAN IS WHAT WOLFMAN DOES. WHAT WOLF-MAN DOES NEXT IS THIS: HE KILLS YOU. DON'T WORRY, IT WON'T HURT. WOLFMAN DOES NOT HURT; JUST DOES WHAT WOLFMAN IS. KNOW THIS, WOMIN, WOLFMAN KNOWS YOU, WHERE YOU LIVE, WHAT YOU LOOK LIKE. JUST TELL THE TRUTH AND NO HARM CAN CUM TO YOU.

On a piece of plain A4-sized paper, folded in four to get it into the small white envelope. The Wolfman had cut a picture of Lisa from one of the newspapers. Then he had cut her head off and drawn a dark pencilled circle on her stomach. And this photograph of her trunk had accompanied the letter.

'Bastard,' Rebus hissed. 'Jesus, you bastard.'

He took the letter along the corridor and up the stairs to the room where Flight was sitting, rubbing at his face again.

'Where's Lisa?'

'Ladies' room.'

'Does she seem . . . ?'

'She's upset, but she's coping. The doctor's given her some tranqs. What have you got there?' Rebus handed over the copy. Flight read through it quickly, intently. 'What the hell do you make of it?' he asked. Rebus sat himself down on a hard chair still warm from Lisa's presence. He reached out a hand and took the paper from Flight, then angled his chair so that both men could inspect the letter together.

'Well,' he said. 'I'm not sure. At first sight, it looks like the work of a near-illiterate.'

'Agreed.'

'But then again, there's something artful about it. Look at the punctuation, George. Absolutely correct, right down to every comma. And he uses colons and semi-colons. What sort of person could spell "woman" as "womin", yet know how to use a semi-colon?'

Flight studied the note intently, nodding. 'Go on.'

'Well, Rhona, my ex-wife, she's a teacher. I remember she used to tell me how frustrating it was that nowadays no one in schools bothered to teach basic grammar and punctuation. She said that kids were growing up now with no need for things like colons and semi-colons and no idea at all of how to use them. So I'd say we're dealing either with someone who has been well educated, or with someone in middle age, educated at a time when punctuation was still taught in every school.'

Flight gave a half-smile. 'Been reading your psychology books again I see, John.'

'It's not all black magic, George. Mostly it's just to do with common sense and how you interpret things. Do you want me to go on?'

'I'm all ears.'

'Well,' Rebus was running a finger down the letter again. 'There's something else here, something that tells me this letter is genuinely from the killer, and not the work of some nutter somewhere.'

'Oh?'

167

'Go on, George, where's the clue?'

He held the paper out towards Flight. Flight grinned for a moment, then took it.

'I suppose,' he said, 'you're talking about the way the writer refers to the Wolfman in the third person?'

'You've just named the tune in one, George. That's exactly what I mean.'

Flight looked up. 'Incidentally, John, what the hell happened to you? Did you get in a fight or something? I thought the Scots gave up wearing woad a couple of years back?'

Rebus touched his bruised jaw. 'I'll tell you the story sometime. But look, in the first sentence, the writer refers to himself in the first person. He's taken our homosexual jibe personally. But in the rest of the letter, he speaks of the Wolfman in the third person. Standard practice with serial murderers.'

'What about the misspelling of homosexual?'

'Could be genuine, or it could be to throw us off the scent. "U" and "a" are at different ends of the keyboard. A two-fingered typist could miss the "a" if he was writing fast, if he was angry.' Rebus paused, remembering the list in his pocket. 'I speak from recent experience.'

'Fair enough.'

'Now look at what he actually says: "Wolfman is what Wolfman does". What the books say is that killers find their identity through killing. That's exactly what this sentence means.'

Flight exhaled noisily. 'Yes, but none of this gets us any closer, does it?' He offered a cigarette to Rebus. 'I mean, we can build up as clear a picture as we like of the bastard's personality, but it won't give us a name and address.'

Rebus sat forward in his chair. 'But all the time we're narrowing down the possible types, George. And eventually we'll narrow it down to a field of one. Look at this final sentence.'

' "Just tell the truth and no harm can cum to you," ' Flight recited.

'Skipping the pun, which is intriguing in itself, don't you

think there's something very, I don't know, official sounding about that construction? Something very formal?'

'I don't see what you're getting at.'

'What I'm getting at is that it seems to me the sort of thing someone like you or me would say.'

'A copper?' Flight sat back in his chair. 'Oh, come on, John, what kind of crap is that?'

Rebus's voice grew quiet and persuasive. 'Someone who knows where Lisa Frazer lives, George. Think about it. Someone who knows that kind of information, or knows how to get it. We can't afford to rule out –'

Flight stood up. 'I'm sorry, John, but no. I simply can't entertain the notion that . . . that someone, some copper, could be behind all this. No, it's just not on.'

Rebus shrugged. 'Okay, George, whatever you say.' But Rebus knew that he had planted a seed now in George Flight's head, and that the seed would surely sprout.

Flight sat down again, confident that this time he had won a point from Rebus. 'Anything else?'

Rebus read the letter through yet again, sucking on his cigarette. He remembered how at school, in his English class, he had loved writing summaries and close interpretations of texts. 'Yes,' he said eventually. 'Actually there is. This letter seems to me more of a warning, a shot across the bows. He starts off by saying that he's going to kill her, but by the end of the letter he's tempered that line. He says nothing will happen if she tells the truth. I think he's looking for a retraction. I think he wants us to put out another story saying he's not gay.'

Flight checked his watch. 'He's in for another fright.'

'How do you mean?'

'The lunchtime edition will be hitting the streets. I believe Cath Farraday's put out the Jan Crawford story.'

'Really?' Rebus revised his idea of Farraday. Maybe she wasn't a vindictive old bat after all. 'So now we're saying we've got a living witness, and he must realise it's a fact. I think it might just be enough to blow what final fuses he's got up here.' Rebus tapped his head. 'To send him barking mad, as Lamb would put it.'

'You reckon?'

'I reckon, George. We need everybody at their most alert. He could try anything.'

'I dread to think.'

Rebus was staring at the letter. 'Something else, George. EC4: where's that exactly?'

Flight thought it over. 'The City, part of it anyway. Farringdon Street, Blackfriars Bridge, all around there. Ludgate, St Paul's.'

'Hmm. He's tricked us before, making us see patterns where none exist. The teeth for example, I'm sure I'm right about them. But now that we've got him rattled –'

'You think he lives in the City?'

'Lives there, works there, maybe just drives through there on his way to work.' Rebus shook his head. He didn't yet want to share with Flight the image which had just passed through his mind, the image of a motorcycle courier based in the City, a motorcyclist with easy access to every part of London. Like the man in leathers he'd seen on the bridge that first night down by the canal.

A man like Kenny Watkiss.

'Well,' he said instead, 'whatever, it's another piece of the jigsaw.'

'If you ask me,' said Flight, 'there are too many pieces. They won't all fit.'

'Agreed.' Rebus stubbed out the cigarette. Flight had already finished his own, and was about to light another. 'But as the picture emerges, we'll know better which bits we can discard, won't we?' He was still studying the letter. There was something else. What was it? Something at the back of his mind, lurking somewhere in memory. . . . Something stirred momentarily by the letter, but what? If he stopped thinking about it, maybe it would come to him, the way the names of forgotten actors in films did.

The door opened.

'Lisa, how are you?' Both men rose to offer her a seat, but she lifted a hand to show she preferred to stand. All three of them stood, a stiff triangle in the tiny box of a room.

'Just been sick again,' she said. Then she smiled. 'Can't

be much more to bring up. I think I'm back to yesterday's breakfast already.' They smiled with her. She looked tired to Rebus, exhausted. Lucky she had slept so soundly yesterday. He doubted she'd get much sleep for the next night ór ten, tranqs or not.

Flight spoke first. 'I've arranged for temporary accommodation, Dr Frazer. The less people who know where, the better. Don't worry, you'll be quite safe. We'll have a guard on you.'

'What about her flat?' asked Rebus.

Flight nodded. 'I've got two men there keeping an eye on the place. One inside the flat itself, the other outside, both of them hidden. If the Wolfman turns up, they'll cope with him, believe me.'

'Stop talking as though I'm not here,' Lisa snapped. 'This affects me too.'

There was a cold silence in the room.

'Sorry,' she said. She covered her eyes with her ringless left hand. 'I just can't believe I was so *scared* back there. I feel –'

She tipped her head back again. The tears were too precious to be released. Flight placed a hand softly on her shoulder.

'It's all right, Dr Frazer. Really it is.' She gave a wry smile at this.

Flight kept on talking, feeding her with comforting words. But she wasn't listening. She was staring at Rebus, and he was staring back at her. Rebus knew what her eyes were telling him. They were telling him something of the utmost importance.

Catch the Wolfman, catch him quickly and destroy him utterly. Do it for me, John. But just do it.

She blinked, breaking the contact. Rebus nodded slowly, almost imperceptibly, but it was enough. She smiled at him, and suddenly her eyes were dry sparkling stones. Flight felt the change and lifted his hand away from her arm. He looked to Rebus for some explanation, but Rebus was studying the letter, concentrating on its opening sentence. What was it? There was something there, something just beyond his line of vision. Something he didn't get.

Yet.

Two detectives, one of them extraordinarily burly, like the prop-forward from a rugby team, the other tall and thin and silent, came to the labs to take Lisa away with them, away to a place of safety. Despite vigorous protests, Rebus wasn't allowed to know the destination. Flight was taking all of this very seriously indeed. But before Lisa could go, the lab people needed her fingerprints and to take samples of fibres from her clothes, all for the purpose of elimination. The two bodyguards went with her.

Rebus and Flight, exhausted, stood together at the drinks machine in the long, brightly-lit hallway, feeding in coins for cups of powdery coffee and powdery tea.

'Are you married, George?'

Flight seemed surprised by the question, surprised perhaps that it should come only now. 'Yes,' he said. 'Have been the past twelve years. Marion. She's the second. The first was a disaster – my fault, not hers.'

Rebus nodded, taking hold of the hot plastic beaker by its rim.

'You said you'd been married, too,' Flight remarked. Rebus nodded again.

'That's right.'

'So what happened?'

'I'm not really sure any more. Rhona used to say it was like the continental drift: so slow we didn't notice until it was too late. Her on one island, me on another, and a great big bloody sea between us.'

Flight smiled. 'Well, you did say she was a teacher.'

'Yes, she still is actually. Lives in Mile End with my daughter.'

'Mile End? Bloody hell. Gentrified gangland, no place for any copper's daughter.'

Rebus smiled at the irony. It was time to confess. 'Actually, George, I've found out she's going out with someone called Kenny Watkiss.'

172

'Oh dear. Who is? Your missus or your daughter?'

'My daughter. Her name's Samantha.'

'And she's going out with Kenny Watkiss? How old is he?'

'Older than her. Eighteen, nineteen, something like that. He's a bike messenger in the City.'

Flight nodded, understanding now. 'He was the one who shouted from the public gallery?' Flight thought for a moment. 'Well, from what I know of the Watkiss family history, I'd say Kenny must be Tommy's nephew. Tommy's got a brother, Lenny, he's doing time just now. Lenny's a big softie, not like Tommy. He's in for fraud, tax evasion, clocking cars, naughty kites, I mean bad cheques. It's all fourth division stuff, but it mounts up, and when there's enough of it against you at any one sitting of the bench, well, it's odds on you'll go inside, isn't it?'

'It's no different in Scotland.'

'No, I don't suppose it is. So, do you want me to find out what I can about this bike messenger?'

'I already know where he stays. Churchill Estate, it's a housing estate in –'

Flight was chuckling. 'You don't have to tell any copper in Greater London where Churchill Estate is, John. They use that place to train the SAS.'

'Yes,' said Rebus, 'so Laine said.'

'Laine? What's he got to do with it?'

In for a penny, thought Rebus. 'I had Kenny's telephone number. I needed an address.'

'And Laine got it for you? What did you tell him it was for?'

'The Wolfman case.'

Flight flinched, his face creasing. 'You keep forgetting, John, you're our *guest* down here. You don't go pulling stunts like that. When Laine finds out –'

'If he finds out.'

But Flight was shaking his head. '*When* he finds out. There's no "if" about it, believe me. When he finds out, he won't bother with you. He won't even bother with who's directly above you. He'll go to your Chief Super back in

173

Edinburgh and give him the most incredible verbals. I've seen him do it.'

Do a good job, John. Remember, you're representing our force down there.

Rebus blew on the coffee. The notion of anyone giving 'verbals' to Farmer Watson was almost amusing. 'I always did fancy getting back into uniform,' he said.

Flight stared at him. The fun was over. 'There are some rules, John. We can get away with breaking a few, but some are sacrosanct, carved into stone by God Almighty. And one of them states that you don't muck around with someone like Laine just to satisfy your own personal curiosity.' Flight was angry, and trying to make a point, but he was also whispering, not wanting anyone to hear.

Rebus, not really caring any more, was half-smiling as he whispered back. 'So what do I do? Tell him the truth? Oh, hello there, Chief Inspector, my daughter's winching with someone I don't like. Can I have the young man's address, please, so I can go and belt him? Is that how I do it?'

Flight paused, then frowned. 'Winching?'

Now he too was smiling, though trying hard not to show it. Rebus laughed aloud.

'It means dating,' he said. 'Next you'll be telling me you don't know what hoolit means.'

'Try me,' said Flight, laughing too.

'Drunk,' explained Rebus.

They sipped their drinks in silence for a moment. Rebus thanked God for the linguistic barrier between them, for without it there would be no easy jokes, jokes which broke the tension. There were two ways to defuse tension: one was to laugh it away, the other was to resort to physical action. It was laugh or lash out. Once or twice now they had come near to trading punches, but had ended up trading grins instead.

Praise be for the gift of laughter.

'Anyway, I went to Hackney last night looking for Kenny Watkiss.'

'And you got those for your pains?' Flight was nodding towards the bruises. Rebus shrugged. 'Serves you right.

Someone once told me hackney's French for a nag. Doesn't sound French, does it? But I suppose it would explain the hackney carriage.'

Hackney. Nag. That horse in the British Museum, no bite. Rebus had to talk to Morrison about the bite marks.

Flight finished his drink first, draining the cup and tossing it into a bin beside the machine. He checked his watch.

'I better find a phone,' he said. 'See what's happening back at base. Maybe Lamb will have found something on that Crawford woman.'

' "That Crawford woman" is a victim, George. Stop making her sound like a criminal.'

'*Maybe* she's a victim,' said Flight. 'Let's get our facts straight before we go for the tea and sympathy routine. Besides, when did you join this little victim support group of yours? You know the way we have to play this sort of thing. It isn't nice necessarily, but it means we don't get it wrong.'

'That's quite a speech.'

Flight sighed and examined the tips of his shoes. 'Look, John, has it ever occurred to you that there might be another way?'

'The way of Zen perhaps?'

'I mean, a way other than your own. Or are the rest of us just thick, and you're the only policeman on the planet who knows how to solve a crime? I'd be interested to know.'

Rebus desperately did not want to blush, which is probably precisely why he did blush. He tried to think of a smart answer, but none came to mind right that second, so he kept silent. Flight nodded approval.

'Let's go find that phone,' he said. Now Rebus found the courage he needed.

'George,' he said. 'I need to know: who brought me here?'

Flight stared at him, wondering whether or not to answer. He pursed his lips as he thought about it, and came up with an answer: what the hell.

'I did,' he said. 'It was my idea.'

'You?' Rebus seemed puzzled. Flight nodded confirmation.

'Yes, me. I suggested you to Laine and Pearson. A new head, fresh blood, that sort of thing.'

'But how in God's name did you know about me?'

'Well,' Flight was beginning to look sheepish. He made a play of examining the tips of his shoes again. 'Remember I showed you that file, the one with all the guesswork in it? On top of that I did some background reading on multiple murderers. Research, you could call it. And I came across that case of yours in some newspaper clippings from Scotland Yard. I was impressed.'

Rebus pointed a disbelieving finger. 'You were reading up on serial killers?'

Flight nodded.

'On the *psychology* of serial killers?'

Flight shrugged. 'And other aspects, yes.' Rebus's eyes had widened.

'And all this time you've been having a dig at *me* for going along with Lisa Frazer's – no, I don't believe it!'

Flight was laughing again. The apparently arch anti-psychologist revealed in his true light. 'I had to examine every angle,' he said, watching as Rebus, having finished his coffee, tossed the cup into a waste-bin. 'Now come on, we really should make that phone call.'

Rebus was still shaking his head as he followed Flight down the hall. But though he appeared to be in good humour, his brain was more active than ever. Flight had pulled the wool over his eyes with consummate ease. How far did the pretence actually stretch? Was he now seeing the real Flight, or yet another mask? Flight whistled as he walked and kicked at an imaginary football. No, not George Flight, Rebus decided in an instant: never George Flight.

There was a telephone in the admin offices. There was also, seated at a desk having a conversation with one of the senior staff, Philip Cousins, immaculate in grey suit and burgundy tie.

'Philip!'

'Hello there, George. How are things?' Cousins spotted Rebus. 'And Inspector Rebus, too. Still lending a Caledonian hand?'

'Trying,' said Rebus.

'Yes, very,' rejoined Flight. 'So what brings you here, Philip? Where's Isobel?'

'Penny's rather tied up, I'm afraid. She'll be sorry to have missed you, George. As for my presence here, I just wanted to double-check some facts on a murder case from last December. You might remember it, the man in the bathtub.'

'The one that looked like suicide?'

'That's right.' Philip Cousins's voice was as rich and slow as double cream. Rebus reckoned that the word 'urbane' had been invented with him in mind. 'I'm in court later today,' Cousins was saying. 'Trying to help Malcolm Chambers pin the deceased's wife for manslaughter at the very least.'

'Chambers?' Flight shook his head. 'I don't envy you that.'

'But surely,' Rebus interrupted, 'you'll be on the same side?'

'Ah yes, Inspector Rebus,' said Cousins, 'you are quite correct. But Chambers is such a scrupulous man. He'll want my evidence to be water-tight, and if it isn't, then he's as likely to undo me as is the defence counsel. More likely, in fact. Malcolm Chambers is interested in the truth, not in verdicts.'

'Yes,' said Flight, 'I remember him having a right go at me once in the witness box, all because I couldn't recall off-hand what kind of clock had been in the living room. The case nearly crumbled there and then.' Flight and Cousins shared a comradely smile.

'I've just been hearing,' said Cousins, 'that there's fresh evidence on the Wolfman case. Do tell.'

'It's beginning to come together, Philip,' said Flight. 'It's definitely beginning to come together, due in no small part to my associate here.' Flight laid a momentary hand on Rebus's shoulder.

'I'm impressed,' said Cousins, sounding neither impressed nor unimpressed.

'It was luck,' said Rebus, as he felt he ought. Not that he believed what he was saying. Cousins's eyes on him were like packs of ice, so that the room temperature seemed to drop with every glance.

'So what do we have?'

'Well,' said Flight, 'we've got someone who claims she was attacked by the Wolfman but escaped from him.'

'Fortunate creature,' said Cousins.

'And,' continued Flight, 'one of the . . . people helping us on the case this morning received a letter claiming to be from the Wolfman.'

'Good God.'

'We think it's kosher,' Flight concluded.

'Well,' said Cousins, 'this *is* something. Wait till I tell Penny. She'll be thrilled.'

'Philip, we don't want it getting out –'

'Not a word, George, not a word. You know it's all one-way traffic with me. But Penny should be told.'

'Oh, tell Isobel by all means,' said Flight, 'only warn her it's not to go any further.'

'Total secrecy,' said Cousins. 'I quite understand. Mum's the word. Who was it, by the way?' Flight appeared not to understand. 'To whom was this threatening letter addressed?'

Flight was about to speak, but Rebus beat him to it. 'Just someone on the case, as Inspector Flight says.' He smiled, trying to alleviate the brusqueness of his response. Oh yes, his mind was working now, working in a fever: nobody had told Cousins the letter was threatening, so how did he know it was? Okay, it was simple enough to work out that it wouldn't exactly have been fan mail, but all the same.

'Well then,' said Cousins, choosing not to press for details. 'And now, gentlemen,' he scooped up two manila files from the desk and tucked them under his arm, then stood, the joints of his knees cracking with the effort, 'if you'll excuse me, Court Eight awaits. Inspector Rebus,' Cousins held out his free hand, 'it sounds as though the case may be drawing towards its conclusion. Should we fail to meet again, give my regards to your delightful city.' He turned to Flight. 'See you soon, George. Bring Marion round for supper some evening. Give Penny a tinkle and we'll try to find one night in the calendar when all four of us are free. Goodbye.'

'Bye, Philip.'

'Goodbye.'

'Goodbye.'

'Oh.' Cousins had stopped in the doorway. 'There is just one thing.' He turned pleading eyes on Flight. 'You don't have a spare driver, do you, George? It's going to be hell getting a taxi at this time of day.'

'Well,' Flight thought hard, then had an idea, 'if you can hang on for a couple of minutes, Philip, I've got a couple of men here in the building.' He turned to Rebus, whose eyes had widened. 'Lisa won't mind, will she, John? I mean, if her car drops Philip off at the Old Bailey?'

Rebus could do little but shrug.

'Excellent!' said Cousins, clasping his hands together. 'Thank you so much.'

'I'll take you to them,' Flight said. 'But first I need to make a phone call.'

Cousins nodded towards the corridor. 'And I must visit the WC. Be back in a tick.'

They watched him leave. Flight was grinning, shaking his head in wonderment. 'Do you know,' he said, 'he's been like that ever since I met him? I mean, the sort of ambassadorial air, the aged aristocrat. Ever since I've known him.'

'He's a gentleman all right,' said Rebus.

'But that's just the thing,' said Flight. 'His background is every bit as ordinary as yours or mine.' He turned to the lab man. 'All right if I use your phone?'

He did not wait for an answer, but started dialling straight away. 'Hello?' he said into the receiver when he was finally connected. 'Who's that? Oh, hello, Deakin, is Lamb there? Yes, put him on, will you? Thanks.' While he was waiting, Flight picked invisible threads from his trousers.

179

The trousers were shiny from too many wearings. Everything about Flight, Rebus noticed, seemed worn: his shirt collar had an edge of grime to it and the collar itself was too tight, constricting the loose flesh of the neck, pinching it into vertical folds. Rebus found himself transfixed by that neck, by the tufts of grey sprouting hair where the razor had failed in its duty. Signs of mortality, as final as a hand around a throat. When Flight got off the phone, Rebus would protest about sending Cousins off with Lisa. *Ambassadorial. Aristocrat.* One of the earlier mass killers had been an aristocrat, too.

'Hello, Lamb? What have you found on Miss Crawford?' Flight listened, his eyes on Rebus, ready to communicate anything of interest. 'Uh-huh, okay. Mm, I see. Yes. Right.' All the time his eyes told Rebus that everything was checking out, that Jan Crawford was reliable, that she was telling the truth. Then Flight's eyes widened a little. 'What's that again?' And he listened more intently, moving his eyes from Rebus to study the telephone apparatus itself. 'Now that is interesting.'

Rebus shifted. What? What was interesting? But Flight had again resorted to monosyllables.

'Uh-hu. Mmm. Well, never mind. I know. Yes, I'm sure.' His voice sounded resigned to something. 'Okay. Thanks for letting me know. Yes. No, we'll be back in about, I don't know, maybe another hour. Right, catch you then.'

Flight held the receiver above the telephone, but did not immediately drop it back into its cradle. Instead, he let it hang there.

Rebus could contain his curiosity no longer. 'What?' he said. 'What is it? What's wrong?'

Flight seemed to come out of his daydream, and put down the receiver. 'Oh,' he said, 'it's Tommy Watkiss.'

'What about him?'

'Lamb has just heard that there isn't going to be a retrial. We don't know why yet. Maybe the judge didn't think the charges were worth all the aggro and told the CPS so.'

'Assault on a woman not worth the *aggro*?' All thought of Philip Cousins vanished from Rebus's mind.

Flight shrugged. 'Retrials are expensive. *Any* trial is expensive. We cocked it up first time round, so we lose a second chance. It happens, John, you know that.'

'Of course it happens. But the idea of a snake like Watkiss getting away with something like that – '

'Don't worry, he can't keep his nose clean for long. Breaking the law's in his blood. When he does something naughty, we'll have him, and I'll see to it there are no balls-ups, mark my words.'

Rebus sighed. Yes, it happened, you lost a few. More than a few. Incompetence or a soft judge, an unsympathetic jury or a rock-solid witness for the defence. And sometimes maybe the Procurator Fiscal thought a retrial not worth the money. You lost a few. They were like toothache.

'I bet Chambers is fuming,' Rebus said.

'Oh yes,' said Flight, smiling at the thought, 'I bet he's got steam coming out of his bloody shirt-cuffs.'

But one person would be happy at least, Rebus was thinking: Kenny Watkiss. He'd be over the moon.

'So,' said Rebus, 'what about Jan Crawford?'

Flight shrugged again. 'She seems straight as a die. No previous, no record of mental illness, lives quietly, but the neighbours seem to like her well enough. Like Lamb said, she's so clean it's frightening.'

Yes, the squeaky clean ones often were. Frightening to a policeman the way an unknown species might be to a jungle explorer: fear of the new, the different. You got to suspect that everyone had something to hide: the schoolteachers smuggled in porn videos from their holiday in Amsterdam; the solicitors took cocaine on their weekend parties; the happily married MP was sleeping with his secretary; the magistrate had a predeliction for underage boys; the librarian kept a real skeleton hidden in the closet; the angelic looking children had set fire to a neighbour's cat.

And sometimes your suspicions were correct.

And other times they weren't. Cousins was standing at the door now, ready to leave. Flight laid a hand softly on his arm. Rebus recalled that he'd meant to say something to Flight, but how to phrase it? Would it do to say that Philip

Cousins seemed almost too clean, with his surgeon's cold, manicured hands and his ambassadorial air? Rebus was wondering now, *seriously* wondering.

Since Flight had gone off with Philip Cousins to find Lisa and her protectors, Rebus went back to the lab to hear the result of the first saliva test.

'Sorry,' said the white-coated scientist. He looked not yet to be out of his teens. Beneath his lab coat, there lurked a black T-shirt decorated with the name of a heavy metal band. 'I don't think we're going to have much luck. All we're finding so far is H_2O, tap water. Whoever stuck the envelope down must have used a wet sponge or a pad or one of those old-fashioned roller things. No traces of saliva at all.'

The breath left Rebus's lungs. 'What about fingerprints?'

'Negative so far. All we've found are two sets which look like they're going to match Dr Frazer's. And we're not having any better luck with fibres or grease stains. I'd say the writer wore gloves. Nobody here has seen such a clean, speck-free job.'

He knows, Rebus was thinking. He knows everything we might try. So damned smart.

'Well, thanks anyway,' he said. The young man raised his eyebrows and spread his palms.

'I wish we could do more.'

You could start by getting a haircut, son, he thought to himself. You look too much like Kenny Watkiss. He sighed instead. 'Just do what you can,' he said. 'Just do what you can.'

Turning to walk away, Rebus felt a mixture of fresh rage and impotence, sudden savage frustration. The Wolfman was too good. He would stop killing before they could catch him; or he would simply go on killing again and again and again. No one would be safe. And most of all, it seemed, Lisa would not be safe.

Lisa.

She was being blamed by the Wolfman for the story

Rebus had invented. It had nothing to do with Lisa. And if the Wolfman should somehow get to her it would be Rebus's fault, wouldn't it? Where was Lisa going? Rebus didn't know. Flight thought it was safer that way. But Rebus couldn't shake off the idea that the Wolfman might well be a policeman. Might well be *any* policeman. Might by the brawny detective or the thin and silent detective. Lisa had gone off with them thinking them her protection. What if she had walked straight into the clutches of. . ? What if the Wolfman knew exactly. . ? What if Philip Cousins. . ?

A loudspeaker sounded from its recess in the ceiling.

'Telephone call for Inspector Rebus at reception. Telephone call for Inspector Rebus.'

Rebus walked quickly down the rest of the corridor and through the swing-door at the end. He didn't know if Flight was still in the building, didn't care. His mind was filling with horrors: Wolfman, Lisa, Rhona, Sammy. Little Sammy, his daughter. She'd seen enough terror in her life. He'd been responsible before. He didn't want her to be hurt ever again.

The receptionist lifted the receiver as he approached, holding it out to him. As he grabbed it, she pressed a button on the dial, connecting him to the caller.

'Hello?' he said, breathlessly.

'Daddy?' Oh Christ, it *was* Sammy.

'Sammy?' Nearly yelling now. 'What is it? What's wrong?'

'Oh, Daddy.' She was crying. The memory flashed in front of him, scalding his vision. Phone calls. Screams.

'What is it, Sammy? Tell me!'

'It's,' a sniff, 'it's Kenny.'

'Kenny?' He furrowed his brow. 'What's wrong with him? Has he been in a crash?'

'Oh no, Daddy. He's just . . . just *disappeared*.'

'Where are you, Sammy?'

'I'm in a call-box.'

'Okay, I'm going to give you the address of a police station. Meet me there. If you have to get a taxi, that's fine. I'll pay for it when you arrive. Understand?'

'Daddy.' She sniffed back tears. 'You've got to find him. I'm worried. Please find him, Daddy. Please. *Please!*'

By the time George Flight reached reception, Rebus had already left. The receptionist explained as best she could, while Flight rubbed his jaw, encountering stubble. He had argued with Lisa Frazer, but by Christ she'd been stubborn. Attractively stubborn, he had to admit. She'd told him she didn't mind bodyguards but that the idea of a 'safe location' was out of the question. She had, she said, an appointment at the Old Bailey, a couple of appointments actually, interviews she was doing in connection with some research.

'It's taken me weeks to set them up,' she said, 'there's no way I'm going to blow them out now!'

'But my dear,' Philip Cousins had drawled, 'that's just where we're headed.' He was, Flight knew, keen for a close to proceedings, glancing at his watch impatiently. And it seemed that Lisa and Cousins knew one another from the murder at Copperplate Street, that they had things in common, things they wanted to talk about. That they were keen to be going.

So Flight made a decision. What did it matter after all if she did visit the Bailey? There were few better protected spots in the whole city. It was several hours yet until the first of her interviews, but that didn't really bother her. She did not, she said, mind hanging around in the 'courthouse'. In fact, she rather enjoyed the idea. The two officers could accompany her, wait for her, then drive her on to whatever safe location Flight had in mind. This, at any rate, was Lisa Frazer's argument, an argument defended by Philip Cousins who could see 'no flaw in the reasoning, m'lud'. So, to smiles on their part and a shrug on Flight's, the course of action was decided. Flight watched the Ford Granada roll away from him – the two officers in the front, Philip and Lisa Frazer in the back. Safe as houses, he was thinking. Safe as bloody houses.

And now Rebus had buggered off. Oh well, he'd catch up with him no doubt. He didn't regret bringing Rebus down here, not a bit. But he knew it had been *his* decision, not one entirely endorsed by the upper echelons. Any balls-ups and it would be Flight's pension on the block. He knew that only too well, as did everyone else. Which was why he'd stuck so close to Rebus in the first few days, just to be sure of the man.

Was he sure of the man? It was a question he would rather not answer, even now, even to himself. Rebus was like the spring in a trap, likely to jump no matter what landed on the bait. He was also a Scot, and Flight had never trusted the Scots, not since the day they'd voted to stay part of the Union . . .

'Daddy!'

And she runs into his arms. He hugs her to him, aware that he does not have to bend too far to accomplish this. Yes, she's grown, and yet she seems more childlike than ever. He kisses the top of her head, smells her clean hair. She is trembling. He can feel the vibrations darting through her chest and arms.

'Sshh,' he says. 'Ssshhh, pet, ssshhh.'

She pulls back and almost smiles, sniffs, then says, 'You always used to call me that. Your pet. Mum never called me pet. Only you.'

He smiles back and strokes her hair. 'Yes,' he says, 'your mum told me off for that. She said a pet was a possession and that you weren't a possession.' He is remembering now. 'She had some funny ideas, your mum.'

'She still does.' Then she remembers why she is here. The tears well up anew in her eyes.

'I know you don't like him,' she says.

'Nonsense, whatever gives you that – '

'But I love him, Daddy.' His heart spins once in his chest. 'And I don't want anything to happen to him.'

'What makes you think something's going to happen to him?'

'The way he's been acting lately, like he's keeping secrets from me. Mum's noticed it, too. I'm not just dreaming. But she said she thought maybe he was planning an engage-ment.' She sees his eyes widen, and shakes her head. 'I didn't believe it. I knew it was something else. I thought, I don't know, I just . . .'

He notices for the first time that they have an audience. Until now they might have been in a sealed box for all the notice he has taken of their surroundings. Now, though, he sees a bemused desk sergeant, two WPCs clutching paperwork to their bosoms and watching the scene with a kind of maternal glow, two unshaven men slumped in seats against the wall, just waiting.

'Come on, Sammy,' he says. 'Let's go up to my office.'

They were halfway to the Murder Room before he remembered that it was not, perhaps the most wholesome environment for a teenage girl. The photos on the walls were only the start of it. A sense of humour was needed on a case like the Wolfman, and that sense of humour had begun to manifest itself in cartoons, jokes and mock-ups of newspaper stories either pinned to the noticeboards or taped onto the sides of computer screens. The language could be choice, too, or someone might be overheard in conversation with someone from forensics.

'. . . torn . . . ripped her right . . . kitchen knife, they reckon . . . slit from ear . . . gouged . . . anus . . . nasty bastard . . . makes some of them seem almost human.' Stories were swapped of serial killers past, of suicides scraped from railway lines, of police dogs playing ball with a severed head.

No, definitely not the place for his daughter. Besides, there was always the possibility that Lamb might be there.

Instead, he found a vacant interview room. It had been turned into a temporary cupboard while the investigation continued, filled with empty cardboard boxes, unneeded chairs, broken desk-lamps and computer keyboards, a heavy-looking manual typewriter. Eventually, the computers in the Murder Room would be packed back into the cardboard boxes, the files would be tidied away into dusty stacks somewhere.

For now, the room had a musty, barren feel, but it still

186

boasted a lightbulb hanging from the ceiling, a table and two chairs. On the table sat a glass ashtray full of stubs and two plastic coffee cups containing a layer of green and black mould. On the floor lay a crushed cigarette packet. Rebus kicked the packet beneath some of the stacked chairs.

'It's not much,' he said, 'but it's home. Sit down. Do you want anything?'

She seemed not to understand the question. 'Like what?'

'I don't know, coffee, tea?'

'Diet Coke?'

Rebus shook his head.

'What about Irn-Bru?'

Now he laughed: she was joking with him. He couldn't bear to see her upset, especially over someone as undeserving as Kenny Watkiss.

'Sammy,' he asked, 'does Kenny have an uncle?'

'Uncle Tommy?'

Rebus nodded. 'That's the one.'

'What about him?'

'Well,' said Rebus, crossing his legs, 'what do you know about him?'

'About Kenny's Uncle Tommy? Not a lot.'

'What does he do for a living?'

'I think Kenny said he's got a stall somewhere, you know, in a market.'

Like Brick Lane market? Did he sell false teeth?

'Or maybe he just delivers to market stalls, I can't really remember.'

Delivers stolen goods? Goods given to him by thieves like the one they'd picked up, the one who had pretended to be the Wolfman?

'Anyway, he's got a few bob.'

'How do you know that?'

'Kenny told me. At least, I think he did. Otherwise how would I know?'

'Where does Kenny work, Sammy?'

'In the City.'

'Yes, but for which firm?'

'Firm?'

187

'He's a courier, isn't he? He must work for a company?'

But she shook her head. 'He went freelance when he had enough regular clients. I remember he said that his boss at the old place was pissed off – ' She broke off suddenly and looked up at him, her face going red. She'd forgotten for a moment that she was talking to her father, and not just to some copper. 'Sorry, Dad,' she apologised. 'His boss was angry with him for taking away so much of the trade. Kenny was good, see, he knows all the shortcuts, knows which buildings are which. Some drivers get confused when they can't find some tiny alleyway, or when the numbers on a street don't seem to make sense.' Yes. Rebus had noticed that; how sometimes the street numbers seemed illogical, as though numbers had been skipped. 'But not Kenny. He knows London like the back of his hand.'

Knows London well, the roads, the shortcuts. On a motorbike, you could cut across London in a flash. Towpaths, alleys –in a flash.

'What kind of bike does he have, Sammy?'

'I don't know. A Kawasaki something-or-other. He's got one that he uses for work, because it's not too heavy, and another he keeps for weekends, a really big bike.'

'Where does he keep them? There can't be too many safe places around the Churchill Estate?'

'There are some garages nearby. They get vandalised, but Kenny's put a reinforced door on. It's like Fort Knox. I keep kidding him about it. It's better guarded than his– ' Her voice falls flat. 'How did you know he lives on Churchill?'

'What?'

Her voice is stronger now, curious. 'How did you know Kenny lives on Churchill?'

Rebus shrugged. 'I suppose he told me, that night I met him round at your place.'

She's thinking back, trying to recall the conversation. But there's nothing there, nothing she can latch onto. Rebus is thinking, too.

Like Fort Knox. A handy place to store stolen gear. Or a corpse.

'So,' he says, pulling his chair a little further in to the table. 'Tell me what *you* think has happened. What do you think he's been keeping from you?'

She stared at the table-top, shaking her head slowly, staring, shaking, until finally: 'I don't know.'

'Well, had you fallen out over anything? Maybe you'd been arguing?'

'No.'

'Maybe he was jealous?'

She gave a desperate laugh. 'No.'

'Maybe he had other girlfriends?'

'No!'

When her eyes caught his, Rebus felt a stirring of shame inside him. He couldn't forget that she was his daughter; nor could he forget that he needed to ask her these questions. Somehow he kept swerving between the two, careering into her.

'No,' she repeated softly. 'I'd have known if there was someone else.'

'Friends, then: did he have any close friends?'

'A few. Not many. I mean, he talked about them, but he never introduced me.'

'Have you tried calling them? Maybe one of them knows something.'

'I only know their first names. A couple of guys Kenny grew up with, Billy and Jim. Then there was someone called Arnold. He used to mention him. And one of the other bike messengers, I think his name was Roland or Ronald, something posh like that.'

'Hold on, let me jot these down.' Rebus took notebook and pen from his pocket. 'Right,' he said, 'so that was Billy, Jim. What was the other one?'

'Roland or Ronald or something.' She watched him writing. 'And Arnold.'

Rebus sat back in his chair. 'Arnold?'

'Yes.'

'Did you ever meet Arnold?'

'I don't think so.'

'What did Kenny say about him?'

She shrugged. 'He was just someone Kenny used to bump into. I think he worked the stalls, too. They went for a drink sometimes.'

It couldn't be the same Arnold, could it? Flight's bald sex-offender snitch? What were the chances? Going for a drink? They seemed unlikely supping companions, always supposing it was the same Arnold.

'All right,' Rebus said, closing the notebook. 'Do you have a recent photo of Kenny? A good one, one that's nice and sharp.'

'I can get one. I've got some back at the house.'

'Okay, I'll get someone to drive you home. Give them the picture and they'll bring it back to me. Let's circulate Kenny's description, that's the first thing to do. Meanwhile I'll do some snooping, see what I can come up with.'

She smiled. 'It's not really your patch, is it?'

'No, it's not my patch at all. But sometimes if you look at something, or some place, for too long, you stop seeing what's there. Sometimes it takes a fresh pair of eyes to see what's staring you in the face.' He was thinking of Flight, of the reason Flight had brought him down here. He was thinking, too, of whether he, Rebus, could muster enough clout to organise a search for Kenny Watkiss. Maybe not without Flight to back him up. No, what was he thinking of? This was a missing person, for Christ's sake. It had to be investigated. Yes, but there were ways and ways of investigating, and he could count on no preferential treatment, no favours, when it came to the crunch. 'I don't suppose,' he asked now, 'you know whether or not his bikes are still in the garage?'

'I took a look. They're both still there. That was when I started to get worried.'

'Was there anything else in the garage?' But she wasn't listening to him.

'He hardly ever goes anywhere without a bike. He hates buses and stuff. He said he was going to name his big bike after . . . after me.'

The tears came again. This time he let her cry, though it hurt him more than he could say. Better out than in, wasn't that how the cliché went? She was blowing her nose when the door opened. Flight looked into the small room. His eyes said it all: *you might have taken her somewhere better than this*.

'Yes, George? What can I do for you?'

'After you left the lab,' the pause showed displeasure at not having been informed or left a message, 'they gave me a bit more gen on the letter itself.'

'I'll be with you in a minute.'

Flight nodded but directed his attention to Samantha. 'Are you okay, love?'

She sniffed. 'Fine, thanks.'

'Well,' he said archly, 'if you *do* want to register a complaint against Inspector Rebus, see the desk sergeant.'

'Ach, get away, George,' said Rebus.

Sammy was trying to giggle and blow her nose at the same time, and making a bit of a mess of both. Rebus winked towards Flight who, having done as much as he could (and for which Rebus was grateful), was now retreating.

'You're not all bad, are you?' said Samantha when Flight had gone.

'What do you mean?'

'Policemen. You're not all as bad as they say.'

'You're a copper's daughter, Sammy. Remember that. And you're a *straight* copper's daughter. Be sure to stick up for your old dad. Okay?'

She smiled again. 'You're not old, Dad.'

He smiled, too, but did not reply. In truth, he was basking in the compliment, whether it was mere flattery or no. What mattered was that Sammy, his daughter Sammy, had said it.

'Right,' he said at last, 'let's get you into a car. And don't worry, pet, we'll track down your missing beau.'

'You called me pet again.'

'Did I? Don't tell your mother.'

'I won't. And, Dad?'

'What?' He half-turned towards her just in time to receive her peck on the cheek.

'Thanks,' she said. 'Whatever happens, thanks.'

* * *

Flight was in the small office of the Murder Room. After the close confines of the interview cupboard, this space had suddenly taken on a new, much larger dimension. Rebus sat himself down and swung one leg over the other.

'So what's this about the Wolfman letter?' he said.

'So,' replied Flight, 'what's this about Kenny Watkiss disappearing?'

'You tell me yours and I'll tell you mine.'

Flight picked up a folder, opened it, took out three or four closely typed sheets of paper, and began to read.

'Typeface used is Helvetica. Unusual for personal correspondence, though used by newspapers and magazines.' Flight looked up meaningfully.

'A reporter?' Rebus said doubtfully.

'Well, think about it,' said Flight. 'Every crime reporter in England knows about Lisa Frazer by now. They could probably find out where she lives, too.'

Rebus considered this. 'Okay,' he said at last, 'go on.'

'Helvetica can be found on some electronic typewriters and electric golfball machines, but is more commonly found on computers and word processors.' Flight glanced up. 'This would corrolate with density of type. The type itself is of very even quality . . . blah, blah, blah. Also, the letters line up neatly, suggesting that a good quality printer has been used, probably a daisywheel, suggesting in turn the use of a high quality word processor or word-processing package. However,' Flight went on, 'the letter K becomes faint towards the tips of its stem.' Flight paused to turn the page. Rebus wasn't really paying a great deal of attention as yet, and neither was George Flight. Labs always came up with more information that was useful. So far, all Rebus had really been hearing was the chaff.

'This is more interesting,' Flight went on. 'Inside the envelope particles were found which appear to be flecks of paint, yellow, green and orange predominating. Perhaps an oil-based paint: tests are still continuing.'

'So we've got a crime reporter who fancies himself as Van Gogh?'

Flight wasn't rising to the bait. He read through the rest of the report quickly to himself. 'That's pretty much it,' he said. 'What's left is more to do with what they failed to find: no prints, no stains, no hair or fibres.'

'No personalised watermark?' Rebus asked. In detective novels, the personalised watermark would lead to a small family business run by an eccentric old man, who would recall selling the paper to someone called . . . And that would be it: crime solved. Neat, ingenious, but it seldom happened like that. He thought of Lisa again; of Cousins. No, not Cousins: it couldn't be Cousins. And besides, he wouldn't try anything with those two gorillas in attendance.

'No personalised watermark,' Flight was saying. 'Sorry.'

'Oh well,' Rebus offered, with a loud sigh, 'we're no further forward, are we?'

Flight was looking at the report, as though willing something, some clue, to grab his attention. Then: 'So what's all this about Kenny Watkiss?'

'He's scarpered under mysterious circumstances. Good riddance, I'd say, but it's left Sammy in a bit of a state. I said we'd do what we could.'

'You can't get involved, John. Leave it to us.'

'I don't want to get involved, George. This one's all yours.' The voice seemed ingenuous enough, but Flight was long past being fooled by John Rebus. He grinned and shook his head.

'What do you want?' he asked.

'Well,' said Rebus, leaning forward in his chair, 'Sammy did mention one of Kenny's associates. Someone called Arnold who worked on a market stall, at least she thinks he works in or around a market.'

'You think it's my Arnold?' Flight thought it over. 'It's possible.'

'Too much of a coincidence, you think?'

'Not in a city as small as this.' Flight saw the look on Rebus's face. 'I'm being serious, actually. The small-time crooks, they're like a little family. If this was Sicily, you could cram every small-timer in London into a village. Everybody knows everybody else. It's the big-timers we

193

can't pin. They keep themselves too much to themselves, never go down the pub shooting their mouths off after a couple of Navy Rums.'

'Can we talk to Arnold?'

'What for?'

'Maybe he knows something about Kenny.'

'Even supposing he does, why should he tell us?'

'Because we're police officers, George. And he's a member of the public. We're here to uphold law and order, and it's his duty to help us in that onerous task.' Rebus was reflective. 'Plus I'll slip him twenty quid.'

Flight sounded incredulous. 'This is London, John. A score can hardly get a round of drinks. Arnold gives good gen, but he'll be looking for a pony at least.' Now he was playing with Rebus, and Rebus, realising it, smiled.

'If Arnold wants a pony,' he said, 'tell him I'll buy him one for Christmas. And a little girl to sit on it. Just so long as he tells me what he knows.'

'Fair enough,' said Flight. 'Come on then, let's go find ourselves a street market.'

The Gallery

Flight was struggling with half a dozen large brown-paper bags, the fruits – literally – of asking for Arnold at three or four market stalls so far. Rebus had refused the offers of free bananas, oranges, pears and grapes, though Flight had prodded him to accept.

'It's a local custom,' Flight said. 'They get annoyed if you don't accept. Like a Glaswegian offering you a drink. Would you turn it down? No, because then you'd offend him. Same with these guys.'

'What would I do with three pounds of bananas?'

'Eat them,' said Flight blandly. Then, cryptically: 'Unless you were Arnold, of course.'

He refused to explain the meaning of this, and Rebus refused to consider the various possibilities. They moved from stall to stall, passing most, stopping at only a few. In their way, they were like the women who crushed in all around them, feeling this or that mango or aubergine, checking prices at the various stalls, pausing only at a few to make their final purchases.

' 'Allo, George.'

'Blimy, George, where you been hiding yourself?'

'All right there, George? How's your love life?'

It seemed to Rebus that half the stall-holders and most of their box- and tray-carrying assistants knew Flight. At one point, Flight nodded behind one of the stalls, where a young man was disappearing rapidly along the street.

'Jim Jessop,' he said. 'He skipped bail a couple of weeks back.'

'Shouldn't we . . . ?'

But Flight shook his head. 'Another time, eh, John? The little bugger was three-A's standard in the thousand metres. I don't feel like a run today, what about you?'

'Fair enough,' said Rebus, aware that here, in this place,

on this 'patch', he was very much the bystander, the tourist. This was Flight's territory. The man moved confidently through the throng, spoke easily with the various vendors, was in every way quite at home. Eventually, after a chat with the man behind the fresh fish counter, Flight returned with a bag of mussels, another of scallops and information on where Arnold might be found. He led Rebus behind the market stalls onto the pavement and then into a narrow alleyway.

'Moules marinière,' he said, holding up one of the white polythene bags. 'Beautiful. Easy to cook, too. It's the preparation that takes up all the time.'

Rebus shook his head. 'You're full of surprises, George. I'd never have taken you for a cordon bleu.'

Flight just smiled, musing. 'And scallops,' he said, 'Marion loves those. I make a sauce with them and serve it with fresh trout. Again, it's all preparation. The cooking's the easy part.'

He enjoyed showing Rebus this other side of his personality, though he couldn't say why. Nor could he exactly say why he hadn't told John Rebus that Lisa had gone to the Old Bailey; had instead mumbled something about seeing her safely on her way. He thought probably his reasoning had to do with Rebus's spring-loaded emotions: if the Scotsman thought Lisa Frazer was *not* in Flight's place of safety, he'd probably go haring off after her, making a fool of himself 'neath blindfolded Justice herself. And Rebus was still Flight's responsibility, still the liability he always had been, if not more so.

They had come out of the alley onto a small-scale housing estate. The houses looked fairly new, but already the paint was flaking from the window sills. There were cries and squeals from just ahead. A kiddies' playground, concrete surrounded by concrete. A huge section of pipe had become a tunnel, a den, a hiding place. There were swings, too, and a see-saw. And a sand-pit which had become second home to the area's cats and dogs.

The children's imaginations knew few bounds: Pretend you're in hospital, and I'm the doctor; And then the spaceman's ship crashed on the planet; Cowboys don't *have* girlfriends; No, you're chasing *me*, because I'm the soldier and you're the guard; Pretend there isn't a pipe.

Pretend. There was no pretend about the energy they were expending. They couldn't stand still, couldn't pause for breath. They had to yell and jump and get involved. It made Rebus tired just to look at them.

'There he is,' said Flight. He was pointing towards a bench on the edge of the playground. Arnold was sitting there, his back very straight, hands clasping his knees. He had an intent look on his face, neither happy nor unhappy. The kind of look you sometimes saw at the zoo, when someone was peering into a particular cage or enclosure. It was best described as an interested look. Oh yes, Arnold was interested. It made Rebus's stomach queasy just to watch him. Flight seemed to take it all quite casually. He walked across the bench and sat down beside Arnold, who turned, his eyes suddenly taking on a hunted, frightened look, his mouth creasing into an O. Then he exhaled noisily.

'It's you, Mister Flight. I didn't recognise you.' He gestured towards the bags. 'Been shopping? That's nice.'

The voice was flat, lacking emotion. Rebus had heard addicts talk like that. Five percent of their brain was fixed on dealing with the external world, the remaining ninety-five concentrating on other things. Well, he supposed Arnold was a kind of addict too.

'Yes,' said Flight, 'just buying a few bits. You remember Inspector Rebus?'

Arnold followed Flight's eyes, staring up from his bench to where Rebus stood, his body purposely shielding Arnold from the children.

'Oh yes,' Arnold said blandly, 'he was in the car with you the other day, Mr Flight.'

'Well done, Arnold. Yes, that's right. You've got a good memory, haven't you?'

'It pays to have, Mr Flight. That's how I remember all the things I tell you.'

'Actually, Arnold,' Flight slid along the bench until his

197

thigh was almost touching that of the other man. Arnold angled his own legs away from the policeman, his eyes intent on Flight's proximity to him. 'Speaking of memory, maybe you can help me. Maybe you can help Inspector Rebus, too.'

'Yes?' The word was stretched almost to breaking point.

'We were just wondering,' said Flight, 'whether you've seen Kenny lately. Only, he doesn't seem to have been around much, does he? I wondered whether he'd maybe gone on holiday?'

Arnold gazed up with milky, childlike eyes. 'Kenny who?'

Flight laughed. 'Kenny Watkiss, Arnold. Your mate Kenny.'

For a moment, Rebus held his breath. What if it was another Arnold? What if Sammy had got the name wrong? Then Arnold nodded slowly.

'Oh, that Kenny. He's not really a mate, Mr Flight. I mean, I see him now and again.' Arnold stopped, but Flight was nodding, saying nothing, expecting more. 'We have a drink together sometimes.'

'What do you talk about?'

The question was unexpected. 'What do you mean?'

'It's a simple enough question,' said Flight with a smile. 'What do you talk about? I wouldn't have thought the two of you would have much in common.'

'We just, we talk. I don't know.'

'Yes, but what do you talk about? Football?'

'Sometimes, yes.'

'What team does he support?'

'I don't know, Mr Flight.'

'You talk about football with him and yet you don't know what team he supports?'

'Maybe he told me and I forgot.'

Flight looked dubious. 'Maybe,' he agreed. Rebus knew his part in the drama now. Let Flight do the talking. Just keep quiet but look ominous, standing over Arnold like a thundercloud, staring down like an avenger onto that gleaming bald dome of a head. Flight knew exactly what he was doing. Arnold was growing nervous, his body jerking, unable to keep his head still, his right knee bobbing up and down.

'So what else do you talk about? He likes motorbikes, doesn't he?'

'Yes,' Arnold answered, guardedly now, for he knew what was happening to him.

'So do you talk about bikes?'

'I don't like bikes. Too noisy.'

'Too noisy? Yes, you've got a point there.' Flight nodded towards the play area. 'But this place is noisy, too, Arnold, isn't it? Yet you don't seem to mind the noise here. Why's that?'

Arnold turned on him, eyes burning. But Flight was ready with a smile, a smile more serious than any grimace. 'What I mean is,' he went on, 'you like some noises but not others. That's fair, isn't it? But you don't like motorbikes. So what else do you talk about with Kenny?'

'We just *talk*,' said Arnold, his face creased with anguish. 'Gossip, how the city's changing, the East End. This used to be all rows of cottages. There was a field and allotments. The families all used to have picnics on the field. They'd bring tomatoes or potatoes or a cabbage to your mum, saying they grew too much, and the kids would all play in the street. There weren't any Bangladeshis or what have you. Just proper East Enders. Kenny's mum and dad didn't live far from here. Two streets away from where I lived. Course, I was older than him. We never played together or anything.'

'And where did Uncle Tommy live?'

'He was over that way.' Arnold pointed with a finger. He had grown a little more confident now. Reminiscences couldn't do any harm, could they? And to talk freely came as such a relief after the careful duel he'd just gone through. So he opened up to them. The good old days. But between his words, Rebus could see a truer picture, a picture of how the other kids used to beat him up, play tricks on him, of how his father used to lock him in his room, starve him. The family breaking apart. Drifting into petty crime. Painfully shy, unable to form relationships.

'Do you ever see Tommy around?' Flight asked suddenly.

'Tommy Watkiss? Yes, I see him.' Arnold was still basking in the past.

'Does Kenny see him?'

'Of course he does. He works for him sometimes.'

'What? Deliveries, that sort of thing?'

'Deliveries, pick-ups –' Arnold halted, aware of what he was saying. This wasn't the past they were talking about any longer. This wasn't safe.

Flight leaned across so that his nose was almost touching Arnold's. All Arnold could do was lean back against the bench, its hard spars stopping him from escaping.

'Where is he, Arnold?'

'Who? Tommy?'

'You know bloody well who I mean! Kenny! Tell me where he is!'

Rebus half-turned, to see that the children had stopped playing and were watching this grown-up game.

'You going to fight, mister?' one of them called. Rebus shook his head and called back, 'Just pretending.'

Flight still had Arnold pinned to the bench. 'Arnold,' he hissed, 'you know me. I've always played fair by you.'

'I know that, Mr Flight.'

'But I'm *not* pretending. What I'm doing is losing my rag. Everything's going to hell in this city, Arnold, and I'm inclined to just shrug my shoulders and join in. Understand me? Why should I play fair when nobody else does, eh? So I'll tell you what I'm going to do, Arnold. I'm going to have to pull you in.'

'What for?' Arnold was terrified now. He didn't think Flight was playing a game. Rebus had the same feeling; either that or Flight was in line for an Oscar.

'For indecent exposure. You were going to expose yourself to those kids. I saw you getting ready. I saw your dick hanging out of your fly.'

'No, no.' Arnold was shaking his head. 'That's a lie.'

'Previous convictions don't lie, Arnold. Inspector Rebus saw you, too. He saw your prick waving in the air like a cocktail sausage. We both saw you, and that's what we'll tell the judge. Now who's he going to believe, eh? Think about that for a moment. Think about solitary. They'll have to hold you in solitary so the other prisoners don't kick the shit out of you. But that won't stop them pissing in your tea and gobbing in your food. You know the score, Arnold. You've been there. And then one night, you'll hear your door being unlocked, and in they'll come. Maybe the screws, maybe the prisoners. They'll come in and they'll hold you down. One of them'll have a brush-handle, and one'll have a rusty old razor blade, won't they, Arnold? Won't they Arnold?'

But Arnold was trembling too violently to speak, trembling and babbling, bubbles of saliva bursting at either side of his mouth. Flight slid back along the bench away from him, then looked up at Rebus with sad eyes. Rebus nodded solemnly. This wasn't a nice business that they were in, not nice at all. Flight lit a cigarette. Rebus refused one. Two words were bouncing around the inside of John Rebus's skull.

Needs must.

And then Arnold started to talk. And when he had finished, Flight dug into a trouser pocket and drew out a pound coin, which he slapped down on the bench beside his shattered victim.

'There you go, Arnold. Get yourself a cup of tea or something. And stay away from playgrounds, all right?' Flight picked up his carrier bags, picked out an apple from one, and tossed it into Arnold's lap, causing the man to flinch. Then he picked out another one and began to crunch on it, starting off back towards the market.

Needs must.

Back at HQ Rebus thought about Lisa. He felt the need for some human contact, for something clean and warm and separate from this other world he chose to inhabit, something to wash out his badly soiled mind.

Flight had warned him on the way back – 'no messing about this time, John. Leave it to us. You've got to stay out of it. It would look bad in court, copper with a grudge, that sort of line.'

'But,' Rebus had replied, 'I do have a grudge, George. This guy Kenny might have been shagging my daughter!'

Flight had glanced from the windscreen into Rebus's face, then had looked away.

'I said leave it to us, John. If you can't play it that way, I'll personally see that you go bouncing back down the ranks like a ball down a fucking stairwell. Got that?'

'Loud and clear.'

'It's not a threat, John. It's a promise.'

'And you always keep your promises, George, don't you? You seem to be forgetting something. It's your fault that I'm down here in the first place. You sent for me.'

Flight had nodded. 'And I can send you back just as quick. Is that what you want?'

Rebus had stayed silent, though he knew the answer. Flight knew it too, and smiled at this small triumph. They drove in silence after that, both men tainted by the memory of a playground and of a silent man, hands clasping his knees, staring ahead of him, his thoughts sweet with corruption.

Now Rebus was thinking of Lisa, thinking of how it would feel to take a shower with her, to scrub away a layer of London from them both. Maybe he would ask George again for the secret address. Maybe he could visit her. He remembered a conversation they'd had in bed. He'd asked if he could see her office in University College sometime.

'Sometime,' she'd said. 'Mind you, it's not a very nice room, nothing like those huge antique Oxbridge rooms you see in television dramas. It's a pokey little hole, to be honest. I hate it.'

'I'd still like you to show me around.'

'And I said okay.' She sounded on edge. Why was that? Why had she been so nervous of letting him see her room? Why had the secretary – Millicent, Lisa had called her – been so vague the day Rebus had visited? No, not just vague. Uncooperative. *Downright* uncooperative, now that he thought of it. What the hell was it they were keeping from him? He knew one way he could find out the answer, one sure and certain way. What the hell: Lisa was safe, and he'd been told to stay out of the Watkiss case, so what was stopping him from following up this latest mystery? He got to his feet. The answer was: nothing was stopping him, nothing at all.

'Where are you going?'

It was Flight, yelling at him from an open door as Rebus stalked down the hall.

'It's personal,' Rebus called back.

'I warned you, John! Don't get involved!'

'It's not what you think!' He stopped, turning to face George Flight.

'Well, what is it then?'

'Like I said, George, it's personal, okay?'

'No.'

'Look,' said Rebus, his emotions suddenly getting the better of him, all those thoughts he'd been keeping on a tight rein – Sammy, Kenny Watkiss, the Wolfman, the threat against Lisa – all boiling up. He swallowed, breathing hard. 'Look, George, you've got plenty to keep you busy, okay?' His finger stabbed at Flight's chest. 'Remember what I said: it could be a copper. Why don't you do some of your careful, precious, nit-picking investigation on *that*. The Wolfman could be here in this building. He could be working on the bloody case, hunting himself!' Rebus heard his voice growing hysterical and calmed quickly, regaining control over his vocal chords if nothing else.

'A sort of wolf in the fold, you mean?'

'I'm serious.' Rebus paused. 'He might even know where you've sent Lisa.'

'For Christ's sake, John, only three people know where Lisa's going. Me, and the two men I sent with her. Now you don't know those guys, but I do. We go back all the way to training college. I'd trust them with my life.' Flight paused. 'Will you trust me?'

Rebus said nothing. Flight's eyes narrowed disbelievingly, and he whistled. 'Well,' he said, 'that certainly answers my question.' He shook his head slowly. 'This case, John. I've been in the force God knows how many years, but this case, it's the worst. It's like every victim was somebody close to me.' He paused again, gathering strength. Now his finger jabbed at Rebus. 'So don't you *dare* think what I know you're thinking! It's the ultimate fucking insult!'

There was a long silence in the corridor. Typewriters chattered somewhere. Male voices were raised in laughter. A hummed tune floated down the hall towards and past them. It was as though the whole world were indifferent to this quarrel. And there they stood, not quite friends, not quite enemies, and not quite sure what to do any more.

Rebus studied the scuff marks on the linoleum. Then: 'Lecture over?'

Flight seemed pained by this response. 'It wasn't a lecture, it was just . . . I want you to see my side of things.'

'But I do, George, I do.' Rebus patted Flight's arm and turned away from him again. He started to walk.

'I want you to stay here, John!' Walking. 'Do you hear me? I'm *ordering* you not to go.'

Rebus kept walking.

Flight shook his head. He'd had enough, absolutely up to his eyes, so that they stung now, stung as though he were in a smoky room. 'You're out on your ear, Rebus,' he called, knowing this to be the final warning. If Rebus kept walking now, Flight would be compelled to keep his word or else lose face, and he was damned if he'd lose face for a hardheaded Jock copper. 'Just keep walking!' he yelled. 'Keep walking and you're finished!'

Rebus walked. He didn't know exactly why, perhaps more out of pride than anything else. Stupid pride, pride he couldn't explain, but pride all the same. The same emotion that made grown men cry at football matches when *Flower of Scotland* was played as the Scots national anthem. All he knew was that he had something to do, and he would do it, like the Scots knew their job was to be footballers with more ambition than ability. Yes, that was him all right: more ambition than ability. They'd put it on his gravestone.

At the end of the corridor, he shoved open the swing doors. He didn't look back. Flight's voice followed him, trailing off as it grew in anger.

'Damn you, you stupid Jock bastard! You've bitten off more than you can chew this time, do you hear me? More than you can bloody well chew.'

FYTP.

Rebus was moving through the entrance hall when he came face to face with Lamb. He made to move past him, but Lamb placed a hand on Rebus's chest.

'Where's the fire?' he said. Rebus was trying to ignore him, was trying to make Lamb invisible. The last thing he needed now was this. His knuckles tingled with anticipation. Lamb was still talking, apparently oblivious to the danger he was in.

'She found you then, your daughter?'

'What?'

Lamb was smiling. 'She phoned here first, and they put her on to me. She sounded a bit upset, so I gave her the lab's number.'

'Oh.' Rebus could feel himself deflating. He managed a grudged 'thanks' and this time succeeded in moving around Lamb. But then Lamb spoke again.

'She sounded a bit tasty though. I like them young. How old is she again?'

Rebus's elbow shot back into Lamb's unprotected stomach, cutting off breath, doubling him over. Rebus studied his work; not bad for an old man. Not bad at all.

He walked.

Because he's on personal business, he stands outside the station and looks for a cab. One of the uniformed officers, who knows him from the scene of Sunday's murder, offers a lift in a patrol car, but Rebus shakes his head. The officer looks at him as if an insult has just been traded.

'Thanks anyway,' says Rebus, trying to sound conciliatory. But all he sounds is mad. Mad with Lamb, with himself, mad with the Wolfman case, mad with Kenny bloody Watkiss, mad with Flight, with Lisa (why did she have to be in Copperplate Street in the first place?) and, most of all, mad with London. Where are all the cabs, all the greedy black cabs, beetling like insects as they try to pick up fares? He's seen thousands of them this past week, but now that he needs one, they're all avoiding him. He waits anyway, eyes slightly unfocussed. And as he waits, he thinks, and as he thinks he calms a little.

What the hell is he doing anyway? He's asking for trouble doing this. He's *begging* for it, like a black-clothed Calvinist pleading to be beaten for his sins. A lash across the back. Rebus had seen them all, all the available religions. He had tasted them and each one tasted bitter in its own particular way. Where was the religion for those who did not feel guilty, did not feel shame, did not regret getting angry or getting even, or, better yet, getting more than even? Where was the religion for a man who believed that good and bad must coexist, even within the individual? Where was the religion for a man who believed in God but not in God's religion?

And where were all the bloody taxis?

'Sod it then.' He walked up to the first patrol car he saw and tapped on the window, flashing his ID.

'Inspector Rebus,' he announced. 'Can you give me a lift to Gower Street?'

The building seemed as deserted as ever and Rebus feared that on this occasion perhaps even the secretary might have scarpered for an early start to the weekend. But no, she was there, like the retainer of some dusty mansion. He cleared his throat, and she looked up from her crochet.

'Yes?' she said. 'Can I help you?' She appeared not to remember him. Rebus brought out his ID and pushed it towards her.

'Detective Inspector Rebus,' he said, his voice stiff with authority. 'Scotland Yard. I want to ask you a few questions about Dr Frazer.'

The woman looked frightened. Rebus feared he had overdone the menace. He tried a don't-worry-it's-not-you-we're-interested-in sort of smile, a peaceable smile. But the woman looked no less afraid, and her fear flustered her.

'Oh, gracious,' she stammered. 'Oh my, oh my.' She looked up at him. 'Who did you say? Dr Frazer? But there's no Dr Frazer in the Department.'

Rebus described Lisa Frazer. The woman suddenly raised her head, recognising the description.

'Oh, Lisa? You mean Lisa? But there's some mistake. Lisa Frazer isn't a member of staff here. Gracious me, no. Though I believe she *may* have taken a tutorial or two, just filling in. Oh dear, Scotland Yard. What, I mean, surely she hasn't . . . What has she done?'

'She doesn't work here?' Rebus needed to be certain. 'Then who is she?'

'Lisa? She's one of our research students.'

'A *student*? But she's –' He was about to say 'old'.

'A mature student,' the secretary explained. 'Oh dear, is she in trouble?'

'I came here before,' Rebus said. 'You didn't tell me any of this then. Why?'

'Came here before?' She studied his face. 'Yes, I remember. Well, Lisa made me promise not to tell anyone.'

'Why?'

'Her project, she said. She's doing a project on, now, what is it exactly?' She opened a drawer of her desk and pulled out a sheet of paper. 'Ah yes, "The Psychology of the Investigation of Serious Crime". She explained it to me. How she needed access to a police investigation. How she needed to gain trust. The courts, police and so on. She told me she was going to pretend to be a lecturer. I told her not to, I warned her, but she said it was the only way. The police wouldn't waste time with a mere student, would they?'

Rebus was stuck for an answer. The answer was no, they wouldn't. Why should they?

'So she got you to cover for her?'

The woman shrugged. 'Lisa is quite a persuasive young woman. She said probably I wouldn't have to tell lies. I could just say things like she's not here, she's not teaching today, that sort of thing. Always supposing anyone bothered to check up on her.'

'And has anybody checked up on her?'

'Oh yes. Why, only today I had a telephone call from someone she had arranged to interview. He wanted to be sure that she really was part of University College, and not just a journalist or a Nosey Parker.'

Today? An interview today. Well, that was one appointment she wouldn't be keeping.

'Who was this person?' Rebus asked. 'Do you remember?'

'I think I wrote it down,' she said. She lifted the thick notepad beside her telephone and flipped through it. 'He did say who he was, but I can't remember. It was at the Old Bailey. Yes, that's right. She'd arranged to meet him at the Old Bailey. I usually write these things down as soon as someone mentions their name, just in case I forget later. No, there's no sign of it. That's funny.'

'Perhaps in the bin?' Rebus suggested.

'Well, perhaps.' But she sounded doubtful. Rebus lifted the small wicker paper-basket onto her desk and sifted through it. Pencil shavings and sweet-wrappers, an empty polystyrene coffee cup and crumpled bits of paper. Lots of bits of paper.

'Too big,' she would say as he started to uncrumple one, or: 'too small.' Until finally, he pulled out a sheet and spread it out on the desk. It was like some bizarre work of art, filled with doodles and hieroglyphs and little notes, phone numbers, names, addresses.

'Ah,' she said, sliding a finger over to one corner where something had been written in very faint, wavering pencil. 'Is that it?'

Rebus looked closer. Yes, that was it. That was most definitely it. 'Thank you,' he said.

'Oh dear,' said the secretary. 'Have I got her into trouble? Is Lisa in trouble? What has she done, Inspector?'

'She lied to us,' said Rebus. 'And because of that, she's ended up having to go into hiding.'

'Hiding? Gracious, she didn't mention anything about that.'

Rebus was beginning to suspect that the secretary was a couple of keys short of a typewriter. 'Well,' he said, 'she didn't know she was in trouble until today.'

The secretary was nodding. 'Yes, but she only phoned a little over an hour ago.'

Rebus's face creased into an all-over frown. 'What?'

'Yes, she said she was calling from the Old Bailey. She wanted to know if there were any messages for her. She told me she had time to kill before her second appointment.'

Rebus didn't bother to ask. He dialled quickly, the receiver gripped in his hand like a weapon. 'I want to talk to George Flight.'

'Just a minute, please.' The ch-ch-ch-ch of a re-routing. Then: 'Murder Room, Detective Sergeant Walsh speaking.'

'It's Inspector Rebus here.'

'Oh yes?' The voice had become as rudimentary as a chisel.

'I need to speak to Flight. It's urgent.'

'He's in a meeting.'

'Then get him out! I told you, this is urgent.'

There was doubt, cynicism in the Sergeant's voice. Everyone knew that the Scotsman's 'urgent' wasn't worth its weight in breath. 'I can leave a message –'

'Don't fuck me around, Walsh! Either get him, or put me on to someone with a spare brain they're not sitting on!'

Ca-click. Brrrrr. The ultimate put-down. The secretary was staring at Rebus in horror. Perhaps psychologists never got angry. Rebus attempted a reassuring smile, but it came out like a clown's drunken greasepaint. He made a bowing motion before turning to leave, and was watched all the way out to the stairwell by a woman mortified almost to the core of her being.

Rebus's face was tingling with a newly stoked anger. Lisa Frazer had tricked him, played him like a fool. Christ, the things he'd told her. Thinking she wanted to help with the Wolfman case. Not realising he was merely part of her project. Christ, the things he had said. What had he said? Too much to recall. Had she been taping everything? Or simply jotting things down after he'd left? It didn't matter. What mattered was that he had seen in her something solid and believable amidst a sea of chaos. And she had been

209

Janus. Using him. Jesus Christ, she had even slept with him. Was that, too, part of the project, part of her little experiment? How could he ever be sure it wasn't? It had seemed genuine enough, but . . . He had opened his mind to her, as she had opened her body to him. It was not a fair exchange.

'The bitch!' he exploded, stopping dead. 'The lying little bitch!'

Why hadn't she told him? Why hadn't she just explained everything? He would have helped her, he would have found time for her. No, he wouldn't. It was a lie. A research student? A project? He would have shown her the door. Instead he had listened to her, had believed her, had learned from her. Yes, it was true. He had learned a lot from her. About psychology, about the mind of the killer. Had learned from her books. Yes, but that wasn't the point. The point was that it had all become crass and diluted, now that he knew her for what she was.

'Bitch.' But his voice was softer, his throat tightening, as though a hand had slid around it and was slowly applying pressure. He swallowed hard, and began to take deep breaths. Calm down, John. What did it matter? What did any of it matter? It mattered, he answered himself, because he felt something for her. Or had felt something for her. No, still did feel something. Something he thought might have been returned.

'Who are you trying to kid?' Look at him, overweight and in his forties. Stuck at Inspector level and going nowhere except, if Flight carried out his promise, down. Divorced. A daughter distraught and mixing with darkness. Someone in London with a kitchen knife and a secret and a knowledge of Lisa. It was all wrong. He'd been clutching at Lisa the way drowning men reached out for a thin snap of straw. Stupid old man.

He stood at the main door to the building, not really sure now. Should he confront her, or let it go, never see her again? Usually he relished confrontation, found it nourishing and exciting. But today, maybe not.

She was at the Old Bailey to interview Malcolm

Chambers. He, too, was at this moment being tricked by her mock credentials, by that falsely prefixed 'Doctor'. Everyone admired Malcolm Chambers. He was smart, he was on the side of the law, and he made pots of money. Rebus had known coppers who were none of these; most could score only one out of three, a few managed two. Chambers would sweep Lisa Frazer off her feet. She would loathe him, until that loathing mingled with awe, and then she'd probably think that she loved him. Well, good luck to her.

He'd head back to the station, say his farewells, pack his bags, and head north. They could get along without him very well. The case was heading nowhere until the Wolf-man bit again. Yet they had so much now, knew so much about him, had come so close to opening him up like a soft fat peach. Maybe he'd bite Lisa Frazer. What the hell was she doing at the Old Bailey when she should be in hiding? He needed to speak to Flight. What the hell was Flight up to anyway?

'Ach, to hell with the lot of you,' he muttered, plunging his hands into his pockets.

Two students, their voices loudly American, were heading towards him. They seemed excited, the way students always did, discussing this or that concept, ready to change the way the world thought. They wanted to get past, wanted to go into the building. He moved aside for them, but they didn't so much move past him as *through* him, as though he were insubstantial as exhaust fumes.

'Like, y'know, I think she likes me, but I'm not sure I'm ready for something like –'

So much for difficult concepts, thought Rebus. Why should students be different from anyone else in the population? Why should they be thinking (and talking), about something other than sex?

'Yeah,' said the other one. Rebus wondered how comfortable he felt in his thick white T-shirt and thicker checked lumberjack shirt. The day was sticky. 'Yeah,' the American repeated. His accent reminded Rebus of Lisa's softer Canadian tones.

'But get this,' continued his companion, their voices fading as they moved deeper into the building, 'she *says* her mother hates Americans because one of them near raped her in the war.'

Get this. Where had Rebus heard that expression before? He fumbled in his jacket pocket and found a folded piece of paper. Unfolded it and began to read.

'GET THIS, I'M NOT HOMOSEXUL, O.K.?' It was the photocopy of the Wolfman's letter to Lisa.

Get this. It did have a transatlantic ring to it, didn't it? A curious way altogether of starting a letter. Get this. Be warned, watch out. There were several ways of starting a letter so that the reader knew he was to pay particular attention to it. But *get this*?

What did they know, or what did they suspect, about the Wolfman? He knew about police procedure (past offender, copper, both were possible). He was a he, if Jan Crawford were to be believed. He was quite tall, she thought. In the restaurant, Lisa Frazer had added her own ideas: he was conservative; most of the time he not only seemed normal, he was normal; he was, in her phrase, 'psychologically mature'. And he had posted a letter to Lisa from EC4. EC4, wasn't that where the Old Bailey was? He recalled his first and only visit to the building. The courtroom, and seeing Kenny Watkiss there. Then meeting Malcolm Chambers. What was it Chambers had said to George Flight?

Royally shafted. Own team. I don't like. Flight, I don't like being royally shafted . . . own team . . . get this. Get this, George.

Jesus Christ! Every ball on the table suddenly fell into a pocket until only the cue ball and the black were left. Every single ball.

'*Get this, George, I don't like being royally shafted by my own team.*'

Malcolm Chambers had studied in the USA for a while. Flight had told Rebus that. You tended to pick up mannerisms when you wanted to fit into a new and strange place. *Get this.* Rebus had tried to avoid the temptation in London, but it was strong. Studied in the USA. And now he was with Lisa Frazer. Lisa the student, Lisa the psychologist, Lisa with her photo in the newspapers. *Get this*. Oh, how the Wolfman must hate her. She was a psychologist after all and the psychologists had pronounced him gay, they had insights into what was wrong with him. He didn't think anything was wrong with him. But something was. Something that was slowly taking him over.

Old Bailey was in EC4. The Wolfman, rattled, had slipped up and posted his letter from EC4.

It was Malcolm Chambers, Malcolm Chambers was the Wolfman. Rebus couldn't explain it, couldn't exactly justify it, but he knew it all the same. It was like a dark polluted wave rolling over him, anointing him. Malcolm Chambers. Someone who knew about police procedure, someone above suspicion, someone so clean you had to scratch beneath the skin to find the filth.

Rebus was running. He was running along Gower Street in what he hoped was the right direction for the City. He was running and he was craning his neck to seek out a taxi. There was one ahead of him, at the corner beside the British Museum, but it was picking up a fare. Students or tourists. Japanese. Grins and cameras. Four of them, two men, two young women. Rebus stuck his head into the back of the cab, where two of them were already seated.

'Out!' he yelled, jerking a thumb towards the pavement.

'Oi, mate, what's your game?' The driver was so fat he could barely turn in his seat.

'I said out!' Rebus grabbed an arm and pulled. Either the young man was surprisingly light, or else Rebus had found hidden strength, for the body fairly flew from its seat, uttering a string of high-pitched comment as it went.

'And you.'

The girl followed obligingly and Rebus hurled himself into the cab, slamming shut the door.

'Drive!' he yelled.

'I'm not moving till I –'

Rebus shoved his ID against the window separating the back seats of the taxi from the front.

'Inspector Rebus!' he called. 'This is an emergency. I

need to get to the Old Bailey. Break every traffic law you like, I'll sort it out later. But get your fucking skates on!'

The driver responded by switching his headlights on full beam before setting out into the traffic.

'Use your horn!' Rebus called. The driver did so. A surprising number of cars eased out of his way. Rebus was on the edge of his seat, gripping it with both hands to stop himself being thrown about. 'How long will it take?'

'This time of day? Ten or fifteen minutes. What's the matter, guv? Can't they start without you?'

Rebus smiled sourly. That was just the problem. Without him, the Wolfman could start whenever he liked. 'I need to use your radio,' he said. The driver slid his window further open.

'Be my guest,' he said, pulling the small microphone up towards Rebus. He'd worked on the cabs for twenty-odd years, but he'd never had a fare like this.

In fact, he was so excited, they were halfway there before he remembered to switch on the meter.

Rebus had told Flight as much as he could, trying not to sound hysterical. Flight sounded dubious about the whole thing, but agreed to send men to the Old Bailey. Rebus didn't blame George Flight for being wary. Hard to justify arresting a pillar of society on the strength of a gut feeling. Rebus remembered what else Lisa Frazer had said about serial killers: that they were products of their environments; that their ambitions had been thwarted, leading them to kill members of the social group above them. Well, that certainly wasn't true in Malcolm Chambers' case, was it? And what had she said about the Wolfman? His attacks were 'non-confrontational', so perhaps he was like that in his working life. Hah! So much for theory. But now Rebus began to doubt his own instincts. Jesus, what if he *was* wrong? What if the theory was right? He was going to look more than a little psychologically disturbed himself.

Then he recalled something George Flight had said. You could build up as neat a picture as you liked of the killer, but it wouldn't give you a name and address. Psychology was all well and good, but you couldn't beat a good old-fashioned hunch.

'Nearly there, guv.'

Rebus tried to keep his breathing regular. Be calm, John, be calm. However, there were no police cars waiting by the entrance to the Old Bailey. No sirens and armed officers, just people milling around, people finishing work for the day, people sharing a joke. Rebus left the cab driver unpaid and untipped – 'I'll settle later' – and pushed open the heavy glass door. Behind more bulletproof glass stood two security personnel. Rebus stuck his ID in front of their noses. One of them pointed towards the two vertical glass cylinders by which people were admitted to the building one at a time. Rebus went to one cylinder and waited. Nothing happened. Then he remembered, pushed the heel of his hand against the button and the cylinder door opened. He walked in, and waited for what seemed an eternity while the door slid shut behind him, before the door in front slid just as slowly open.

Another guard stood beside the metal detection equipment. Rebus, still holding open his ID, walked quickly past until he found himself behind the bulletproof glass of the reception area.

'Can I help?' said one of the security men.

'Malcolm Chambers,' said Rebus. 'He's a barrister. I need to see him urgently.'

'Mr Chambers? Hold on, I'll just check.'

'I don't want him to know I'm here,' Rebus warned. 'I just want to know where I can find him.'

'Just one moment.' The guard moved off, consulting with one of his companions, then slowly going through a sheet of paper attached to a clipboard. Rebus's heart was pounding. He felt like he was about to explode. He couldn't just stand here. He had to *do* something. Patience, John. Less haste, more speed, as his father had always said. But what the hell did that mean anyway? Surely haste was a kind of speed?

The guard was coming back.

'Yes, Inspector. Mr Chambers has a young lady with him at present. I'm told they're sitting together upstairs.'

Upstairs meant the concourse outside the courtrooms. Rebus flew up the imposing flight of steps two at a time. Marble. There was a lot of marble around him. And wood. And glass. The windows seemed huge. Bewigged counsels came down a spiral staircase, deep in conversation. A frayed-looking woman smoked a cheap cigarette as she waited for someone. It was a quiet pandemonium. People were moving past Rebus, moving in the opposite direction from him. Juries, finished for the day. Solicitors and guilty-looking clients. The woman rose to greet her son. The son's solicitor had a bored, drawn look. The concourse was emptying rapidly, the stairs taking people down to more glass cylinders and to the outside world.

About thirty yards from where Rebus stood, the two men were sitting, legs crossed, enjoying a cigarette. The two men Flight had sent with Lisa. Her bodyguards. Rebus ran to them.

'Where is she?'

They recognised him, seemed to realise immediately that something was wrong, and rose to their feet.

'She's interviewing some barrister – '

'Yes, but *where*?'

The man nodded towards one of the courtrooms. Court Eight! Of course: hadn't Cousins been due to give evidence in Court Eight? And wasn't Malcolm Chambers the prosecuting counsel?

Rebus pushed through the doors into the courtroom, but, cleaners apart, it was completely empty. There had to be another exit. Of course there was: the green padded door to the side of the jury-box. The door leading to the judges' rooms. He ran across the court and up the steps to the door, pulling it open, finding himself in a bright carpeted corridor. A window, flowers in a pot on a table. A narrow corridor, doors only on one side, the other wall a blank. Judges' names above the doors. The doors themselves locked. There was a tiny kitchenette, but it too was empty. One door eventually gave, and he peered into a jury room. Empty. Back into the corridor again, hissing now with frustration. A court usher, cradling a mug of tea, was coming towards him.

'No one's allowed – '

'Inspector Rebus,' he said. 'I'm looking for an advocate . . . I mean, a barrister. Malcolm Chambers. He was here with a young woman.'

'They've just left.'

'Left?'

She gestured along towards the far end of the corridor. 'It leads to the underground car park. That's where they were headed.' Rebus made to squeeze past her. 'You won't catch them now,' she said. 'Not unless they're having trouble with the car.'

Rebus thought about it, gnawing at his bottom lip. There wasn't time. His first decision had to be the right one. Decision made, he turned from the usher and ran back towards the court, back across the court itself and out into the concourse.

'They've gone!' he yelled to the bodyguards. 'Tell Flight! Tell him they're in Chambers' car!' And then he was off again, down the steps towards the exit, pausing only to grab at a security man's sleeve. 'The car park exit, where is it?'

'Round the other side of the building.'

Rebus stuck a finger in the guard's face. 'Buzz down to the car park. Don't let Malcolm Chambers leave.' The guard stood there dumbly, staring at the finger. '*Do it!*'

And then he was off again, running, taking the stairs down three at a time, great leaps which almost sent him flying. He pushed his way to the front of the crowd waiting to leave.

'Police,' he said, 'emergency.' Nobody said anything. They were like cows, patiently waiting to be milked. Even so, it took a silent scream of an age for the cylinder to empty its cargo, close its doors, then open them again for Rebus.

'Come on, come on.' And then the door sucked itself open and he was out, out in the foyer, bursting through the main doors. He ran up to the corner, took a right, and ran again along the face of the building. Another right. He was on the other side of the building now. Where the car park exit was. A slope of road down into darkness. The car screeched as it came to the surface, hardly slowing as it climbed the hill to Newgate Street. It was a long gloss-black BMW. And in the passenger seat sat Lisa Frazer, looking relaxed, smiling, talking to the driver, not realising.

'Lisa!' But he was too far away, the traffic around him too loud. 'Lisa!' Before he could reach it, the car had turned into a flow of traffic and disappeared. Rebus cursed under his breath. Then looked around him for the first time and saw that he was standing next to a parked Jaguar, in the front of which sat a liveried chauffeur, staring out of the window at him. Rebus yanked at the doorhandle and threw open the door, reaching in with one hand to pull out the bemused driver. He was getting to be a dab hand at this: relieving people of their vehicles.

'Hoi! What the bleedin' 'ell – '

The man's cap rolled along the ground, given force by a gust of wind. For a moment, he knelt on the pavement, undecided whether to rescue the cap or the car. The moment was enough. Rebus gunned the engine and pulled away from the kerb, horns sounding behind him as he did so. At the top of the slight incline, he pressed his hand hard on the horn and careered left into the main road. A squeal of brakes. More horns. The pedestrians looking at him as though he were mad.

'Need lights,' he said to himself, glancing at the dashboard. Eventually, he found the headlamp switch and flipped them to full beam. Then took a hard right to bring himself into the middle of the road, passing the traffic, scraping the passenger side against an oncoming red bus, clipping a central bollard, uprooting the flimsy plastic construction and sending it flying into the path of the oncoming traffic.

They couldn't be too far ahead of him. Yes! He caught a glimpse of the BMW's tail-lights as it braked to turn a corner. He'd be damned if they'd lose him.

'Excuse me?'

Rebus flinched, startled, and nearly pulled the car onto the pavement. He looked in the rear-view mirror and saw an elderly gentleman sitting in the back seat, arms spread so as to keep himself upright. He appeared calm as he leaned forward towards Rebus.

'Would you kindly mind telling me what's going on? Am I being kidnapped?'

Rebus recognised the voice before he remembered the face. It was the judge from the Watkiss case. Jesus Christ, he'd run off with a judge!

'Only, if you are kidnapping me,' the judge went on, 'perhaps you'd allow me to call my wife. She'll burn the chops otherwise.'

Call! Rebus looked down again. Below the dashboard, between the driver's and front passenger seats, there was a neat black carphone.

'Do you mind if I use your phone?' he asked, grinning with a face full of adrenaline.

'Be my guest.'

Rebus grabbed at the contraption and fiddled as he drove, his steering becoming more erratic than ever.

'Press the button marked TRS,' the judge suggested.

'Thank you, your honour.'

'You know who I am? I thought I recognised the face. Have I had you before me recently?'

But Rebus had dialled and was now waiting for the call to be answered. It seemed to take forever. And meantime, the BMW had nipped across an amber traffic light.

'Hold tight,' Rebus said, baring his teeth. The horn was a banshee wail as they pushed past the waiting traffic and flew across the intersection, traffic from left and right braking hard. One car dented the back of another. A motorcycle slewed on the greasy road. But they were across. The BMW was still in sight, less than half a dozen cars ahead now, yet still apparently unaware of the pursuing demon.

Finally, the call was answered.

'It's Rebus here.' Then, for his passenger's sake: 'Detective Inspector Rebus. I need to speak to Flight. Is he there?' There was a long pause. The connection crackled wildly, as though about to short out altogether. Rebus gripped the handset between hunched shoulder and angled cheek, driving with both hands to take first one bend and then another.

'John? Where are you?' Flight's voice sounded metallic and distant.

'I'm in a car,' said Rebus, 'a car I commandeered. I'm following Chambers. He's got Lisa Frazer with him. I don't think she knows he's the Wolfman.'

'But for Christ's sake, John, *is* he the Wolfman?'

'I'll ask him when I catch him. Did you send any cars to the Old Bailey?'

'I sent one, yes.'

'That was generous.' Rebus saw what was ahead. 'Oh shit!' He braked hard, but not hard enough. The old lady was shuffling slowly across the zebra crossing, her shopping trolley a step behind her like a pet poodle. Rebus swerved but couldn't avoid winging the trolley. It flew into the air as though fired from a cannon, dispensing groceries as it went: eggs, butter, flour, cornflakes raining down on the road. Rebus heard the woman screaming. At worst she'd have a broken arm. No, at worst the shock would kill her.

'Oh shit,' he said again.

The judge was staring out of the rear window. 'I think she's all right,' he said.

'John?' It was Flight's tin-can voice on the line. 'Who was that speaking?'

'Oh,' said Rebus. 'That was the judge. It's his Jaguar I've commandeered.' He had found the windscreen wiper switch and was letting them deal with the pancake mixture on the windscreen.

'You *what*?' So that was what a roar sounded like. The BMW was still in sight. But it had slowed a little, perhaps aware of the incident behind it.

'Never mind,' said Rebus. 'Look, just get some patrol cars up here. We're on . . .' He glanced out of windscreen and side window, but could see no street signs.

'High Holborn,' said the Judge.

'Thanks,' said Rebus. 'We're on High Holborn, George.'

'Wait a second,' said Flight. There was a muffled exchange at his end of the line. Then he came back on again. He sounded tired. 'Please, John, tell me it isn't you behind these reports we're getting. The switchboards are lighting up like Christmas trees.'

'That's probably us, George. We took a bollard out a

little way back, caused a couple of accidents and now we've just sent an old woman's messages flying everywhere. Yes, that's us.'

If Flight groaned, he did so quietly. Then: 'What if it's not him, John? What if you're wrong?'

'Then it's all a bit of a balls-up, George, and I'll probably get to see what the inside of a dole office looks like, if not a prison cell. Meanwhile, get those coppers down here!' Rebus looked at the handset. 'Judge, help me. How do I – '

'Just press Power.' Rebus did, and the illuminated digits faded.

'Thanks,' he said.

The traffic was slowing, a jam of lights up ahead. 'And,' the judge was saying, 'if you intend using the apparatus again, I should probably inform you that it can be used in hands-free mode. Just dial and leave it in its little compartment there. You'll be able to hear the caller and they'll be able to hear you.' Rebus nodded his thanks. The judge's head was close to Rebus's ear, peering over his shoulder at the road ahead.

'So,' he said excitedly, 'you think Malcolm Chambers is behind all these killings?'

'That's right.'

'And what evidence do you have, Inspector?'

Rebus laughed, and tapped his head. 'Just this, your lordship, just this.'

'Remarkable,' said the Judge. He seemed to be considering something. 'I always thought Malcolm was rather an odd young man. Fine in court, of course, very much the star prosecutor, playing to the gallery and what have you. But outside the courtroom, he seemed very different. Oh, very different indeed. Almost sullen, as though his mind were wandering.'

His mind had wandered all right, thought Rebus, wandered all the way over the edge.

'Would you like to speak to him?'

'You think I'm chasing him for a bet?'

The judge chuckled, pointing to the car-phone. 'I meant talk to him right now.'

Rebus went rigid. 'You mean you've got his number?'

'Oh yes.'

Rebus thought it over, but shook his head. 'No,' he said. 'He's got someone with him. An innocent woman. I don't want to panic him.'

'I see,' said the judge, settling back again. 'Yes, I suppose you're right. I hadn't thought of that.'

And then there was an electric purring inside the car. It was the phone, its display illuminated now and flashing. Rebus handed the set to the judge.

'Probably for you,' he said drily.

'No,' said the judge, 'just put it back and press Receive.' Rebus did so. Only then did the judge speak. 'Hello?'

The voice was clear, the reception signal strong. 'Edward? Is that you following me?'

It was Chambers' voice, sounding amused about something. The judge stared at Rebus, who could offer no suggestion for an answer.

'Malcolm?' said the judge, his composure intact. 'Is that you?'

'You should know. You're only about twenty yards behind me.'

'Am I? Which road are you on?'

The voice altered, taking on an edge of sudden viciousness. 'Don't fuck with me, Ted! Who's driving the fucking car? Can't be you, you haven't even got a licence. Who is it?'

The judge looked to Rebus again, seeking guidance. They listened together in silence and heard Lisa's faint voice.

'What's going on?' she was saying. 'What's happening?'

Then Chambers's voice. 'Shut up, bitch! You'll get yours.' The voice rose a chilling octave, sounding like a bad female impersonator, making the hairs on Rebus's neck bristle. 'You'll get yours.' Then it dropped again, speaking into the handset. 'Hello? Who's that? Who's there? I can hear you breathing, you little shit.' Rebus bit his lip. Was it better to let Chambers know, or to stay silent? He stayed silent.

'Oh well,' said Chambers with a sigh, as though resigned to this stalemate. 'Out she goes.'

Ahead, Rebus saw the BMW's passenger door swing open as the car veered onto the pavement.

'What are you doing!' screamed Lisa. 'No! No! Let me go!'

'Chambers!' Rebus yelled towards the handset. 'Leave her!' The BMW swerved back into the road, the door drifting shut. There was a pause.

'Hello,' said Chambers's voice. 'To whom am I speaking?'

'My name's Rebus. We met at – '

'John!' It was Lisa's voice, very afraid now, almost hysterical. The sound of the slap was a static crack in Rebus's ear.

'I said leave her!' Rebus yelled.

'I know you did,' said Chambers, 'but then you're hardly in a position to give orders. Anyway, now that I know you two know each other, that makes things interesting, doesn't it, Inspector?'

'You remember me?'

'I have an intimate knowledge of everyone on the Wolfman case. I've taken an interest in it from the start – for obvious reasons. There was always someone around willing to tell what they knew.'

'So you could keep one step ahead?'

'*One* step?' Chambers laughed. 'You flatter yourself. So tell me, Inspector, what do we do now? Do you stop your car – Edward's car, I should say – or do I kill your friend here? Do you know, she wanted to ask *me* about the psychology of court trials. She couldn't have picked better, could she, the little bitch?' Lisa was sobbing. Rebus could hear her, and every sound cut him a little deeper. 'Picture in the paper,' Chambers was cooing. 'Picture in the paper with the big tough detective.'

Rebus knew he had to keep Chambers talking. By keeping him talking, he was keeping Lisa alive. But the traffic had stalled. Red lights ahead. The BMW only a few cars in front, prevented from jumping the lights by another car directly in front of it. Could he. . . ? Should he even be thinking of it? The judge was still gripping Rebus's headrest, staring out towards the gleaming black car, the car that was so close to them. So close . . . and so stationary.

'Well?' It was Chambers's voice. 'Do you pull over, Inspector, or do I kill her?'

Rebus was staring hard at Chambers's car. He could see that Lisa was leaning away from Chambers, as though making to escape. But Chambers was gripping her with his left arm, his right presumably resting on the steering-wheel. So the man's attention would be focussed on the passenger side of the car, leaving the driver's side un-guarded.

Rebus made up his mind and quietly opened his door, slipping out onto the reassuringly solid surface of the road. Horns were sounding around him. He paid them no heed. The lights were still at red. He began to move forward, crouching, but moving quickly. Chambers's driver's-side mirror! If Chambers looked into it, he'd have a clear view of Rebus's approach. Make it fast, John, make it.

Amber.

Shit!

Green.

He had reached the BMW, had gripped the doorhandle. Chambers looked out at him, a stunned expression on his face. And then the car in front moved off, and Chambers gunned the engine, the car accelerating forwards, tearing itself free of Rebus.

Shit! Car horns all around. Angry. Angry drivers rolling down their windows and yelling at him as he ran back to the Jaguar. Started the car, moved off. The judge's hand patted his shoulder.

'Good try, my boy. Good try.'

And Chambers's laughter on the car-phone. 'Hope I didn't hurt you, Inspector.' Rebus examined his hand, flexed it painfully. The fingers had nearly been pulled out of their joints. His little finger was swelling already. A break? Perhaps.

'So,' said Chambers, 'for the last time I make you an offer you can hardly refuse. Stop the car, or I kill Dr Frazer.'

'She's not a doctor, Chambers. She's just a student.' He

swallowed: now Lisa knew that he knew. Not that it mattered one way or the other, not now. He took a deep breath. 'Kill her,' he said. Behind him, the judge gasped, but Rebus shook his head, reassuring him.

'What did you say?' asked Chambers.

'I said kill her. I'm not really bothered. She's led me a merry little dance this past week. It's her own fault she's in this deep. And after you've killed her, I'll take great pleasure in killing you, Mr Chambers.'

He heard Lisa's faint voice again. 'God, John, please no!' And then Chambers, seeming to grow calmer as Rebus grew more excited: 'As you wish, Inspector. As you wish.' The voice was as cold as a mortuary floor, any vestige of humanity gone. Perhaps partly it was Rebus's fault, taunting him with newspaper stories, with fabrications. But Chambers hadn't picked on Rebus: he had picked on Lisa. Had Rebus arrived a minute later at the Old Bailey, she would be on her way to certain death. At it was, nothing was certain.

Nothing but the fact of Malcolm Chambers's madness.

'He's turning onto Monmouth Street,' said the judge, his voice level. He had grasped the fact of Chambers's guilt, the horror of what had happened and what might still happen.

Rebus heard a flapping sound overhead, and glanced up towards where a helicopter was shadowing the chase. A police helicopter. He could hear sirens, too. So, it seemed, could Chambers. The BMW spurted ahead, slashing the side of another car as it squeezed into space. The injured car stopped dead. Rebus braked, pulled on the steering wheel, but still clipped it with his driver's-side bumper, the headlamp shattering.

'Sorry about that.'

'Never mind the car,' said the judge. 'Just don't let him get away.'

'He won't get away,' said Rebus, with sudden confidence. Now where the hell had that come from? The moment he thought about it, it disappeared again, leaving behind a quivering vapour.

They were on St Martin's Lane now. People mingling,

pre-theatre or after work. The busy West End. Yet the traffic ahead had thinned for no apparent reason and the crowds gawped as first the BMW, then the Jaguar sped past.

As they approached Trafalgar Square Rebus saw, to right and left, police officers in luminous yellow jackets holding up the traffic in the side streets. Now why would they do that? Unless . . .

Road block! One entrance to the Square left open, all exits blocked, the Square itself kept empty for their arrival. In a moment they'd have him. God bless you, George Flight.

Rebus picked up the handset, his voice a snarl, specks of saliva dotting the windscreen as he spoke.

'Stop the car, Chambers. There's no place to go.'

Silence. They were skidding into Trafalgar Square now, traffic blaring in queues all around them, held back by the gloved, raised hand of authority. Rebus was buzzing again. The whole West End of London, brought to a standstill so that he might race a Jaguar against a BMW. He could think of friends who'd give whole limbs to be in his place. Yet he had a job to do. That was the bottom line. It was just another job to be cleared up. He might as well have been following teenage Cortina thieves through the streets of some Edinburgh housing-scheme.

But he wasn't.

They'd done one full circuit around Nelson's Column. Canada House, South Africa House and the National Gallery were just blurs. The judge was being thrown against the door behind Rebus.

'Hang on,' Rebus called.

'To what, pray?'

And Rebus laughed. He roared with laughter. Then he realised the line was still open to Chambers's BMW. He laughed even harder, picking up the handset, his knuckles white against the steering-wheel, left arm aching.

'Having fun, Chambers?' he yelled. 'Like the TV programme used to say, there's no hiding place!'

And then the BMW gave a jolt, and Rebus heard Chambers gasp.

'You bitch!' Another jolt, and sounds of a struggle. Lisa was retaliating, now that Chambers was intent on this speeding circuit without end.

'No!'

'Get off!'

'I'll – '

And a piercing scream, two piercing screams, both high-pitched, feminine in their intensity, and the black car didn't take the next bend, flew straight for the pavement, mounted it and bounced into a bus shelter, crumpling the metal structure and driving on into the walls of the National Gallery itself.

'Lisa!' Rebus cried. He brought the Jaguar to a sudden, pivoting stop. The driver's door of the BMW creaked open and Chambers stumbled out, slouching off in a half-run, clutching something in his right hand, one leg damaged. Rebus struggled with his own door, finally finding the handle. He ran to the BMW and peered in. Lisa was slumped in the passenger seat, a seatbelt passing in a diagonal across her body. She was groaning, but there were no signs of blood. Whiplash. Nothing more serious than whiplash. She opened her eyes.

'John?'

'You're going to be all right, Lisa. Just hang on. Somebody will be here.' Indeed, the police cars were closing in, uniforms running into the Square. Rebus looked up from the car, seeking Chambers.

'There!' The judge was out of the Jaguar and pointing with a rigid arm, pointing upwards. Rebus followed the line to the steps of the National Gallery. Chambers had reached the top step.

'Chambers!' Rebus yelled. 'Chambers!'

But the body disappeared from view. Rebus started towards the steps, finding his own legs to be less than solid. As though rubber instead of bone and cartilage were keeping him upright. He climbed the steps and entered the building by its nearest door – the exit door. A woman in a staff uniform was lying on the ground in the foyer, a man standing over her. The man gestured towards the gallery's interior.

'He ran inside!'

And where Malcolm Chambers went, Rebus would surely follow.

*   *   *

He ran and he ran and he ran.

The way he used to run from his father, running and climbing the steps to the attic, hoping to hide. But always caught in the end. Even if he hid all day and half of the night, eventually the hunger, the thirst, would force him back downstairs, to where they were waiting.

His leg hurts. And he's cut. His face is stinging. The warm blood is trickling down his chin, down his neck. And he's running.

It wasn't all bad, his childhood. He remembers his mother delicately snipping away at his father's nosehairs. 'Long nosehairs are so unbecoming in a man.' It wasn't his fault, was it, any of it? It was theirs. They'd wanted a daughter; they'd never wanted a son. His mother had dressed him in pink, in girls' colours and girls' clothes. Then had painted him, painted him with long blonde curls, imagining him into her paintings, into her landscapes. A little girl running by a riverbank. Running with bows in her hair. Running.

Past one guard, past two. Lunging at them. The alarm is ringing somewhere. Maybe it's just his imagination. All these paintings. Where have all these paintings come from? Through one door, turn right, through another.

They kept him at home. The schools couldn't teach him the way they could. Home taught. Home made. His father, some nights, drunk, would knock over his mother's canvases and dance on them. 'Art! Fuck art!' He'd do his little dance with a chuckle in his throat and all the time his mother would sit with her face in her hands and cry, then run to her room and bolt shut the door. Those were the nights when his father would stumble through to *his* bedroom. Just for a cuddle. Sweet alcoholic breath. Just for a cuddle. And then more than a cuddle, so very much more.

228

'Open wide, just like the dentist tells you.' Christ, it hurt so much. A probing finger . . . tongue . . . the wrenching open . . . And even worse was the noise, the dull grunting, the loud nasal breathing. And then the sham, pretending it had been just a game, that was all. And to prove it, his father would bend down and take a big soft bite out of his stomach, growling like a bear. Blowing a raspberry on the bare flesh. And then a laugh. 'You see, it was only a game, wasn't it?'

No, never a game. Never. Running. To the attic. To the garden, to squeeze behind the shed, where the stinging nettles were. Even their bite was not so bad as his father's. Had his mother known? Of course she had known. Once, when he had tried to tell her in a whispered moment, she had refused to listen. 'No, not your father, you're making it up, Malcolm.' But her paintings had grown more violent: the fields now were purple and black, the water blood-red. The figures on the riverbank had grown skeletal, painted stark white like ghosts.

He'd hidden it all so well for so long. But then she'd come back to him. And now he was mostly 'she', consumed by her, and by her need for . . . Not revenge, it couldn't really be called revenge. Something deeper than revenge, some huge and hungry need without a name, without a form. Only a function. Oh yes, a function.

This way and that. The people in the gallery make way for him. The alarm is ringing still. There's a hissing in his head like a child's rattle. Sss-sss-sss. Sss-sss-sss. These paintings he is running past, they're laughable. *Long nosehairs Johnny*. None mimicked real life, and less so the life beneath. None could ape the grim caveman thoughts of every human being on the planet. But then he pushes open another door and it's all so very different. A room of darkness and shadowplay, of skulls and frowning bloodless faces. Yes, this is how it is. Velasquez, El Greco, the Spanish painters. Skull and shadow. Ah, Velasquez.

Why couldn't his mother have painted like this? When they died. (*Together, in bed. A gas leak. The police said the child was lucky to be alive. Lucky his own bedroom window*

229

had been open a couple of inches.) When they had died, all he'd taken with him from the house had been her paintings, every single one of them.

'Only a game.'

'Long nosehairs, Johnny.' Snipping with the scissors, his father asleep. He'd pleaded with his eyes, pleaded with her to stick the point of the scissors into his father's fleshy noiseless throat. She'd been so gentle. Snip. So kind and gentle. Snip. *The child was lucky.*

What could they know?

* * *

Rebus walked up the stairs and through the bookshop. Other officers were close behind him. He motioned for them to spread out. There would be no escape. But he also warned them to keep their distance.

Malcolm Chambers was *his.*

The first gallery was large, with red walls. A guard pointed through the doorway on the right and Rebus strode towards it. By the side of the doorway, a painting showed a headless corpse, spouting blood. The painting mirrored Rebus's thoughts so well that he smiled grimly. There were spots of rust-coloured blood on the orange carpet. But even without these, he would have had no difficulty following Chambers's trail. The tourists and attendants stood back from him, pointing, showing him the way. The alarm bell was bright and sharp, focussing his mind. His legs had become solid once again and his heart pumped blood so loudly he wondered if others could hear it.

He took a right, from a small corner room into another large gallery, at the far end of which stood a set of hefty wooden and glass doors. Near them another attendant stood nursing a wounded arm. There was a bloody hand-print on one door. Rebus stopped and looked through into the room itself.

In the furthest corner, slouched on the floor, sat the Wolfman. Directly above him on the wall was a painting of a monastic figure, the face cowled and in shadow. The figure looked to be praying to heaven. The figure was holding a skull. A smear of blood ran down and past the skull.

Rebus pushed open the door and walked into the room. Next to this painting was another, of the Virgin Mary with stars around what was left of her head. A large hole had been punched through her face. The figure beneath the paintings was still and silent. Rebus took a few paces forward. He glanced to his left and saw that on the opposite wall were portraits of unhappy looking noblemen. They had every right to be unhappy. Slashes in each canvas almost ripped their heads from their bodies. He was close now. Close enough to see that the painting next to Malcolm Chambers was a Velasquez, 'The Immaculate Conception'. Rebus smiled again. Immaculate indeed.

And then Malcolm Chambers's head jerked up. The eyes were cold, the face stippled with glass from the BMW's windscreen. The voice when it spoke was dull and tired.

'Inspector Rebus.'

Rebus nodded, though it had not been a question.

'I wonder,' Chambers said, 'why my mother never brought me here. I don't remember being taken anywhere, except perhaps Madame Tussaud's. Have you ever been to Madame Tussaud's, Inspector? I like the Chamber of Horrors. My mother wouldn't even come in with me.' He laughed, and leaned against the foot-rail behind him, ready to push himself to his feet. 'I shouldn't have torn those paintings, should I?' he was saying. 'They were probably priceless. Silly really. They're only paintings, after all. Why should paintings be priceless?'

Rebus had reached out a hand to help him up. At the same time, he saw the portraits again. Slashed. Not torn, *slashed*. Like the attendant's arm. Not by human hand, but with an instrument.

Too late. The small kitchen-knife in Chambers's hand was already pushing through Rebus's shirt. Chambers had leapt to his feet and was propelling Rebus backwards, back towards the portraits on the far wall. Chambers was infused with the strength of madness. Rebus felt his feet catch on the foot-rail behind him, his head fell back against one painting, thudding into the wall. He had his own right hand clasped around Chambers's knife-hand now, so that the tip of the knife was still gouging at his stomach but could go no deeper. He jerked a knee into Chambers's groin, at the same time jamming the heel of his left hand into Chambers's nose. There was a squeal as the pressure lessened on the knife. Rebus twisted Chambers's wrist, trying to shake free the knife, but Chambers's grip held fast.

Upright again, away from the wall now, they wrestled for control of the knife. Chambers was crying, howling. The sound chilled Rebus, even as he grappled with the man. It was like fighting with darkness itself. Unwanted thoughts sped through his mind: crammed tube trains, child molesters, beggars, blank faces, punks and pimps, as everything he'd seen and experienced in London washed over him in a final rolling wave. He dare not look into Chambers's face for fear that he would freeze. The paintings all around were blurs of blue, black and grey as he danced this macabre dance, feeling Chambers growing stronger and himself growing more tired. Tired and dizzy, the room spinning, a dullness coursing through his stomach towards the hole made by the knife.

The knife which is moving now, moving with new-found power, a power Rebus feels unable to counter with anything more than a grimace. He dares himself to look at Chambers. Does so, and sees the eyes staring at him like a bull's, the mouth set defiantly, the chin jutting. There is more than defiance there, more than madness, there is a resolution. Rebus feels it as the knife-hand turns. Turns one hundred and eighty degrees. And then he is being pushed backwards again. Chambers is rearing up, driving him on, powerful as an engine, until Rebus slams into another wall, followed by Chambers himself. It is almost an embrace. The bodies seemingly intimate in their contact. Chambers is heavy, a dead weight. His cheek rests against Rebus's. Until Rebus, recovering his breath, pushes the body away. Chambers staggers backwards into the room, the knife buried in his chest all the way up to the hilt. He angles his head to look down, dark blood dribbling from the corners of his mouth. He touches at the handle of the knife. Then looks up at Rebus and smiles, almost apologetically.

'So unbecoming . . . in a man.' Then falls to his knees. Trunk falls forward. Head hits carpet. And stays like that. Rebus is breathing hard. He pushes himself up from the wall, walks to the centre of the room, and pushes at the body with the toe of his shoe, tipping Chambers sideways. The face looks peaceful, despite the welts of blood. Rebus touches two fingers to the front of his own shirt. They come away moist with blood. That didn't matter. What mattered was that the Wolfman had turned out to be human after all, human and mortal, mortal and dead. If he wanted to, Rebus knew he could take the credit. He didn't want the credit. He'd get them to take away the knife and check it for fingerprints. They would find only Chambers's. That didn't mean much, of course. The likes of Flight would still think Rebus had killed him. But Rebus hadn't killed the Wolfman, and he couldn't be sure exactly what had: cowardice? guilt? or something deeper, something never to be explained?

So unbecoming . . . in a man. What kind of obituary was that?

'John?'

It was Flight's voice. Behind him stood two officers armed with pistols.

'No need for silver bullets, George,' said Rebus. He stood there, surrounded by what he supposed would be millions of pounds' worth of damaged works of art, alarm bells ringing, while outside the traffic in central London would be backed up for miles until Trafalgar Square could be opened again.

'I told you it'd be easy,' he said.

Lisa Frazer was fine. Shock, a few bruises, whiplash. The hospital wanted to keep her in overnight, just to be sure. They wanted to keep Rebus in, too, but he refused. They gave him painkillers instead, and three stitches in his stomach. The cut, they said, was fairly superficial, but it was best to be safe. The thread they used was thick and black.

By the time he arrived at Chambers's huge two-storey flat in Islington, the place was crawling with police, forensics, photographers and the usual retinue. The reporters outside were desperate for a quote, some recognising him from the impromptu conference he had given outside the house on Copperplate Street. But he pushed past them and into the Wolfman's lair.

'John, how are you?' It was George Flight, looking bemused by the day's proceedings. He had placed a hand on Rebus's shoulder. Rebus smiled.

'I'm fine, George. What have you found?'

They were standing in the main hall. Flight glanced back into one of the rooms off this hall. 'You won't believe it,' he said. 'I'm still not sure I do.' There was a tang of whisky on Flight's breath. The celebrations had begun already.

Rebus walked to the door and into the room. This was where the photographers and forensics people were busiest. A tall man rose to his feet from behind a sofa and looked across to Rebus. It was Philip Cousins. He smiled and nodded. Near him stood Isobel Penny, sketchbook in hand. But Rebus noticed that she wasn't drawing, and her face had lost all traces of liveliness. Even she, it seemed, could still be shocked.

The scene was certainly shocking. But worst of all was the smell, the smell and the buzzing of flies. One wall was covered in what had been paintings – very crudely done paintings, as even Rebus could tell. But now they had been slashed into tatters, some of which lay across the floor. And on the opposite wall was as much graffiti as would befit any tower block in Churchill Estate. Venomous stuff: FUCK ART. FEEL THE POOR. KILL PIGS. The stuff of madness.

There were two bodies thrown casually behind the sofa, and a third lying under a table, as though some rudimentary effort had been made to tidy them out of sight. Carpet and walls were stained with fine sprays of blood and the cloying smell told Rebus that at least one of the bodies had been here for several days. Easy to confront this now, now that it was at an end. Not so easy to work out the 'why?'. That was what worried Flight.

'I just can't find a motive, John. I mean, Chambers had everything. Why the hell did he need to. . . ? I mean, why would he just. . . ?' They were in the flat's living room. No clues were being offered up. Chambers's private life seemed as tidy and innocuous as the rest of his home. Just that one room, that one secret corner. That apart, they might have been in any successful barrister's apartment, poring over his books, his desk, his correspondence, his computer files.

It didn't really bother Rebus. It wouldn't bother him supposing they never found out why. He shrugged.

'Wait till the biography's published, George,' said Rebus, 'maybe then you'll get your answer.' Or ask a psychologist, he thought to himself. He didn't doubt there would be plenty of theories.

But Flight was shaking his head, rubbing at his head, his face, his neck. He still couldn't believe it had come to an end. Rebus touched a hand to his arm. Their eyes met. Rebus nodded slowly, then winked.

'You should have been in that Jag, George. It was magic.'

Flight managed to pull a smile out of the air. 'Tell that to the judge,' he said. 'Tell that to the judge.'

Rebus ate that night at George Flight's home, a meal cooked by Marion. So at last they were having the promised dinner together, but it was a fairly sombre occasion, enlivened only by an interview with some art historian on the late-night news. He was talking about the damage to the paintings in the National Gallery's Spanish Room.

'Such pointless waste . . . vandalism . . . sheer, wanton . . . priceless . . . perhaps irreparable . . . thousands of pounds . . . heritage.'

'Blah, blah, blah,' said Flight sneeringly. 'At least you can patch up a bloody painting. These people talk half the time out of their arses.'

'George!'

'Sorry, Marion,' said Flight sheepishly. He glanced towards Rebus, who winked back at him.

Later, after she had gone to bed, the two men sat together drinking a final brandy.

'I've decided to retire,' said Flight. 'Marion's been nagging me for ages. My health's not what it was.'

'Not serious, I hope?'

Flight shook his head. 'No, nothing like that. But there's a security firm, they've offered to take me on. More money, nine till five. You know how it is.'

Rebus nodded. He'd seen some of the best of his elders drawn like moths to a lightbulb when security firms and the like came to call. He drained his glass.

'When will you be leaving?' Flight asked.

'I thought I'd go back tomorrow. I can come back down again when they need me to give evidence.'

Flight nodded. 'Next time you come, we've got a spare bedroom here.'

'Thanks, George.' Rebus rose to his feet.

'I'll drive you back,' said Flight. But Rebus shook his head.

'Call me a cab,' he insisted. 'I don't want you done for D and D. Think what it would do to your pension.'

Flight stared into his brandy glass. 'You've got a point,' he said. 'Okay then, a cab it is.' He slipped a hand into his pocket. 'By the way, I've got you a little present.'

He held the clenched fist out to Rebus, who placed his own open palm beneath it. A slip of paper dropped from Flight's hand into his. Rebus unfolded the note. It was an address. Rebus looked up at Flight and nodded his understanding.

'Thanks, George,' he said.

'No rough stuff, eh, John?'

'No rough stuff,' agreed Rebus.

Family

He slept deeply that night, but woke at six the next morning and sat up in bed immediately. His stomach hurt, a burning sensation as though he had just swallowed a measure of spirits. The doctors had told him not to drink alcohol. Last night he had drunk just the one glass of wine and two glasses of brandy. He rubbed the area around the wound, willing the ache to go away, then took two more painkillers with a glass of tap-water before dressing and putting on his shoes.

His taxi-driver, though sleepy, was full of tales of yesterday's action.

'I was on Whitehall, wasn't I? An hour and a quarter in the cab before the traffic got moving again. Hour and a bleedin' quarter. Didn't see the chase either, but I heard the smash.'

Rebus sat back in silence, all the way to the block of flats in Bethnal Green. He paid the driver and looked again at the slip of paper Flight had given him. Number 46, fourth floor, flat six. The elevator smelled of vinegar. A crumpled paper package in one corner was oozing under-cooked chips and a tail-end of batter. Flight was right: it made all the difference having a good network of informers. It made for quick information. But what a good copper's network could get, so too could a good villain's. Rebus hoped he'd be in time.

He walked quickly across the small landing from the open lift to the door of one of the flats where two empty milk bottles stood to attention in a plastic holder. He picked up one bottle and hurried back to the lift just as its doors were shuddering to a close to place the milk bottle in the remaining gap. The doors stayed where they were. So did the lift.

You never knew when a quick getaway would be needed.

Then he walked along the narrow corridor to flat six,

braced himself against the wall and kicked at the door-handle with the heel of his shoe. The door flew open and he walked into a stuffy hall. Another door, another kick and he was face to face with Kenny Watkiss.

Watkiss had been asleep on a mattress on the floor. He was standing now, clad only in underpants and shivering, against the furthest wall from the door. He pushed his hair back when he saw who it was.

'Jee-Jesus,' he stammered. 'What are you doing here?'

'Hello, Kenny,' said Rebus, stepping into the room. 'I thought we'd have a little chat.'

'What about?' You didn't get as frightened as Kenny Watkiss was by having your door kicked in at half past six in the morning. You only got that frightened by the idea of *who* was doing it and *why*.

'About Uncle Tommy.'

'Uncle Tommy?' Kenny Watkiss smiled unconvincingly. He moved back to the mattress and started pulling on a pair of torn denims. 'What about him?'

'What are you so scared of, Kenny? Why are you hiding?'

'Hiding?' That smile again. 'Who said I was hiding?'

Rebus shook his head, his own smile one of apparent sympathy. 'I feel sorry for you, Kenny, really I do. I see your kind a hundred times a week. All ambition and no brain. All talk but no guts. I've only been in London a week, and already I know how to find you when I want you. Do you think Tommy *can't*? You think maybe he'll lay off? No, he's going to nail your head to the wall.'

'Don't talk daft.' Now that he was dressed, having pulled on a black T-shirt, Kenny's voice had lost some of its trembling. But he couldn't hide the look in his eyes, the haunted, hunted look. Rebus decided to make it easy for him. He reached into a pocket and brought out a packet of cigarettes, offered one to Kenny and lit it for him before taking one himself. He rubbed at his stomach. Jesus, it was hurting. He hoped the stitches were holding.

'You've been ripping him off,' Rebus said casually. 'He handled stolen goods, you were his courier, passing it down the chain. But you've been skimming a little off the top, haven't you? And with each job you'd take a little more than he knew about. Why? Saving for that Docklands flat? So you could start your own business? Maybe you got greedy, I don't know. But Tommy got suspicious. You were in court that day because you wanted to see him go down. It was the only thing that could have saved you. When he didn't, you still tried putting one over on him, yelling out from the public gallery. But by then it was only a matter of time. And when you heard that the case had been dropped altogether, well, you knew he'd come straight after you. So you ran. You didn't run far enough, Kenny.'

'What's it to you?' The words were angry. But it was the anger that came of fear. It wasn't directed at Rebus. He was merely the messenger.

'Just this,' Rebus said calmly: 'keep away from Sammy. Don't ever go near her again, don't even try to talk to her. In fact, your best bet right now is to get on a train or a bus or whatever and get the hell out of London. Don't worry, we'll pin Tommy for something sooner or later. Then maybe you can come back.' He had slipped a hand into his pocket again. It came out holding a fold of ten pound notes, four of which he peeled off and threw onto the mattress. 'I'm offering you a one-way ticket, and I'm suggesting you take it right now, this morning.'

The eyes and voice were wary. 'You're not going to take me in?'

'Why should I?'

The smile this time was more confident still. He looked at the money. 'It's just family, Rebus. That's all. I can take care of myself.'

'Can you?' Rebus nodded, taking in the room with its peeling wallpaper and boarded up window, the mattress with its single rumpled sheet. 'Fair enough.' He turned to go.

'It wasn't just me, you know.'

Rebus stopped but didn't turn. 'What?' He tried not to sound interested.

'There was a copper, too. He was on a cut from the robberies.'

Rebus sucked in air. Did he need to know? Did he *want* to know? Kenny Watkiss didn't give him the choice.

'A detective called Lamb,' he said. Rebus exhaled silently, but, saying nothing, showing nothing, walked back out of the flat and, pulling open the lift doors, kicking away the milk bottle, pressed the button for the ground floor and waited for the slow descent.

Outside the block, he paused to stub out his cigarette. He rubbed at his stomach again. Stupid not to have brought the painkillers with him. From the corner of his eye, he could see the unmarked transit van in the car park. Six forty-five. There could be a perfectly rational explanation for it, for the fact that two men sat stonily in its front seats. They might be about to go to work, mightn't they?

In fact, Rebus knew damned fine that's what they were doing. And he had another choice now. He could let them go to work, or he could stop them. It took him another second or two to decide, but finally, with a picture of Samantha's face in his head, he walked across nonchalantly to the van and, the men still ignoring his existence, thumped hard on the passenger-side window. The passenger looked at him with undisguised enmity, but, seeing that Rebus was undeterred, rolled down the window.

'Yeah?'

Rebus stuck his ID so far into the man's face that the plastic coating brushed against his nose.

'Police,' he snapped. 'Now get the fuck out of here. And tell Tommy Watkiss we've got his nephew under twenty-four hour watch. Anything happens, we'll know where to come and who to charge.' Rebus stood back and looked carefully at the man. 'Think you can remember all that, or do you want me to write it down?'

The passenger was growling audibly as he rolled the window back up. The driver was already starting the van. As it began to move off, Rebus gave its side a farewell kick. Maybe Kenny would leave and maybe he'd stay. It was up to him. Rebus had given him a chance. Whether the young man took it or not was out of Rebus's hands.

'Like Pontius Pilate,' he mumbled to himself as he made

for the main road. Standing by a lamppost, waiting and praying for a black cab to come along, he saw Kenny Watkiss emerge from the flats, a duffel-bag slung across his shoulder, and, looking around him, start to jog towards the far end of the estate. Rebus nodded to himself. 'That's my boy,' he said, as, with protesting brakes, a cab slowed to a halt beside him.

'You're in luck, mate,' said the driver. 'I'm just starting my shift.' Rebus clambered in and gave the name of his hotel, then settled back, enjoying the city at this quiet hour. The driver, though, was in practice for the day ahead.

'Here,' he said, 'did you hear about that rumpus yesterday at Trafalgar Square? I was in a queue for an hour and a half. I mean, I'm all for law and order, but there must've been another way of going about it, mustn't there?'

John Rebus shook his head and laughed.

His suitcase sat closed on the bed beside the little-used briefcase and the bag of books. He was squeezing the last few items into his sports bag when there was a soft tapping at his door.

'Come in.'

She did. She was wearing a solid-foam neck-brace, but grinned it away.

'Isn't it stupid? They want me to wear it for the next few days, but I –' She saw the cases on the bed. 'You're not leaving already?'

Rebus nodded. 'I came here to help with the Wolfman case. The Wolfman case is finished.'

'But what about –'

He turned to her. 'What about us?' he guessed. She lowered her eyes. 'That's a good question, Lisa. You lied to me. You weren't trying to help. You were trying to get your bloody PhD.'

'I'm sorry,' she said.

'Me too. I mean, I can understand why you did it, why you think you *had* to do it. Really I can. But that doesn't make it any better.'

She straightened her back and nodded. 'Fair enough

241

then,' she said. 'So, Inspector Rebus, if all I was doing was using you, why did I come here straight from the hospital?'

He zipped shut the bag. It was a good question. 'Because you got found out,' he said.

'No,' she said. 'That was bound to happen eventually. Try again.' He shrugged his shoulders. 'Oh,' she said, sounding disappointed. 'I was hoping you could tell me. I'm not really sure myself.'

He turned towards her again and saw that she was smiling. She looked so stupid in the neck-brace that he had to return the smile eventually. And when she came towards him he returned her hug, too.

'Ouch!' she said. 'Not too hard, John.'

So he relaxed his muscles a little, and they kept on hugging. He was actually feeling mellow; the painkillers had seen to that.

'Anyway,' he said at last, 'you weren't much help.'

She pulled away from him. He was still smiling, but archly. 'What do you mean?'

'I mean all that stuff we talked about in the restaurant. All those index cards.' Rebus recited the list. 'Thwarted ambition. Victims from a social class above the killer. No confrontation . . .' He scratched his chin. 'None of it fits Malcolm Chambers.'

'I wouldn't say that. We've still got to look at his home life, his background.' She sounded defiant rather than merely defensive. 'And I was right about the schizophrenia.'

'So you'll still do your project?'

She tried to nod; it wasn't easy. 'Of course,' she said. 'There's plenty of work to be done on Chambers, believe me. There must be clues there somewhere in his past. He must have left something.'

'Well, let me know what you find out.'

'John. Before he died, did he say anything?'

Rebus smiled. 'Nothing important,' he said. 'Nothing important.'

After she'd gone, after the promises of return trips and of

weekends in Edinburgh, promises of postcards and phone calls, he took his luggage down to reception. George Flight was at the desk. Rebus put his key down next to where Flight was signing his name to several forms.

'Do you realise how much this hotel costs?' Flight said, not looking up. 'Next time you visit, you really will have to bunk at my place.' Then he glanced towards Rebus. 'But I suppose you were worth it.' He finished with the forms and handed them to the receptionist, who checked them before nodding that everything was in order. 'You know the address to send them to,' Flight called back as the two men started towards the hotel's swing-doors.

'I really must get the lock on the boot fixed,' Flight said, shutting the car's back door on Rebus's luggage. Then: 'Where to? King's Cross?'

Rebus nodded. 'With one slight detour,' he said.

The detour, in Flight's words, turned out to be more than slight. They parked across from Rhona's flat in Gideon Park and Flight pulled on the handbrake.

'Going in?' he said. Rebus had been thinking about it, but shook his head. What could he tell Sammy? Nothing that would help. If he said he'd seen Kenny, she'd only accuse him of scaring him off. No, best leave it.

'George,' he said, 'could you maybe have someone drop in and tell her Kenny's left London. But stress that he's okay, that he's not in trouble. I don't want him lingering too long in her memory.'

Flight was nodding. 'I'll do it myself,' he said. 'Have you seen him yet?'

'I went this morning.'

'And?'

'And I was just in time. But I reckon he'll be all right.'

Flight studied the face next to him. 'I *think* I believe you,' he said.

'Just one thing.'

'Yes?'

'Kenny told me one of your men is involved. The baby-faced redneck.'

'Lamb?'

'That's the one. He's on Tommy Watkiss's payroll, according to Kenny.'

Flight pursed his lips and was silent for a moment. 'I think I believe that, too,' he said at last, very quietly. 'Don't worry, John. I'll deal with it.'

Rebus said nothing. He was still staring out at the windows of Rhona's flat, willing Sammy to come to one of them and see him. No, not see him, just so that *he* might see *her*. But there was no one at home. The ladies were out for the day with Tim or Tony or Graeme or Ben.

And it was none of Rebus's business anyway.

'Let's go,' he said.

So Flight drove him to King's Cross. Drove him through streets paved with nothing so very different from any other city. Streets ancient and modern, breathing with envy and excitement. And with evil. Not much evil, perhaps. But enough. Evil, after all, was pretty well a constant. He thanked God that it touched so few lives. He thanked God that his friends and family were safe. And he thanked God he was going home.

'What are you thinking about?' Flight asked as they idled at yet another set of traffic lights.

'Nothing,' said Rebus.

He was still thinking about nothing when he boarded the busy Inter City 125, and sat down with his newspapers and his magazines. As the train was about to move off, someone squeezed into the seat opposite him and deposited four large cans of strong lager on the table. The youth was tall and hard-looking with shorn hair. He glared at Rebus and turned up his personal cassette player. Tscchh-tscchh-tscchh it went, so loud Rebus could almost make out the words. The youth was grasping a ticket denoting Edinburgh as his destination. He put the ticket down and pulled on a ring-pull. Rebus shook his head wearily and smiled. His own personal hell. As the train pulled away, he caught its rhythm and beat that rhythm out silently in his head.

FYTP
FYTP

FYTP
FYTP
FYTP
FYTP
All the way home.

Acknowledgements

Thanks for help with facts, figures, psychopaths and
   garden paths (*viz* leading the reader up the . . .) go to
   the following:

In London: Dr S. Adams, Ms Fiona Campbell, Chris
   Thomas, Mr Andrew Walker, the officers of
   Tottenham Police Station
In Newmarket: L. Rodgers
In Edinburgh: Professor J. Curt, Ms Alison Girdwood
In Fife: Mr & Mrs Colin Stevenson
In Glasgow: Alex Blair
In Canada: Mr Tiree Macgregor, Dr D. W. Nichol
In the USA: Dr David Martin, Ms Rebecca Hughes

Suggested further reading:

Elliott Leyton, *Hunting Humans* (Penguin)
Clive R. Hollin, *Psychology and Crime* (Routledge)
Professor Keith Simpson, *Forty Years of Murder* (Grafton)
Martin Fido, *Murder Guide to London* (Weidenfeld)
R. M. Holmes & J. DeBurger, *Serial Murder* (Sage)
R. H. C. Bull *et al.*, *Psychology for Police Officers* (Wiley)
David Canter, 'To Catch a Rapist', *New Society*, 4 March
   1988
David Canter, 'Offender Profiles', *The Psychologist*, Vol
   2, No 1, January 1989